READING DISABILITY:

DIAGNOSIS

AND TREATMENT

READING DISABILITY

Diagnosis and Treatment

FLORENCE ROSWELL
AND GLADYS NATCHEZ

Foreword by
Katrina de Hirsch

Basic Books, Inc., Publishers
NEW YORK · LONDON

NINTH PRINTING

© 1964 by Basic Books, Inc., Publishers

Library of Congress Catalog Card Number: 63–19292

Manufactured in the United States of America

Designed by *Sophie Adler*

TO OUR HUSBANDS AND CHILDREN

⁂ FOREWORD

⁂ In a field beset by emotional controversies and evangelical fervor, *Reading Disability* is a much-needed and highly desirable book. It does not press a theory. It does not assume that children's difficulties with printed words are necessarily the result of intrapsychic conflict or that significant neurophysiological factors are easily separable from a child's total social and emotional experience. It does take cognizance of the complexity of the problem and the multidimensional aspects of maturation. The authors' respect for the individual rhythm of growth and their insight into the problems of the classroom teacher, who all too often feels threatened by the "expert," demonstrate an awareness and wisdom which is lacking in much of the literature on the subject.

The chapter on diagnosis is exemplary of the authors' fortunate handling of the problems. Their recommendations that reading tests be evaluated qualitatively in addition to quantitatively, that trial lessons be part of the diagnostic procedure, and that the child be given a sympathetic explanation as to his specific strength and weakness after tests are completed are as yet by no means standard procedure. Of utmost importance also is their emphasis on involving the pupil in searching for the remedial measures most appropriate to his needs. Beyond the wealth of practical suggestions which should be immensely helpful to remedial therapists and teachers, the book has a spirit of warmth and empathy. It is this spirit which is so essential in handling children with reading problems.

KATRINA DE HIRSCH
Director, Pediatrics
Language Disorder Clinic
Columbia Presbyterian Medical Center
New York City

ぺ PREFACE

ぺ The purpose of this book is to set forth what the authors have learned with regard to diagnosis and treatment of children with reading disability. Few books on reading are directed exclusively toward those children who have already drifted into trouble. Therefore, we describe the ways in which such children can be speeded toward firmer learning and self-realization. We focus on the various aspects related to reading disability—its causes, diagnosis, and treatment.

There are several unique features of this book which should make it useful for teachers, reading specialists, and psychologists who handle children with reading problems; it should also be of assistance in both graduate and undergraduate professional training programs. One distinction is that diagnosis is discussed from two angles. Chapter 2 shows how a teacher might make a reading diagnosis of an individual or a group; Chapter 3 considers how a psychologist investigates a child with a severe reading problem. Second, this book concerns pupils at widely differing stages of achievement. Thus, Chapter 6 includes three pupils of nine, twelve, and sixteen years, respectively, all reading at primary levels. The differences in approach and use of materials are discussed. On the other hand, Chapter 8 deals with the older pupil who is almost a non-reader, whereas Chapter 9 describes a bright high school student who reads on grade level, but who is not reaching his capabilities.

These major categories by no means cover all the combinations and permutations that occur in reading disability. Each individual presents his own pattern. To give a deeper understanding of the kinds of pupils that come to the attention of a reading clinician, the authors have included in Chapter 10 six cases representative of a varied practice. We show how we dealt with the problems of a delinquent adolescent, a boy with maturational lag, two girls with study-skill difficulties, a boy with brain damage, and a bright high school boy who was underachieving.

Throughout the text, we list many children's books, workbooks, teaching devices, and games. A special bibliography on neurophysiological and emotional factors follows Chapter 1, and one on phonics, phonic systems, and individualized reading follows Chapter 5. The appendixes offer tests, word lists, and further materials. Appendix B is divided into books which contain short stories, simplified classics, and fiction for independent reading.

The authors have been influenced by many writings, teachers, and colleagues. Reflections and thoughts from all of them have become so interwoven with our own that it is difficult to separate them or recognize their source. Certain influences, however, have been so profound that we wish to acknowledge our indebtedness. We are particularly grateful to Dean Harold H. Abelson and Dr. Herbert Nechin, who have been sources of constant encouragement in our work at City College. Dr. Albert J. Harris and Dr. Nila B. Smith have contributed to our thinking and enhanced our knowledge in the field of reading.

Finally, to all those students, parents, and children who unknowingly helped to develop our understanding and from whom we learned, we offer our deep appreciation. Any examples that we have taken from them have been used to illustrate general, rather than unique, problems. If many readers are reminded of similar individuals and situations in their own experience, we will feel that our examples were satisfactorily drawn.

FLORENCE G. ROSWELL
GLADYS NATCHEZ

November 1963

৯ CONTENTS

READING DISABILITY:

DIAGNOSIS

AND TREATMENT

৯৵ INTRODUCTORY
CHAPTER

৯৵ Today both laymen and professionals are concerned about the large numbers of children who, because of their difficulties in reading, cannot cope with schoolwork. Authorities have variously estimated the number of children with inadequate reading skills to be as high as thirty percent of the total school population,[1] over fifteen percent,[2] or between ten and fifteen percent.[3] Whatever the percentage, most educators agree that the number of children who read less effectively than they should—and could—is far too high.

Whether there are more reading problems today than there were formerly has not been clearly demonstrated. There are many possible explanations for the supposed increase in recent years. Formerly, many children who had reading difficulties might have left school at an early age, found employment, and lived out their lives satisfactorily. They most likely experienced a minimum of regret over their departure because work opportunities were plentiful and there was less need for formal schooling. Also, many children who might have had reading problems remained undetected before concentrated mass testing was inaugurated. Today, with a high premium placed on high school and college achievement, education is mandatory. Reading, the crux of most learning, is indispensable in the modern era, which depends on written communication for both personal growth and national survival.

It is the purpose of this book to examine the complex causes of reading disability and to suggest methods for its diagnosis and treatment. Frequently, the disciplines of education, psychology, and psychiatry tend to approach the problem from their own perspectives. Here we are attempting to combine the pertinent theory and methodology of each area; such integration

---

[1] J. Deboer and Martha Dallmann, *The Teaching of Reading* (New York: Henry Holt, 1960), p. 267.

[2] D. Smith and Patricia Carrigan, *The Nature of Reading Disability* (New York: Harcourt Brace, 1959), pp. 1–2.

[3] A. Harris, *How to Increase Reading Ability*, 4th ed. (New York: Longmans, Green, 1961), p. 18.

of knowledge and skills may prevent or alleviate a reading difficulty that otherwise might have been impervious to treatment.

What Is Reading Disability?

Reading disability must always be defined in terms of intelligence. A reading disability exists where there is a significant discrepancy between reading ability and intellectual potential. Thus, this term should not be applied to children who, although reading below grade level, are reading as well as their intellectual capacity allows. Quantitative evaluation, however, must be used with caution because all tests are subject to a certain amount of error. Furthermore, test scores alone do not provide a complete appraisal of a process as complex as reading.

In reality, a pupil with a reading disability is one who has suffered years of despair, discouragement, and frustration. He may be any pupil between the ages of seven and seventeen and possibly older who cannot cope with schoolwork because he cannot read successfully. Feelings of rejection, failure, and hopelessness about the future are always present. In expressing such feelings, one nine-year-old wished he were all grown up and ready to die so he would not have to struggle with reading any more. A fifteen-year-old claimed that he felt like a blind man because he could not even read job applications, whereas a seventeen-year-old with an I.Q. of 135 recounted how he sat staring at the college board examinations one afternoon, concluding that his low score would ruin his entire career.

A student with a reading disability, then, is a lost and frightened person. The wider the discrepancy between achievement and ability, the more seriously will he be affected. Not only does his reading disability prevent him from developing sufficient knowledge for his studies, but it also deprives him of the intellectual enjoyment and stimulation of books.

Unlike the child who is poor only in sports or Latin or science, the child with a reading disability is usually hindered in every subject. For twelve long years of school and after, he contends with a situation for which he can find no satisfactory solution. When schoolwork becomes insurmountable, the child has no resources from which to fortify himself. An adult dissatisfied with his job may seek a position elsewhere, find solace outside his work, or be able to tolerate the difficulties because of high salary or other compensations. For a child who fails, however, there is no escape. He is subjected to anything from degradation to long-suffering tolerance. Optimum conditions may lessen the child's misery, but proof of his inadequacies appears daily in the classroom. In the end, he is held in low esteem not only by his classmates, but also by his family, on whom he depends for love and comfort. Thus poor reading influences every aspect of a child's world.

Varied Characteristics of Children with Reading Disability

Despite their common feelings, children with reading disability do not fall into set categories.[4] They are found in all age groups, all ranges of intelligence, all cultural groups, and all types of physical and personality make-ups. Pupils who read poorly grow up in diverse environments; they may live with understanding or punitive parents in happy or broken homes. Some may be seriously affected by these conditions; others remain untouched. In some instances, a child with reading problems shows severe emotional maladjustment at the outset; sometimes the maladjustment manifests itself only after the appearance of poor achievement. But that all students with reading disability are to some extent emotionally disturbed seems to be inevitable. Those whose disturbance goes back to preschool years often develop increased emotional problems if they cannot acquire academic skill. Those who demonstrate a fairly stable background react to school failure with varying degrees of emotional upset.

How Can Pupils with Reading Problems Be Helped?

What can we do to help such pupils? Is psychotherapy necessary for all? Should specialized methods be used in each case? Many believe that proper techniques are the solution; some even trust in a particular phonics system. Some recommend remedial reading; others advocate various forms of therapy. So far, however, there is no evidence to substantiate any one treatment.

Rather than depend for treatment on any one educational technique or on psychotherapy alone, the authors believe that a combined approach is the most effective. However, the reading problem itself needs close attention, no matter what other procedures are indicated. Rarely do causative factors, singly or in combination, have a totally disabling effect on learning. The more rapidly the reading problem is corrected, the stronger the pupil becomes, and the more he may be able to withstand any other adverse aspects of his life.

We also find that all but a small minority of children can improve their

---

[4] A. Gates, "The Role of Personality Maladjustment in Reading Disability," *Journal of Genetic Psychology*, 69 (1941), pp. 77–83.

reading through proper help and guidance in the school. There are always the exceptional cases which are so severe that they cannot be treated successfully in this way. It is the school's prerogative to identify such pupils and refer them out for suitable assistance. In most cases, however, the reading disability can be alleviated to a large extent in the regular school setting, and in many cases it can be overcome completely.

Throughout this book we propound our theory regarding the diagnosis and treatment of reading disability. We have set forth what we believe to be effective practice in remedial treatment. In those cases where we have been specific in describing treatment, we have not meant the description to be duplicated exactly. We hope rather that the techniques cited will be used as a guide. Because the aim of treatment is to liberate the pupil so that he may learn and grow, remedial instruction must be based on each pupil's unique requirements and qualities.

We recognize that there is still much that is not known about the causes of reading disability and much to be learned about its treatment, and so we continue to question, to investigate, and to try to deepen our understanding.

PART I

৯ 1

Causes of Reading Disability

৯ The causes of reading disability can never be pinpointed accurately. They are complex, often obscure, and always interrelated. One cannot isolate a single cause, diagnose it, treat it, and then dismiss a child as "cured" of his disability. Often the reading disability itself may be a symptom of some more deep-seated emotional problem. The more teachers and psychologists understand the multiple causes of reading disability, the greater possibility will there be in coping with it successfully or at the very least alleviating it. In the end, perhaps a more thorough knowledge of the causes of it will be able to effect an almost total prevention of the disability.

Reading disability is rarely caused by a single isolated factor. It is more likely to be an integral part of some inconsistency or imbalance in the forces governing the child's whole life. Such forces, which are major ones, include the child's innate constitutional make-up as it affects his growth and intellectual capacity, as well as the environment in which he develops. The interplay of these forces influences his social and emotional growth. The child brings this whole pattern with him to any situation, which of course includes the learning situation.

Thus investigation of causation is extremely complicated. For purposes of clarity, we shall discuss separately the major areas contributing to reading disability, whether singly or in combination. These include intellectual, physical, social, emotional, and educational factors. After that we shall show how all the separate components are likely to act and react upon one another to produce further complexities.

Intellectual Factors

Obviously, intellect ultimately determines learning ability. As a result, the level of intelligence is used as a criterion for determining the level of reading achievement to be expected of a child. Thus, a third grader who is above average in intelligence should be reading above third grade level, while a child of the same age who is below average in ability might be achieving adequately if he read at second grade level. However, estimates of intelligence or achievement can never be completely valid or reliable; the testing instruments themselves are always subject to a degree of error. Also, such factors as the child's physical, environmental, and emotional condition affect test results. Therefore, any quantitative scores are useful as rough measures only. They merely suggest the level at which a child may be expected to read. Intelligence is a determinant of reading achievement, but intelligence test scores do not necessarily predict the level of reading achievement.

Physical Factors

Physical ailments, even those of a minor or temporary nature, affect efficiency and reading performance. Consider, for example, how an adult's powers of concentration are reduced by hay fever, a cold, or even an irritating rash. Children are generally less well equipped to overcome such discomfort. Such factors as lack of sleep and even inadequate clothing can also make it difficult or impossible for a child to profit fully from school instruction.

Obviously some physical factors are of more importance than others in causing reading disability and need special medical attention. For example, defects in hearing, speech, or vision, brain damage, and endocrine or neurophysiological dysfunction are particularly pertinent. Adequate vision is so essential that it will be discussed further below. Slow or atypical patterns of neurophysiological and physical growth are considered by the authors to be of such major causal significance in a large proportion of children with reading difficulty that they need extensive elaboration and explanation. They are discussed in detail in a separate section, "Developmental Factors as Related to Reading Disability" on pages 12–20 of this chapter.

Vision

Visual defects may affect the child's ability to learn to read or cause such a degree of discomfort that the act of reading produces eye strain and fatigue. Some of the more common defects found in children with reading disability are farsightedness, nearsightedness, various forms of eye muscle imbalance, and astigmatism. Most of these conditions do not show up on the tests of vision generally used in schools. Nevertheless they impede the child's reading performance in different ways.

A farsighted child may have considerable difficulty reading printed matter close up. This condition is often undetected because the child shows no difficulty in seeing objects or printed matter at a distance. The near-sighted child may be able to see well at close range but may not see printed material on charts or on the chalk board. Eye muscle imbalance can interfere with the child's ability to receive a single image as he focuses on the printed page. Astigmatism often prevents clearness of perception. There are, of course, many other visual conditions which, in addition to those just mentioned, require diagnosis by an eye specialist.

Research investigators differ as to the incidence of visual defects in children with reading disabilty.[1] But if a child's visual efficiency seems to be impaired in any way, it is important that he be referred for an examination of his vision.

Emotional Factors

The relationship of emotional factors to reading disability is extremely intricate. Despite investigation and research, knowledge in this area is still conflicting and incomplete. Some ways in which emotional factors appear to affect reading ability are summarized here. For those interested in further study, see *Selected Research on Emotional Factors* listed at the end of this chapter.

Rarely can emotional difficulties be isolated in order to determine precisely how they interfere with learning. First of all, emotional disturbances vary not only in nature and degree, but also in complexity. Secondly, the fundamental issues with regard to the functioning and malfunctioning of personality are still only in their infancy.[2] The theories of the different psychoanalytic schools, the separate schools of psychology, as well as the fields of physiology, cultural anthropology, and the like, differ from psychologist to psychologist and from discipline to dis-

---

[1] The research on visual defects is too extensive to relate here. See summaries by Helen Robinson and C. Huelsman, "Visual Efficiency and Progress in Learning to Read," in *Clinical Studies in Reading*, II, pp. 31–63. Supplementary Educational Monographs, No. 77 (Chicago: University of Chicago Press, 1953), and D. Cleland, "Seeing and Reading," *American Journal of Optometry*, 30 (1953), pp. 467–81.

[2] H. Sullivan, *Conceptions of Modern Psychiatry* (New York: Norton, 1953), Lecture II.

cipline. Furthermore, personality factors exist as only one feature in a much more complex and intricate amalgam of physical, environmental, and social forces. Despite the advances made by gifted and renowned authorities, our understanding is incomplete and may easily be "regarded two or three generations hence, as minor, fragmentary contributions. . . ."[3] Finally, even though maladjustment is found in most children with reading disability,[4] it is uncertain whether it arises as a cause or effect of the disability. Since investigation of reading disability usually does not occur until after the school failure appears, it is most difficult to determine whether frustrations, insecurity, lowered motivation, lack of application, or other personality maladjustments cause the reading disability or are a direct reaction to it.

In general, however, there are three major ways in which emotional disturbance arises in children with reading disability. First, a child who suffers emotional upset as he is growing up may face the school situation with heightened anxiety or similar psychic disturbances. In many cases, distracting, unconscious conflicts diminish his concentration in class. The disturbance can be so overwhelming that he learns little. It can be less massive but still powerful enough to distort his perceptions and thought processes, so that he learns incorrectly or ineffectively; or it can be mild and play only a minor role. A variety of symptoms can emerge, ranging from open resistance against learning to avoidance of reading through daydreaming, dawdling, or apathy.

Secondly, although the child may be fairly free from emotional maladjustment at the outset, it may evolve as a direct outgrowth of his frustration in schoolwork. For example, he may be learning at a pace slower than that of the other pupils in his class, either because he is one of the youngest, or because he is less bright, or simply because he is developing more slowly. His comparatively poor performance can cause feelings of inadequacy and discouragement. These feelings can become intense enough to handicap his learning.

Finally, both conditions can be present and reinforce each other. That is, a pupil's negative reactions from poor schoolwork can cause emotional difficulties or increase any that were already present. The personality disturbance then heightens the reading problem and creates a vicious circle.

---

[3] G. Murphy, *Personality* (New York: Harper & Brothers, 1947), p. 918.

[4] A. Gates, "The Role of Personality Maladjustment in Reading Disability," *Journal of Genetic Psychology*, 59 (1941), pp. 77–83; H. Smith, *Psychology in Teaching Reading* (Englewood Cliffs, N.J.: Prentice-Hall, 1961), Ch. 11.

It is the cyclical nature itself of this condition that makes it so difficult to determine whether or not emotional disturbance is at the root of the trouble. Yet in terms of treatment it is important to attempt a distinction. Thus the etiology of the personality maladjustment and its relation to reading disability will be explored to the extent possible.

Background Factors

It is well known that the milieu and the setting in which children live have an important influence on their lives.[5] With regard to learning, parents' attitudes are particularly important. Some place a higher premium on education than others.

Environmental conditions also affect learning. When parents are in no position to offer their children a variety of experiences, they tend to alienate them from reading and other academic pursuits. In homes where there are few opportunities for discussion, storytelling or reading, children lack incentive for formal learning. The children's meager background then hinders their understanding basic concepts in books and subject matter. For example, the authors found sixth graders from deprived families who had no idea what faucets and pipelines were, or scenery, or landscapes. The stories and books that they encountered at school had slight appeal for these children because their contents were so foreign to them.

On the other hand, there are home environments which stimulate children's intellectual curiosity and promote their general knowledge of people and the world around them. Such pupils are often eager to widen their horizons. They ask endless questions; they experiment in many different areas; their interests seem boundless. Provided there are no interfering factors, these children usually learn to read easily and bring joy and delight to the process.

Hence, in searching for causal factors, it is well to consider background and environmental elements in order to gain insight and understanding of the entire problem. If there are such features as a lack of intellectual stimulation in the family, or if a foreign language is spoken exclusively in the home, it may have a direct bearing on reading ability.

---

[5] M. Deutsch, *Minority Groups and Class Status as Related to Social and Personality Factors in Scholastic Achievement* (New York: Society for Applied Anthropology, 1960); Helen Davidson, F. Riessman, and E. Myers, "Personality Characteristics Attributed to Various Occupational Groups," *Journal of Social Psychology*, 57 (1962), pp. 155–60; F. Riessman, *The Culturally Deprived Child* (New York: Harper & Brothers, 1962).

Educational Factors

Ineffective teaching methods and inappropriate reading materials can retard a child's reading. For example, a child may be given materials so difficult or even so easy that he becomes either discouraged on the one hand or bored on the other. Teaching methods often are not suited to a particular child. Or the teacher may not have adequate professional training in the teaching of reading.

Also, the climate of the classroom may be unsuited to learning. The teacher may be so permissive that the entire class lacks appropriate discipline or structure; this can be extremely disconcerting to an anxious child. Or the classroom situation may be so inflexible that a child becomes tense under the strain. If the teaching is inappropriate, it can adversely affect reading ability.

Irregular attendance and frequent changes of school or teachers can prevent adequacy in learning too. If the child had excessive absences in the early grades, or if he moved frequently from one school district to another, he may never have had the opportunity to acquire the proper training.

Developmental Factors as Related to Reading Disability

Maturational Factors

The process of slow maturation is extremely complicated and research is still needed before its implications can be fully understood.[6] In general, maturation refers to the multifarious facets of a child's growth in such areas as height, weight, responsiveness, control of behavioral reactions, intelligence, perception, and integrative capability, which is the ability to organize stimuli into an ordered pattern. Development of certain of these factors is crucial to learning and is described below. First a summary of general developmental factors is presented, next the ways in which slow maturation can delay reading ability, then the consequences of more serious delay in maturational factors, and finally the severe problems that arise from irregular neurological growth.

However, before any discussion of maturational factors proceeds, it is important to clear up a misconception that often arises. Because deviant growth is frequently intertwined with emotional disturbance, one factor can easily be mistaken for the other. For example, a slowly developing child

---

[6] For further information and research on neurophysiological factors as related to reading disability, see "Selected Research on Developmental and Neurophysiological Factors" at the end of this chapter.

may incorrectly be considered emotionally immature if no reference is made to the rate of his physiological development. Or a child who has not yet attained the physiological growth necessary for learning to read may be mislabeled emotionally disturbed. The so-called emotional immaturity or disturbance may be a direct outgrowth of the slow maturation, as we shall have occasion to point out later, or it may stem from a host of other factors. To explain the phenomenon of maturation more clearly, we shall refer throughout this section to those children with irregular development who are fairly free from emotional disturbance except as it arises from discrepant development. (The presence of emotional disturbance in other connections is covered in this chapter under the sections "Emotional Factors" and "Interaction of Causative Factors.")

Let us first examine the general factors in maturation. Human development usually proceeds in an orderly and calculable fashion. Most children teethe, talk, walk, learn the social amenities, and so forth within a predictable period of time. The factors necessary for these accomplishments are inherent in them as a part of nature's unfolding design, and they depend upon a favorable environment to develop optimally. Hence both nature and nurture contribute to growth.

Obviously a variety of individuals will show a variety of rates of growth as they develop.[7] Irregularities in maturation are found in differing degrees from extremely mild to the more severe ones that verge on minimal brain damage—then on through all types of neurophysiological dysfunctions.[8] Between the two extremes—slow maturation and brain damage—there is a distinct and clear difference. However, in between are found a number of variable conditions which are difficult to identify or categorize, yet which influence an individual's functioning in many ways.

Everyone realizes that each particular stage of physiological development affects the tasks that an individual can master. For example, a one-year-old baby rarely can hold an intelligible conversation of any length; a two-year-old is unlikely to be able to ride a two-wheeler. No amount of training, practice, or encouragement at such early ages is likely to accelerate the fundamental maturation necessary for these skills. When discrepancies in growth processes occur, they affect these and other tasks in different ways, depending on the nature and severity of the irregularity.

---

[7] Many terms are used in referring to delay in maturation, as *maturational lag, developmental lag,* or *delayed development.*

[8] In their most severe form, they are referred to as brain damage, organic injury or disease, dyslexia, irregular functioning, or disturbance of the central nervous system.

So it is with learning to read. If a child has not yet reached sufficient physiological growth, he cannot profit from reading instruction nor can he yet attain "reading readiness." Implied in this concept is the fact that he will reach "readiness" in the near future.

Reading Readiness as Related to Growth Factors

Reading readiness is the point at which learning to read proceeds with a minimum of difficulty. Readiness has long been a familiar concept in education. It describes so-called normal children, all of whose abilities are intact. Although they develop slowly, no pathology is present.[9] Many separate factors contribute to reading readiness. The major ones are sufficient mental age,[10] understanding of language, background of experience, social and emotional development, and maturation in the areas directly related to word recognition, such as visual and auditory discrimination and the ability to blend separate sounds into words.

These abilities are highly dependent on the level of the child's physiological development. Therefore, those who develop slowly will be at a disadvantage when they are given reading instruction, particularly if they are placed with those who mature more rapidly. If slow growth is overlooked and reading instruction is imposed too early, reading disability is likely to result. Hence, Olson[11] stresses the need for adjusting educational procedures to the child's level of development rather than risking the disastrous consequences of forcing impossible learning tasks too soon. He suggests that many of these pupils may be expected to catch up with their peers eventually, as a matter of course. If they are handled properly in the interim by being given appropriate educational preparation for reading and are helped to avoid inferiority feelings with reference to their less rapid achievement, they will in all probability read in accordance with their capacity at a later date. In this way, suitable teaching will avoid many of the secondary emotional consequences of early failure. However, if reading is delayed six to twelve months and the child still does not show sufficient readiness to read, it is quite possible that a much more severe form of maturational lag is present.

---

[9] G. Pearson, *Psychoanalysis and the Training of the Child* (New York: Norton, 1954), p. 28.

[10] Authorities differ on the mental age necessary for success in learning to read. This depends on such variables as the materials and the methods of teaching used.

[11] W. Olson, *Child Development* (Boston: D. C. Heath, 1959), p. 3.

Extremely Slow Maturation

Children who reach the second, third, and fourth grades,[12] or even higher without acquiring the basic word-analysis skills due to slow maturation are bound to show deviant development in the areas of perception, integration, and differentiation.[13] (How these deficiencies interfere with their learning words is discussed in this chapter in the sections "Visual Discrimination," "Auditory Discrimination," "Blending Ability," and "Dominance and Directional Confusion" on pages 16–17.) These difficulties may be a part of a general language disorder,[14] so that a child may show difficulty in forming words, in expressing himself both orally and in written work, as well as in figuring out words and in reading. The language disorder may persist for many years so that these pupils may have difficulty not only in conceptualizing in these areas, but in spelling and other studies and skills as well. Foreign languages in particular could be extremely difficult for them to learn.

There is often evidence of poor motor coordination, general awkwardness, restlessness, and hyperactivity. Sometimes these children have trouble controlling their impulses. They may show outbursts of temper; they may not be able to sit quietly for any length of time; they may be quick to shove or push. Finer muscle integration can also be affected and cause poorly formed or illegible handwriting. There may be, in addition, a residual ambidexterity and a tenuous establishment of left to right progression which is so essential to speaking, reading, or writing in accurate sequences. Hence the well-known reversal errors that these children make.

Children with pronounced developmental lag are likely to show emotional disturbance as a direct result of their condition. For example, long before he enters school, a child may become aware of the superiority of his contemporaries in such things as playing games, handling crayons, paints, blocks, or scissors, or in expressing themselves easily. Perhaps he is always chosen last for the "team," rejected on the playground, or made to feel like an outsider to the group. As a result, he forms a low opinion of himself. Continued negation from parents, brothers, sisters, playmates, and others

---

[12] If this problem persists beyond elementary grades, we are probably dealing with a much more serious form of deviant development which borders on or is frank brain damage.

[13] Katrina de Hirsch, "Tests Designed to Discover Potential Reading Difficulties at the Six-year-old Level," *American Journal of Orthopsychiatry*, 27 (1957), p. 574.

[14] For further discussion on language disorder see Bender, Benton, de Hirsch, Orton, Schilder, and Vernon, listed at the end of this chapter under Selected Research on Developmental and Neurophysiological Factors.

will lower his self-esteem and heighten still further his anxiety. If on top of all this he is exposed to reading instruction and does not learn, his feelings of inadequacy increase even more.

Maturational Factors Interfering with Word Analysis

What are the major factors in maturational lag which directly interfere with word-analysis skill? Children who have persistent trouble with word recognition usually show at least some minor difficulty with visual and auditory discrimination, but they are apt to have even more trouble blending separate sounds together and establishing sufficient dominance and directionality to analyze words into proper letter sequences. It is not with the meanings of words that they have a problem; they are usually bright enough to grasp literal meanings; they can understand passages that are read to them. But they simply cannot read comparable material independently.

VISUAL DISCRIMINATION. Reading requires instant recognition of printed symbols. Many symbols differ only in minute details. Some letters are exactly alike except that they face in opposite directions, such as *b* and *d*, *p* and *q*, *u* and *n*, *b* and *p*. Numbers present similar problems, as 6 and 9, *81* and *18*. A child with immature perceptual functioning in all probability will have difficulty discriminating between them. Insufficient visual discrimination and poor spatial orientation[15] also interfere with recognizing words. Thus the child might not be able to see the difference between words, particularly if their configurations are similar, like *went* and *want*, *where* and *there*. Those who are familiar with such children know how difficult it is for them to render a printed page accurately. They persist in misreading, substituting extraneous words, or adding or omitting words. This seems to be due to their primitive perceptual organization, which is so diffuse that parts of words are poorly differentiated. They are unable to retain a strong grasp of visual patterns made up of discrete elements.

AUDITORY DISCRIMINATION. Inadequate perceptual functioning also makes it difficult for children with delayed maturation to detect differences in sounds of letters even though they have adequate hearing. Thus a child who cannot tell the difference between the beginning sounds of such words as *sad* and

---

[15] It has not been established whether difficulty in distinguishing such symbols is due to visual discrimination, directional confusion or spatial orientation. The latter factors are discussed on pp. 17–18 of this chapter.

tan, or hears no distinction between *beg* and *bag,* will find it virtually impossible to learn to read when taught by a method requiring him to associate sounds with letters.

BLENDING ABILITY. Children with developmental lag find great difficulty not only in distinguishing separate sounds, but in blending them to form words. This apparently requires a high degree of physiological integration. Extensive research has been carried out to discover the nature of this difficulty, but no clear evidence has so far emerged. Agreement at present has it that "severe cases of disability seem to have a deep-rooted incapacity to perform the process of analysis with facility and to synthesize or blend phonetic units to form complete words."[16]

This means that if a teacher pronounces slowly a simple word such as *s-a-t,* enunciating clearly and being careful not to put extraneous vowel sounds between the letters, the pupils with severe disability cannot put the sounds together so that they recognize aurally the word *sat.* When these pupils are taught by a phonic approach, which requires synthesizing sounds to form words, they cannot learn. Even if they have developed sufficient auditory discrimination to associate letters and sounds correctly, they cannot synthesize them to decipher unknown words. It is disheartening to observe them struggling unsuccessfully with this procedure. Exhorting them to put forth more effort, sending home report cards with "U" for unsatisfactory, drilling the child over and over again, merely aggravate the problem. (Alternate methods which may be used with such children are discussed in Chapters 5 and 6.)

DOMINANCE AND DIRECTIONAL CONFUSION. To complicate further the acquiring of academic techniques, children with deviant physiological functioning will perhaps show difficulty in establishing dominance and directionality. This can interfere with their learning to read. Lateral dominance and directional confusion have for many years been in the forefront of discussions on reading disability. Let us examine what has been discovered so far as to their nature. Harris[17] defines lateral dominance as "the preferred use and superior functioning of one side of the body over the other." A person who habitually uses his right hand more skillfully than his left is considered to have right-hand dominance. Similarly, one who uses his left hand consistently

[16] M. Vernon, *Backwardness in Reading* (London, England: Cambridge University Press, 1958), p. 71.

[17] A. Harris, *How to Increase Reading Ability* (New York: Longmans, Green, 1961), pp. 249 ff.

and with greater skill has left-hand dominance. People also show eye dominance by favoring one eye over the other in such monocular tasks as looking through a telescope, microscope, or kaleidoscope and foot dominance by showing preference of one foot over the other in kicking or hopping, although little study has been devoted to the latter. An individual is said to have mixed dominance when he is right-handed and left-eyed or vice versa. A person may also have mixed hand or mixed eye dominance when he does not show a distinct preference for using one hand or eye more decidedly than the other. It should be noted that children with mixed dominance are often called ambidextrous. However, they are not ambidextrous in the usual sense of the term. Rather than using both hands skillfully, they use them equally poorly. In this connection, Orton's[18] theories continue to receive considerable attention. He proposed that if an individual fails to develop consistent dominance of one side in preference to the other, reversal tendencies will result and reading will be seriously affected. He suggested the term *strephosymbolia* (literally, *twisted symbols*) to describe the reading disability.

Directionality is the awareness of right and left outside the body and seems to develop after laterality has been established. Harris[19] considers that evidence of directional confusion in reading disability cases is of far greater significance than any pattern of lateral dominance which may appear.

What is the relationship between dominance and directionality? The child first develops awareness of the two sides of his body. As already stated, consistent use of one side of the body indicates that dominance has been established. However, when the child is able to project directional concepts into external space, he has developed adequate directionality and orientation.[20] For example, in attempting to grasp an object, a child experiments with movement. He learns that to reach it he must move one way or the other. When concepts of sidedness in the world around him have been established, directionality has become stable. However, many children and even some adults remain uncertain as to directionality, When some people try to open a car door, for instance, and are given the order "Turn the handle to the right," they automatically move it to the left. They report

---

[18] S. Orton, *Reading, Writing and Speech Problems in Children* (New York: Norton, 1937), Ch. 2.

[19] Harris, *op. cit.*, p. 255.

[20] N. Kephart, *The Slow Learner in the Classroom* (Columbus, Ohio: Charles E. Merrill, 1960), p. 46.

that they often experience directional confusion in following left-right directions.

While the nature of dominance and directionality remain obscure, investigators[21] have shown that they are related to physiological growth. This directly interferes with their recognizing letter or word sequences correctly. Benton[22] points out the significance of dominance and directionality. He states that "both impressionistic observation and systematic study indicate that disturbance in right-left discrimination may be shown by children with reading disability. . . . There is a possibility that within the broad category of children with reading disability, there may be a special group characterized by confusion in handedness, impaired right-left discrimination and other evidence of body-schema disturbance and neurologic abnormality and whose reading disability may reasonably be interpreted as the resultant of a global neurologic maldevelopment."

Children with problems of directionality or spatial orientation may have trouble distinguishing between *on* and *no, was* and *saw*. They may also reverse letters and numbers in writing, speaking, or reading. For example, pupils of that kind might write *clam* for *calm*, say *aminal* for *animal*, or read *scared* for *sacred*. These errors are usually due not to inattention or lack of effort, but to a more basic, language disorder. This tendency not only interferes with early learning, but often persists for many years. This is evidenced in the poor spelling, writing, and reading of some bright high school and college students who were found to have experienced earlier developmental difficulties.

Severe Problems of Irregular Growth

Closely related to and often indistinguishable from maturational lag are neurophysiological factors of a more serious nature, which frequently include actual brain damage. Children who suffer from such severe difficulty are apt to show more obvious impairment in all the characteristics and symptoms discussed under "Extremely Slow Maturation." Difficulty with comprehension is also more apparent, especially on material involving abstract thinking and with questions which require making inferences and

---

[21] M. Vernon, *op. cit.*, Ch. 5; G. Forlano, Julia Martin, J. Reswick, and N. Tieman, "Assessing Mirror Reading Techniques for Children with Mixed Dominance," *Bureau of Educational Research*, J. Wayne Wrightstone, Dir., New York: Board of Education (May, 1960).

[22] A. Benton, *Right-left Discrimination and Finger Localization* (New York: Hoeber, 1959), p. 57.

the like.[23] Manifestations relating to a general language disorder of the kind that has already been described are even more prevalent.

Learning to read can be a particularly slow process for these children because of the extreme difficulty some of them experience in mastering phonics. The cases of Frank and Lloyd in Chapter 10 illustrate these points. How long the problem is likely to persist would depend on its nature and severity. Frequently the condition does improve with the child's maturation. Also, there is some evidence pointing to the possibility of restoration, rehabilitation, or compensation of the impaired physiological areas as the child develops.[24] If the teacher understands why the pupil is having trouble, and recognizes that his pace of progress will be slow and that his performance is likely to show wide fluctuations from day to day, some of the negative reactions can be avoided, and the child can gradually improve.

Interaction of Causative Factors

Although we have attempted for purposes of discussion to isolate the separate causes of reading disability, the authors believe that these factors rarely act independently. More often one is tangential upon the other. The entire focus then shifts, and a whole new constellation arises. Thus the interrelationships are far greater in complexity than are any of the factors taken individually. Furthermore, no matter what the significant causal factors—intellectual, physical, environmental, or emotional—failure in school will cause negative reactions to appear. As already stated, these reactions will produce emotional disturbance or heighten any that was already present. This is why there is such a preponderance of personality maladjustment found in children with reading disability.

Suppose, for example, that a child is socially immature, "whiny," and helpless. The parents are told not to overprotect or overindulge him. This may create guilt and conflict on their part and may even deprive the child of appropriate warmth and affection. He may then resort to demanding more and more attention. If this is denied, he could conceivably develop strong resistance, which would eventually lead to his not learning in school. The school failure then would create repercussions: upset in the parents, and apprehension, disappointment or dissatisfaction in the teacher, and in

---

[23] A. Silver, "Behavioral Syndrome Associated with Brain Damage in Children," *Pediatrics Clinics of North America* (Philadelphia: W. B. Saunders, 1958), pp. 687–98.

[24] R. Masland, S. Sarason, and T. Gladwin, *Mental Subnormality* (Basic Books, 1958), Ch. 7; J. Money, *Reading Disability* (Baltimore: Johns Hopkins Press, 1962), p. 14.

the child, increased anxiety and agitation due to lack of approval and con-fidence from those he wishes so much to please. All of these conditions perpetuate the circular constellation of forces.

The same repercussions might occur with a child who is developing slowly and because of growth factors fails to learn. If he has a teacher who is unfamiliar with maturational lag and who employs inappropriate methods, she can add to his problem. For example, if she requires him to blend sounds together to figure out words, he may be unable to do this because his physiological growth simply has not reached this level of integrative capacity. The frustration on the part of the teacher and the child then becomes serious. The parent, in turn, becomes anxious over the child's failure. The mother may rush out to buy popular books offering as a panacea the employment of the phonic method. She may enthusiastically begin teaching the child herself. But the learning problem by this time has become so intensified by futile, misdirected efforts that the pattern becomes extremely complicated.

Different classroom environments can have a positive or negative effect also. Consider two children who have a similar emotional disturbance and similar reading problems. One is placed in a class where provision is made for giving him each day five to ten minutes of individual attention, in which he is taught the skills he needs; the class is composed of pupils not too far ahead of him in achievement, and he is able to make progress. The other child is placed in a class where the pupils are far ahead of him in achievement; the teacher feels she should not be expected to cope with such deviant achievement. She has no time to give him special treatment. Al-though neither of these environments is aimed at curing the basic problem, it is likely that the first child will become better able to cope with school-work and may even develop a stronger ego through academic accomplish-ment, while the other is likely to recede more and more into negative patterns of defense.

Examples could be cited ad infinitum. The cause of reading disability, then, whatever its basic origin (if indeed this can be determined), is not an entity in and of itself but is interrelated with and acted upon by many factors, all of which need evaluation for the problem to be properly under-stood.

Thus we can see the interplay of both obvious and subtle forces on a child's reading ability. The complicated patterns and far-reaching con-sequences of all the varying possibilities affect the life of the child, the teacher, and the parent. The authors believe that one is never dealing here with a separate school problem or an exclusively emotional or developmental one. All these factors are interdependent and all-encompassing in their influence. The continued search for causes of reading disability will throw light on the problem and may help to avoid certain pitfalls. But, as has been stated throughout this chapter, knowledge in this area is still incomplete. New dimensions will arise, and so the quest for more definitive formulations persists as the pursuit of a broader understanding continues.

Suggestions for Further Reading

HEBB, D., *The Organization of Behavior: A Neuropsychological Theory*. New York: John Wiley & Sons, 1949.

HEILMAN, A., *Teaching Reading*. Columbus, Ohio: Charles E. Merrill, 1961, pp. 375–82.

HUNT, J., *Intelligence and Experience*. New York: Ronald Press, 1961, pp. 362 ff.

MONROE, MARION, *Children Who Cannot Read*. Chicago: University of Chicago Press, 1932.

RABINOVITCH, R., *Reading and Learning Disabilities*, in S. Arieti, *American Handbook of Psychiatry*. New York: Basic Books, 1959.

ROSWELL, FLORENCE, "Observations on Causation and Treatment of Learning Disabilities." *American Journal of Orthopsychiatry, 24*, No. 4 (1954), pp. 784–8.

SCHWEBEL, M., "Individual Differences in Learning Abilities." *American Journal of Orthopsychiatry, 33*, No. 1 (1963), pp. 60–70.

SMITH, H., and DECHANT, E., *Psychology in Teaching Reading*. Englewood Cliffs, N.J.: Prentice-Hall, 1961, Chs. 2, 11.

Selected Research on Emotional Factors

AXLINE, VIRGINIA, "Non-directive Therapy for Poor Readers." *Journal of Consulting Psychology, 11* (1947), pp. 61–9.

BILLS, R., "Non-directive Play Therapy with Retarded Readers." *Journal of Consulting Psychology, 14* (1950), pp. 140–9.

BLANCHARD, PHYLLIS, "Psychoanalytic Contributions to the Problem of Reading Disabilities." *The Psychoanalytic Study of the Child, 2* (1946), pp. 163–86.

BOUISE, LOUISE, "Emotional and Personality Problems of a Group of Retarded Readers." *Elementary English, 32* (1955), pp. 544–8.

EPHRON, BEULAH, *Emotional Difficulties in Reading*. New York: The Julian Press, 1953, Chs. 1, 6.

FABIAN, A., "Reading Disability: An Index of Pathology." *American Journal of Orthopsychiatry, 25* (1955), pp. 319–29.

GANN, EDITH, *Reading Difficulty and Personality Organization.* New York: Kings Crown Press, 1945.

GATES, A., "The Role of Personality Maladjustment in Reading Disability." *Journal of Genetic Psychology, 59* (1941), pp. 77–83.

HARRIS, I., *Emotional Blocks to Learning.* New York: The Free Press of Glencoe, 1961, Parts 1, 3.

HILGARD, E., *Theories of Learning.* New York: Appleton-Century-Crofts, 1948, Chs. 1, 12.

KUNST, MARY, "Psychological Treatment in Reading Disability." *Supplementary Educational Monographs,* No. 68. Chicago: University of Chicago Press, 1949, Ch. 7.

LISS, E., "Learning Difficulties: Unresolved Anxiety and Resultant Learning Patterns." *American Journal of Orthopsychiatry, 11* (1941), pp. 520–4.

———, "Psychiatric Implications of the Failing Student." *American Journal of Orthopsychiatry, 19* (1949), pp. 501–19.

LOUTTIT, C., "Emotional Factors in Reading Disabilities: Diagnostic Problems." *Elementary School Journal, 56* (1955), pp. 68–72.

McKILLOP, ANNE, *The Relationship between the Reader's Attitude and Certain Types of Reading Response.* New York: Teachers College, Columbia University, 1952.

MONEY, J., *Reading Disability.* Baltimore: Johns Hopkins Press, 1962, Ch. 5.

NATCHEZ, GLADYS, *Personality Patterns and Oral Reading.* New York: New York University Press, 1959, Ch. 2.

OSBURN, W., "Emotional Blocks in Reading." *Elementary School Journal, 42* (1951), pp. 23–30.

PEARSON, G., *Psychoanalysis and the Education of the Child.* New York: Norton, 1954, Part 2.

PRESTON, MARY, "Reading Failure and the Child's Security." *American Journal of Orthopsychiatry, 10* (1940), p. 252.

"Reading and the Emotions." *The Reading Teacher,* entire issue, 7 (1955).

ROBINSON, HELEN, *Why Pupils Fail in Reading.* Chicago: University of Chicago Press, 1946, Ch. 7.

RUSSELL, D., "Interrelationships of the Language Arts and Personality," in *Child Development and the Language Arts.* Research Bulletin of the National Conference on Research in English. Champaign, Ill.: National Council of Teachers of English, 1953, pp. 29–40.

SCARBOROUGH, OLIVE, *et al.,* "Anxiety Level and Performance in School Subjects." *Psychological Reports, 9* (1961), pp. 425–30.

SILVERMAN, J., FITE, MARGARETTE, and MOSHER, MARGARET, "Learning Problems." *American Journal of Orthopsychiatry, 29* (1959), pp. 298–314.

SMITH, NILA, "Research on Reading and the Emotions." *School and Society, 81* (1955), pp. 8–10.

SOLOMON, R., "Emotions and Perceptions." *Claremont College Reading Conference,* 1953, pp. 69–81.

SPACHE, G., "Personality Patterns of Retarded Readers." *Journal of Educational Research, 50* (1957), pp. 461–9.

STAUFFER, R., "Basic Problems in Correcting Reading Difficulties." *Corrective Reading in Classroom and Clinic.* Compiled and edited by Helen Robinson. *Supplementary Educational Monographs,* No. 79. Chicago: University of Chicago Press, 1953, pp. 118–26.

WHITEHORN, J., "The Concepts of Meaning and Cause in Psychodynamics." *American Journal of Psychiatry, 104* (1947), pp. 289–95.

YOUNG, N., and GAIER, E., "Implications in Emotionally Caused Reading Retardation." *Elementary English, 28* (1951), pp. 271–5.

ZOLKOS, HELEN, "What Research Says about Emotional Factors in Retardation in Reading." *Elementary School Journal, 11* (1951), pp. 512–8.

Selected Research on Developmental and Neurophysiological Factors

BAKWIN, H., "Psychiatric Aspects of Pediatrics: Lateral Dominance, Right- and Left-handedness." *Journal of Pediatrics, 36* (1950), pp. 385–91.

BARGER, W. C., LAVIN, R., and SPEIGHT, F. S., "Constitutional Aspects in Psychiatry of Poor Readers." *Diseases of the Nervous System, 18* (1957), pp. 289–94.

BENDER, LAURETTA, *Psychopathology of Children with Organic Brain Disorders.* Springfield, Ill.: Charles C Thomas, 1956.

BENTON, A., *Right-left Discrimination and Finger Localization.* New York: Hoeber, 1959.

BILLS, R. E., "Non-directive Play Therapy with Retarded Readers." *Journal of Consulting Psychology, 14* (1950), pp. 140–9.

COHN, R., "Delayed Acquisition of Reading and Writing Abilities in Children: A Neurological Study." *Archives of Neurology, 4* (1961), pp. 153–64.

DE HIRSCH, KATRINA, "Gestalt Psychology as Applied to Language Disturbance." *Journal of Nervous and Mental Disease, 120* (1954), pp. 257–61.

EAMES, T. H., *Some Neural and Glandular Bases of Learning.* Boston: Boston University School of Education, 1960.

FREUD, S., *On Aphasia.* New York: International Universities Press, 1953.

GELLHORN, E., *Physiological Foundations of Neurology and Psychiatry.* Minneapolis: University of Minnesota Press, 1953.

GESELL, A., and AMATRUDA, CATHERINE, *Developmental Diagnosis.* New York: Hoeber, 1941.

GESELL, A., ILG, FRANCES, and BULLIS, G., *Vision—Its Development in Infant and Child.* New York: Hoeber, 1941.

GOINS, J., *Visual Perception and Early Reading Progress. Supplementary Educational Monographs,* No. 87. Chicago: University of Chicago Press, 1958.

GOLDBERG, H. K., "The Ophthalmolgist Looks at the Reading Problem." *American Journal of Orthopsychiatry, 47* (1959), pp. 69–74.

GOLDSTEIN, K., *The Organism.* New York: American Book, 1939.

HINSHELWOOD, J., *Congenital Word-Blindness.* London: Lewis, 1917.

LACHMAN, F., "Perceptual Motor Development in Children Retarded in Reading Ability." *Journal of Consulting Psychology,* 24 (1960), pp. 427–31.

LANGMAN, MURIEL, "The Reading Process: A Descriptive, Interdisciplinary Approach." *Genetic Psychology Monographs,* 62 (1960), pp. 3–40.

MALMQUIST, EVE, *Factors Related to Reading Disabilities in the First Grade.* Stockholm: Almqvist & Wiskell, 1958.

MILES, T., "Two Cases of Developmental Aphasia." *Journal of Child Psychiatry* (Great Britain) June, 1961.

MONEY, J., *Reading Disability.* Baltimore: Johns Hopkins Press, 1962, Chs. 6, 7, 8, 10.

ORTON, S. T., *Reading, Writing and Speech Problems in Children.* New York: Norton, 1937.

O'SULLIVAN, M. A., and PRYLES, C. V., "Reading Disability in Children." *Journal of Pediatrics,* 60 (1962), pp. 369–75.

PENFIELD, W., and ROBERTS, L., *Speech and Brain Mechanisms.* Princeton, N.J.: Princeton University Press, 1959.

RABINOVITCH, R., DREW, A., DEJONG, R., INGRAM, W., and WITTEY, L., "A Research Approach to Reading Retardation." *Neurology and Psychiatry in Childhood,* Proceedings of the Association. Baltimore: Williams & Wilkins, 34 (1954), pp. 363–96.

SCHILDER, P., "Congenital Alexia and Its Relation to Optic Perception." *Journal of Genetic Psychology,* 65 (1944), pp. 67–88.

SILVER, A., "Postural and Righting Responses in Children." *Journal of Pediatrics,* 41 (1952), pp. 493–8.

SILVER, A., and HAGIN, ROSE, "Specific Reading Disability: Delineation of the Syndrome and Relationship to Cerebral Dominance." *Comprehensive Psychiatry,* 1 (1960), pp. 126–34.

SMITH, D., and CARRIGAN, PATRICIA, *The Nature of Reading Disability.* New York: Harcourt Brace, 1959, Ch. 2.

STATTEN, T., "Behaviour Patterns, Reading Disabilities and EEG Findings." *American Journal of Psychiatry,* 110 (1953), pp. 205–6.

STRAUSS, A., and KEPHART, N., *Psychopathology and Education of the Brain Injured Child.* New York: Grune & Stratton, 1955.

STRAUSS, A., and LEHTINEN, LAURA, *Psychopathology and Education of the Brain Injured Child.* New York: Grune & Stratton, 1947.

TIMME, A., "What Has Neurology to Offer Child Guidance?" *Neurology,* 2 (1952), pp. 435–40.

VERNON, M., *Backwardness in Reading.* London, England: Cambridge University Press, 1957, Ch. 6.

WEPMAN, J. M., "The Interrelationship of Hearing, Speech and Reading." *The Reading Teacher,* 14 (1961), pp. 245–7.

‍2

Evaluation of Reading Disability

‍ Most of the cases of reading disability are of necessity handled by teachers. Therefore this chapter deals with the approaches which a classroom teacher, remedial reading teacher, or reading consultant might use in evaluating the disability. There is only a very small proportion of cases with problems so severe that they require referral to a psychologist for diagnosis. Chapter 3 describes the type of comprehensive psychological examination which is indicated in such cases.

Investigation of Reading Disability

When a teacher suspects that a child has a reading problem, she tries to identify the contributing factors, find out if he doing as well as he is able, and discover his specific reading deficiencies. On the basis of her findings, she plans a program for remedial instruction.

Exploring Background Information

The teacher confers with any individuals who might be familiar with the child's background, such as former teachers or the school nurse. She consults available records for information regarding intelligence and achievement test results, the child's absences, number of schools attended, the school physician's notations, and other relevant matter.

In many instances such exploration might suggest the need for referral for further diagnosis and treatment. For example, if there are indications of a defect in vision, the teacher might confer with the school physician or nurse so that suitable arrangements can be made for an eye examination.[1]

---

[1] Most schools use an instrument such as the Snellen Chart for detecting difficulty in visual acuity. However, this does not identify other visual factors of causal significance, such as eye muscle imbalance, astigmatism, and so on. Some screening instruments for school use, which are more comprehensive in scope include:

Other available specialists, such as a psychologist or guidance counselor, might be consulted on the efficacy of other forms of treatment, including those that deal specifically with emotional and neurophysiological problems.

Whether or not the causative factors are alleviated, the problem of helping the child overcome his reading difficulty nevertheless remains. Thus the teacher analyzes whatever data she has and administers the necessary tests in order to understand the ways in which the reading difficulty is manifested.

Estimating Intelligence

One or more I.Q. scores are usually listed on the child's record card. In most instances, these scores are based on group tests which may or may not require reading. Those administered above third grade level usually require the ability to read. Obviously the results of such tests cannot be relied upon when given to children with reading deficiencies. Furthermore, the teacher must bear in mind that even those group intelligence tests which do not require reading yield at best an approximate estimate of intelligence. Therefore, in addition to using such ratings, the teacher can form some idea of the child's intellectual ability from his general responsiveness in class. She notes his understanding of current events and the kind of general information he has acquired from outside sources. She observes the level of insight he displays during class discussions pertaining to subject matter presented orally or visually. His ability in arithmetic computation (not arithmetic problems, which require reading) provides another indication of intellectual functioning.

Determining the Extent of the Reading Disability

By definition, a reading disability exists where there is a discrepancy of one or more years between the child's current reading level and his intel-

---

The *Keystone Visual Survey* or *Telebinocular Test,* Keystone View Co., Meadville, Pennsylvania.

The *Orthorater Test,* American Optical Co., New York.

The *Sight Screener Test,* American Optical Co., New York.

The *Massachusetts Vision Test,* Massachusetts State Department of Public Health, Welch Allyn, Inc., Boston, Mass.

For further discussion of the use of screening devices see M. Crane, R. Scobee, F. Foote, and E. Green, "Study of Procedures Used for Screening Elementary School Children for Visual Defects: Referrals by Screening Procedures *vs.* Ophthalmological Findings," *The Sight Saving Review,* 22 (1952), pp. 141–53; H. Robinson, "An Analysis of Four Visual Screening Tests at Grades Four and Seven," *American Journal of Optometry and Archives of the Academy of Optometry,* 30 (1953), pp. 177–87.

lectual level. Thus the teacher compares the pupil's intelligence with his reading level. Reading ability is more easily estimated if the teacher is familiar with a child's reading performance. From observing his classroom work, she knows which books he can read easily for pleasure and at what level he can read to obtain information. If she is uncertain about his abilities she might do well to undertake a more extensive investigation. Tests and techniques for such investigation can be chosen from those described on pages 30 ff. of this chapter.

In determining the extent of the reading disability, the teacher uses her best judgment to arrive at representative scores for both intellectual capacity and reading ability, recognizing that at best, given scores can only approximate a pupil's capabilities.

In order to ascertain the extent of the discrepancy between the child's capacity and his achievement, a simple procedure to follow is the one developed by Harris.[2] He subtracts five years from the mental age; this is the reading expectancy.[3] The teacher then compares this "expected" grade level score with the child's current achievement. If the mental age level is not available, the teacher multiplies the child's chronological age by his I.Q. to obtain it. For example, if a child is aged 10 years 6 months, and his I.Q. score is estimated as 100, multiply 10.5 (10½ years) by 1.00. (I.Q. scores are always computed in hundredths.) The result is his present mental age (M.A.). In this example, the M.A. is 10.5 (10 years 6 months). In order to determine the child's reading expectancy in terms of grade level, subtract five years from the M.A. The result— in this case 5.5—is the grade level (middle fifth grade) at which a child of the given age and intellectual capacity can be expected to read. This estimate is compared with his actual reading achievement to determine the extent of retardation.

It cannot be overemphasized that the quantitative scores and formulas for determining reading disability, although they can be useful, should not be relied on exclusively. They must always be interpreted in the light of the teacher's judgment and as much background information as can be gathered about the child so as not to neglect any child who may profit from individual reading instruction.

---

[2] A. Harris, *How to Increase Reading Ability* (New York: Longmans, Green, 1961), pp. 299 ff.

[3] It is assumed that the normal child enters kindergarten at five years of age and is not exposed to any reading instruction until first grade. Thus, the five years during which no reading achievement has been accomplished are subtracted from the M.A. The resultant figure is called the expected reading grade level, or the reading expectancy.

Analysis of Reading Achievement

Not all pupils will need the extensive reading analysis to be described in the rest of this chapter. The choice of techniques depends upon the severity of the problem that the child presents and the amount of time the teacher has available. Thus the teacher can make as simple or as detailed an investigation as is warranted. Suggestions are offered for using informal procedures when, for various reasons, standardized tests cannot be administered.

In order to obtain a comprehensive evaluation of a child's reading ability, the teacher appraises mastery of oral reading, word-analysis techniques, and silent reading. From these tests she decides at what level he can profitably handle different types of reading material. This is discussed further under "Interpreting Oral Reading Test Results" on pages 33 ff. and under "Interpreting Silent Reading Test Results" on pages 39 ff. of this chapter.

Oral Reading Tests

Oral reading tests are designed to provide an indication of the level at which the child can read, his competence in word-analysis techniques, his attitudes toward his difficulty, and his fluency, articulation, and expressiveness in reading aloud. They also suggest the level of silent reading test that should be administered. This is especially important, for the teacher or psychologist frequently has no other clue to an appropriate silent reading test. Obviously the child's chronological age and the grade in which he is enrolled are of no use as criteria, for a child of any given age may be reading at virtually any level.

Both standardized and informal instruments are available to test the pupil's ability to read aloud. Whereas standardized oral reading tests yield a grade-level score, results of the informal tests provide an approximation of the grade level at which the child can actually handle a book.

Standardized and informal tests also facilitate detailed analysis of the types of errors a child makes in oral reading. Analysis of errors can, of course, suggest his needs in remedial work. For example, examination of errors can reveal whether the child used any systematic method for figuring out unfamiliar words, what word recognition skills he has mastered, and which still need to be developed.

Standardized Oral Reading Tests

Standardized tests are convenient to use because they contain a number of paragraphs of increasing difficulty, from first grade up as high as eighth grade level, in some tests. The more familiar the teacher is with a test, the more useful it is to her. It is therefore recommended that she use the same battery regularly, particularly when retesting a group of pupils. Increasing familiarity will enable her to compare a given child's responses, not only with the standardized norms, but also with the responses of other pupils whom she has examined. This procedure helps to develop insight into the strengths and weaknesses of the instrument.

The most commonly used standardized tests of oral reading are the oral reading subtest of the *Durrell Analysis of Reading Difficulty*, new edition (grades 1–6), and of the *Gates Reading Diagnostic Tests* (grades 1–8); the *Gilmore Oral Reading Test* (grades 1–8); and the *Gray Standardized Oral Reading Paragraphs Test* (grades 1–8).[4]

Informal Oral Reading Tests

If standardized tests are not available, the teacher might devise her own instrument, choosing appropriate paragraphs from a series of graded readers or from a single book, such as Smith's *Graded Selections for Informal Reading Diagnosis*,[5] which includes material in a wide range of difficulty. If the teacher thinks that the child is reading at about second grade level, for example, she might choose three selections—one at high first, one at low second, and one at high second grade level. (If the teacher finds that she has misjudged the pupil's ability, she can of course add lower or higher level books.) The child reads aloud until he finds a book he can read with relative ease. How to judge ease of readability on informal tests is discussed in the following section.

Administering the Informal Test

It is helpful to approach the oral reading inventory (or any other testing situation) as a collaborative venture in which teacher and pupil together attempt to assess the child's strengths and weaknesses in reading

---

[4] These tests are listed and described in Appendix A, as are tests of reading readiness, spelling proficiency, silent reading, word-analysis skills, and intelligence.

[5] Nila Smith, *Graded Selections for Informal Reading Diagnosis* (New York: New York University Press, 1959).

in order to bolster the former and remedy the latter. The teacher begins by explaining the test and the reasons for giving it. She might say something like, "You know you seem to be having some trouble with reading. By listening to you read several different things, I will be able to tell which books are best for you. After you finish reading, I can show you where your greatest difficulties lie, and I'll know the kind of help you'll need. This test has nothing to do with any marks for classwork or for your report card."

The teacher might describe briefly the general content of each selection to be read. Then the child begins to read aloud at sight. If he makes more than five significant errors per 100 words,[6] he is given an easier book. Ultimately the examiner should know which book or books (if any) the child can read with ease, which with assistance, and which with difficulty or not at all.

Although many examiners ask content questions after the pupil has read aloud, the authors do not advocate this practice. Many children, particularly those with reading disability, find the mechanics of reading aloud so absorbing or trying that they are unable to attend to content, just as most adults, asked to read aloud during an eye examination, would be unable to answer detailed questions concerning the meaning of the reading matter. Some children experience such anxiety in struggling to pronounce words that they cannot possibly pay attention to their meaning, regardless of their ability to understand them. Their inability to answer questions on content is therefore not necessarily an indication of a lack of comprehension.

Recording Errors

It is important to establish a systematic method of recording errors so that the examiner can analyze the child's performance and compare it with his performance on tests administered previously or subsequently.

When a standardized oral reading test is used, a duplicate copy is usually available on which the teacher can record errors. This convenience is lacking when an informal test is used, but the teacher might request permission of the publishers to reproduce the selected passages so that

---

[6] Significant errors are renderings which are highly inaccurate and distort the meaning—i.e., *wagon* for *capon*, *family* for *father*, and so on. Mispronouncing the names of people and places is considered insignificant, as is saying *wouldn't* for *would not*, *a* for *the*, and the like.

she can mark her copy as the child is reading the material. The symbols that the authors find most convenient are presented below.[7]

> If a word or portion of a word is mispronounced or read incorrectly, it is underlined, and the word the child said is written above it.
>
> A wavy line indicates repetitions. Two or more consecutive words must be repeated one or more times to count as an error.
>
> A capital *P* is written over words that the child has failed to recognize. (After a lapse of five seconds, the teacher pronounces the word in order to minimize the child's frustration.)
>
> Omissions are encircled.
>
> Parentheses are placed around self-corrected mistakes, with the mispronunciation written above the word. These do not count as errors in scoring.
>
> A caret indicates insertions made in error.

The paragraph below illustrates the use of these symbols.

Mother said, "Now we can go to work. The house is quiet." Tom did not want to work. He wanted to go outside and play.

How to evaluate these errors is described on pages 33–35, in the section "Interpreting Oral Reading Test Results."

If the teacher cannot reproduce passages from the readers as we have suggested, she can record the child's errors on a separate sheet of paper, as follows:

Word Said	for	*Word in Book*	*Nonrecognitions*	*Repetitions*	*Insertions*
how		now	not	he wanted	to go
home		house	outside		

In addition to his errors, it is sometimes useful to record any unusual aspects of the child's behavior as he reads aloud, so that the teacher can assess the degree of discouragement that the child has experienced and his resultant attitude toward reading. If the teacher is to reduce the child's negative behavior, she must be aware not only of the mechanical aspects of his reading but also of how he feels, how he tries to cope

---

[7] These symbols have been adapted by Harris (*op. cit.*, p. 202) from those used in the *Gray Standardized Oral Reading Paragraphs Test* (see Appendix A).

with the subject, and what interactions are taking place. The teacher should understand the meaning of these reactions so that she can handle the child in the most effective way possible.

Interpreting Oral Reading Test Results

As we have implied, some mistakes on oral reading tests indicate relatively severe reading difficulty, while others need not be considered important. Merely counting the errors overlooks the most valuable part of the examination. For example, such mistakes as reading *a* for *the* or *Annie* for *Anne* and repeating a word usually do not alter meaning. Children with reading disability tend to make a large number of errors of all varieties. It is therefore wise to exercise wide latitude in interpreting mistakes as indications of proficiency level. Weighting all errors equally, regardless of their nature, yields a distorted picture of the book that the child can handle. Naturally, inaccurate reading is not desirable, but if mistakes are interpreted too rigidly, the pupil might be assigned reading material on a much lower level than is desirable in light of his maturity, interests, and need for information.

From the specific types of error that the child makes while he is reading aloud, the teacher can ascertain which techniques of word recognition the child has already mastered and which he lacks. Does the child know the basic sight words, such as *want, anyone, same,* for example? Does he have difficulty with initial consonants, combinations of consonants, or vowel sounds? Does he understand the rule for the silent *e* and the rule for double vowels? Is he able to make use of context clues, or is he just guessing wildly? With a little experience, the teacher will begin to perceive a definite pattern. She might ditto a list of the major skills and use it as a check list to indicate each pupil's deficiencies and progress. Such a list is illustrated below, based on the sequence of instruction for pupils with reading disability suggested in Chapter 5. It has been filled out to show one pupil's needs in word-analysis skills.

The teacher can also gain valuable information about the child by observing his approach to the reading material. Is it markedly different from his approach to other tests and other situations? Does the child overestimate or underestimate his ability? Is he reluctant to expose what he considers poor achievement? Many children attempt to cover up for inadequate skills. For example, a child might read accurately but repeat words or groups of words frequently. This tendency might be due to insecurity in reading, or he might be stalling for time because he cannot

CHECK LIST OF MAJOR WORD-ANALYSIS SKILLS

PUPIL'S NAME——————————

DATE——————————

SIGHT WORDS
Fails to recognize *want, talk, anyone, pull, same.*

INITIAL CONSONANTS
Needs to learn sounds of *l, h, g.*

CONSONANT COMBINATIONS
Needs to learn *tr, fl, sc, ch.*

SHORT VOWEL SOUNDS
Unfamiliar with *i, o, e.*

LONG VOWEL SOUNDS (SILENT *e* AND
DOUBLE VOWEL)
Cannot apply either rule.

SYLLABICATION
Cannot divide words into syllables.

USE OF CONTEXT
Demonstrates good use of context.

ADDITIONAL COMMENTS
Mistakes words of similar configuration.
Cooperative, willing to practice.

---

easily recognize some of the words that follow. Perhaps he often loses his place and has difficulty focusing his attention on the line. Natchez[8] investigated children's approaches to oral reading and found that hesitations, such interruptions as the child's asking, "Is that right?," long pauses with no attempt to figure out the word, and angry outbursts were related to the pupil's characteristic reactions to frustrating situations in general. Thus, observing a child during oral reading sessions can yield clues to his personality pattern. In this sense, oral reading tests can be useful projectively.

---

[8] Gladys Natchez, *Personality Patterns and Oral Reading* (New York: New York University Press, 1959).

Fluency of reading is also taken into consideration. However, the rate at which a child "should" read aloud cannot be determined. In an informal test, the teacher simply uses her judgment as to the degree of fluency. (It is true that paragraphs in standardized oral reading tests are generally timed. However, the timing factor is usually provided to yield a bonus for fluent reading rather than impose a penalty for slowness.)

Tests of Word Recognition Skills

The ability to figure out unfamiliar words is basic to all reading. Children with reading disability at all levels, even through high school, are commonly deficient in this ability. Obviously inaccurate word recognition techniques interfere seriously with reading comprehension, for misreading words changes the meaning of the material. Although some evidence of the pupil's word recognition difficulties can be gathered from oral reading tests, word-analysis tests specify the skills he lacks more precisely.

Widely used oral tests of word-analysis skills include the *Durrell Analysis of Reading Difficulty,* new edition; the *Gates Reading Diagnostic Tests;* the *Roswell-Chall Diagnostic Reading Test;* and the *Roswell-Chall Auditory Blending Test.* All these tests include items testing the pupil's knowledge of letters of the alphabet, sounds of consonants and consonant combinations, sounds of vowels and vowel combinations, and the application of this knowledge in reading words of one syllable and more. All are administered orally and individually. The Gates and Durrell tests each contain subtests for more extensive analysis of reading ability, including items on visual memory for forms and auditory blending, as well as oral and silent reading subtests. The *Roswell-Chall Diagnostic Test,* although short, yields data concerning the pupil's mastery of sounds of consonants and consonant combinations, one-syllable words, long and short vowel sounds, and syllabication. The *Roswell-Chall Auditory Blending Test* is a brief test that measures the pupil's ability to combine separate sounds to form words. There are, of course, other diagnostic tests available (see Appendix A).

When many children have to be tested and the teacher does not have the time to administer a test of word-analysis skills to each child individually, she can gain some impression of the children's basic knowledge of phonics through a group test which she can make up containing an inventory of initial consonants, consonant blends, and short vowel sounds.

The teacher can prepare a master sheet with key words to be used in associating the letter sounds to be tested. Each pupil would need a duplicate sheet, subdivided into spaces and numbered according to the way the master sheet is planned.

In presenting initial consonants, for example, the teacher might use key words such as *hill, match, table, lamp,* and so on. As she pronouunces each word, she asks the pupils to write in the designated space the letter corresponding to the very first sound they hear. She proceeds in a similar way with words that begin with consonant blends such as *spill, tree, blue, stop,* and so on. In presenting these words, she asks the children to write the first two letters that represent the sounds they hear. To judge the pupils' knowledge of short vowels, the teacher dictates words such as *bag, top, mud, sip,* and *pet.* The children are instructed to write the whole words.

The results of this informal test will give the teacher a general idea of her pupils' needs. For example, errors on the test records will reveal which pupils should be grouped for help with particular initial consonants or consonant combinations and which ones need training with certain vowel sounds. She can plan a word-analysis skills program accordingly.

Silent Reading Tests

Silent reading tests are used to determine the level at which the child can read silently with comprehension. Among the most widely used silent reading batteries are the *California Achievement Tests* (available for grades 1–2, 3–4, 4–6, 7–9, and 9–14); the *Gates Reading Tests,* revised edition (available in several versions, for grades 1–10); the *Metropolitan Achievement Tests* (for grades 1, 2, 3–4, 5–6, and 7–9); and the *Stanford Achievement Tests* (for grades 1–3, 3–4, 5–6, and 7–9). The subtests usually administered to determine the extent and nature of reading disability include paragraph meaning, vocabulary, and sometimes spelling. As we have pointed out, the results of an oral reading test suggest the level of the silent reading test to be administered subsequently. For example, if the pupil can read aloud only first grade material, a silent reading test designed for primary levels should be used, regardless of the pupil's age or grade. If his score puts him at fifth grade level in reading ability, a test designed for children reading at fifth grade level should be administered, and so on. This method of selecting silent reading tests produces a more accurate assessment of the silent reading skills of children with reading disability than does the routine administration of standardized tests chosen on the basis of the child's grade.

Interpreting Silent Reading Test Results

Some test results frequently seem to underestimate or overestimate the child's ability. Pupils whose reading ability is poor may mark items indiscriminately. The results in such cases may be more indicative of their good fortune in guessing correctly than of their proficiency in reading. Conversely, when a pupil misses many of the relatively easy items at the beginning of a test, because of initial anxiety in the test situation, but gets the harder ones right, or when he becomes so frustrated that he gives up, the score may underestimate his reading ability. Grade scores alone, therefore, do not provide sufficient information about a pupil's silent reading skills. The test results must be analyzed qualitatively for additional information that may shed light on the nature of the reading problem.

Analysis of test patterns at primary levels is somewhat different from analysis at advanced levels. At primary levels, the tests for the most part measure the degree to which the pupil uses word recognition skills and his accuracy in using them. The teacher looks for consistent errors. For example, some tests contain illustrations, each followed by a list of words of which one is the correct designation. Children may use a variety of skills in selecting the word that represents the picture. Let us suppose that a picture of a book is followed by the choices *look, bat, farm,* and *book.* If the child selects *look,* he may be using similar configuration; if he chooses *bat,* he may be relying on initial consonants; a choice of *farm* would probably indicate pure guesswork. Similar errors on sentence and paragraph reading subtests indicate which skills the child has mastered and which he still lacks. Consistency in errors suggests the area in need of instruction.

At higher levels, word recognition is still important, but comprehension plays a greater role. Thus the pupil's ability to use context influences his test results, as does the extent of his background information. Previous knowledge of the subject and adept use of context enable him to supply a particular word (or one close in meaning) even if he were unable to recognize it in isolation. For example, a pupil who uses context skillfully could probably answer questions on the following paragraph even if he were not able to recognize the italicized words.

> It's over an hour until the *scheduled* takeoff, but there is plenty for us to do. We don't have any *particular* worries about the plane. After every 900 hours of flying time each engine is *completely* rebuilt.

General background information also influences the ability to use context even when every word is known. For example, each word in the following title is probably familiar to the reader: "Experimental Study of the Quenched-In Vacancies and Dislocations in Metals"; yet without an engineering background, few can decipher its meaning. Thus the way in which a pupil answers questions may reveal deficiencies in word recognition, comprehension, use of context clues, or background. If the teacher is uncertain as to the nature of the reading problem, it might be advisable to allow the student to go beyond the time limits of the standardized test and answer as many questions as he can. (The results in this case can be used for qualitative evaluation only, not as actual test results.) If he sustains a high accuracy score, his problem is probably related to slow rate. Or the teacher might have the pupil read some of the paragraphs aloud. Discussion can help in locating where the difficulties lie.

In analyzing vocabulary subtests, it is important to try to determine whether low scores are due to poor word recognition skills, difficulty in word meaning, or slowness in handling the test. The vocabulary score on a reading test might be compared with the score obtained on the vocabulary subtest of an individually administered intelligence scale, if available. If the latter is considerably higher, it might be inferred that the lower score on the reading test was due to poor word recognition skills rather than to inability to understand meanings. If a child misreads words (e.g., *profession* for *possession*), he cannot possibly find the required synonyms. The examiner can determine whether or not this is the case by checking some of the incorrect responses orally, after the test has been completed. Pupils who appear to be deficient in vocabulary are frequently found to know the words very well when they are presented orally; the pupils simply cannot read them accurately. This, then, is evidence of word recognition difficulties—not meager vocabulary. Also, the errors might be analyzed to see whether or not they tend to occur in highly technical words related to specific subjects rather than in more general words. Even pupils who have no reading difficulties tend to miss words in areas in which their background is weak. Since many pupils with reading disability have done little or no reading in the content areas, they are likely to miss such words as *resource, ingredient,* and *metallic* with greater frequency than words of a more general character.

Upper-Level Tests

When the pupil is above sixth grade level in reading achievement, a more accurate evaluation of his silent reading skills may be obtained through the use of instruments which include subtests designed to yield percentiles in rate of reading along with comprehension, vocabulary, and other skills. Tests of this type include the *Cooperative Sequential Tests of Educational Progress—Reading* (available in forms designed for grades 4–6, 7–9, and 10–12, and for college freshmen and sophomores); the *Iowa Silent Reading Tests* (for grades 4–8 and 9 through college); the *Nelson-Denny Reading Test,* Revised (for grade 9 through college); the *Traxler Silent Reading Test* (for grades 7–10); and the *Traxler High School Reading Test* (for grades 10–12).

Additional tests are available to determine the adequacy of the pupil's study skills. If, for example, there is an unaccountable discrepancy between results on oral and on silent reading tests or between reading scores and reports from teachers, the examiner must attempt to find the possible reasons. Often lack of motivation, short attention span, or resistance to learning play as important a role as skill deficiencies. Let us consider, as an example, the case of George, an eleven-year-old boy at the beginning of the sixth grade. He is doing mediocre work in school, although his I.Q. is 115. Psychological test data has ruled out serious personality maladjustment, although there is some evidence of lack of concentration, mild anxiety, and insecurity. Achievement test scores are as follows:

Gray Standardized Oral Reading Paragraphs Test	6.2
Metropolitan Achievement Test—Intermediate	
Word Knowledge	5.9
Reading	6.4

These scores might be considered just about adequate for the grade in which George has been placed—perhaps slightly lower than one might expect in view of his intelligence, but not low enough to account for his poor schoolwork. What is holding him back? The boy is given the first two subtests of the *Iowa Silent Reading Test—Elementary,* with the following results: rate, 18th percentile; comprehension, 40th percentile. This test is a more critical measure of reading ability, since it does not permit the testee to look back at the paragraph while answering the questions. In going over this test with the pupil, the teacher learns that (1) he has difficulty when dealing with factual material, (2) he is lost when he has to choose responses without having the text in front of him, (3) his rate is very slow, and (4) he is not interested in any voluntary reading other than an occasional light short story. Remedial treatment is instituted to help him handle subject matter material more efficiently, speed up his performance, become more flexible in his reading, and support and encourage him in his schoolwork.

Spelling

Analyzing the pattern of errors on a spelling test and other written work helps the teacher to plan effective instruction for an individual child. Most standardized achievement batteries have separate spelling subtests from which the teacher can assess the level of spelling proficiency and the types of error the pupil makes. Some of the most widely used include the *Metropolitan Achievement Tests*, the *Stanford Achievement Tests*, and the *California Reading Tests*. Other batteries as well as specific spelling tests are listed in Appendix A. Quantitative analysis of the results will indicate the level at which to start instruction; qualitative analysis, the skills that should be emphasized for each child.

Errors generally fall into the following categories: lack of knowledge of phonic elements, spelling nonphonetic words phonetically, omitting or adding syllables, reversing or transposing letters, and other misspellings too inconsistent to classify. If errors are due to inadequate phonic skills, the examiner can discover the child's areas of weakness by inspecting results on the previously administered diagnostic test of word-analysis skills. Where words with irregular spelling are written phonetically, the examiner should try to determine whether the child is able to learn nonphonetic words by the visual-motor method (described on pages 43–44). If the child shows considerable difficulty learning the words this way, the kinesthetic method (see pages 82–83) should be tried. (Treatment of spelling problems is discussed in Chapter 5.)

Trial Lessons as a Diagnostic Technique

When formal testing has been completed and the results analyzed, a fairly clear picture of the child's achievement pattern should emerge. Essential as it is to administer these standardized tests, the teacher or examiner still does not know, at their conclusion, which methods and materials to recommend for remedial instruction. Also, the child himself has little understanding of what is actually wrong with his reading and in all probability remains apprehensive about his difficulty. The teacher tries to relieve the pupil's anxiety in any way she deems appropriate. It is also vital that the teacher and pupil discover ways in which he can overcome his problem. Enlisting the pupil's participation not only is therapeutic in and of itself, but it serves as powerful motivation for future learning in remedial sessions and in school. Therefore, trial lessons are recommended as an integral part of the diagnostic examination to give the teacher a definite guide as to which procedures will be most effective and to demonstrate to the pupil those methods most suited to his learning.[9]

In contrast to the controlled standardized test situation, trial lessons are conducted in an informal, spontaneous atmosphere. The teacher tells the pupil that there are several methods and many kinds of reading matter especially designed to teach those who have difficulty similar to his. Several appropriate readers or stories are made available to the pupil.[10] He chooses any he wishes. The teacher and pupil try them out to decide which ones are most suitable. In presenting reading materials, the teacher encourages the pupil to react as freely as possible and designate which stories he likes and dislikes. When the pupil realizes that he can really say that a selection is dull or uninteresting, he often experiences immense relief at finding someone who understands how he feels. No longer does he have to resist, suffer, or pretend that he likes meaningless exercises.

The teacher observes whether the pupil is slow or quick to grasp salient points, whether he needs a great deal of repetition, support, and encouragement, how well he recalls what he has read, how much effort he puts forth, and so on. However, the whole session is a collaborative one. The teacher explains which techniques seem suitable and helps the pupil understand his problem. The more insight a pupil gains, the more likely it is that he will summon the strength he needs to improve. Trial lessons contribute to such insight in a way that the regular test situation cannot. They may be used with pupils at all levels, from beginning reading through high school. The areas to be investigated at the different stages can be divided roughly into reading levels 1 through 3, 4 through 6, 7 through 9, and 10 through 12.

Reading Levels 1 through 3

For a nonreader or one who has mastered a minimum of word-analysis techniques, the three major word-recognition approaches—visual, phonic, and visual-motor[11]—should be tried. If none of these methods is success-

---

[9] Trial lessons geared to children reading at primary levels were developed by Albert J. Harris and Florence G. Roswell and published in Harris and Roswell, "Clinical Diagnosis of Reading Disability," *Journal of Psychology*, 3 (1953), pp. 323–40. The present authors have revised and extended these lessons upward for older pupils.

[10] The teacher can choose selections from the list of books in Appendix B.

[11] All of these methods are fully described in Chapter 5. The teacher should be familiar with the way in which each method is taught. However, for use as a diagnostic technique, they are summarized succinctly in this chapter.

ful, the kinesthetic approach might be used.[12] (If it is found that the child can learn by only one of these methods, it is used in treatment merely as a starting point to ensure a successful experience. Before long it must be supplemented by other procedures because a successful reader needs a variety of techniques at his command.) In addition to finding suitable methods for word recognition, the teacher offers several readers or short stories to find the type of reading material that is most acceptable to the child. (See Appendix B for appropriate books at primary levels.)

Visual Method

The simple visual approach to word recognition involves learning words by means of picture clues. If the child reads at a second grade level or above, this procedure is omitted, for it has already been established that he is able to use this method.

Several cards are needed, each with a picture illustrating a well-known object, like a book, man, coat, and so on. The identifying noun is printed under the picture. On another set of cards the words are printed without pictures. The child is first tested on the cards with the word alone to make sure that he does not already know them. After the unknown words are selected, the teacher presents a picture card, pointing to the word and pronouncing it. The child is asked to say the word several times while looking at it. He then finds the corresponding nonillustrated card containing the same word. After five words have been studied in this manner, the child is tested with the nonillustrated cards. (If time allows, he is retested after a short interval.)

If the child can grasp a visual procedure readily and shows some knowledge of letter sounds, the teacher immediately proceeds with Step One of the phonic approach.

Phonic Approach

STEP ONE: WORD-FAMILY METHOD. A rudimentary blending technique, sometimes called the word-family method, is especially useful with children who are not yet able to cope with a letter-by-letter blending procedure. It affords a limited degree of independence in word analysis. For example, a known word such as *book* may be changed into *took*, *look*, or *hook* by substituting different initial consonants. Several initial consonants are taught, studied, and combined with the appropriate word ending. Other words

---

[12] The kinesthetic method is described on p. 82. It will not be described here because it is a laborious way to learn and requires continued individual instruction.

learned in the visual lesson may be developed in the same way: *boat, goat.* If the child cannot learn initial sounds readily, he needs practice in auditory discrimination of letter sounds (see pages 86–87) before he can profit from the word-family or phonic method.

STEP TWO: COMBINING SEPARATE SOUNDS. In order for a pupil to master the phonic method, he must be able to combine separate sounds to form whole words. To determine this, the teacher first tries an informal auditory blending test without written words. She pronounces one syllable words slowly and distinctly, emphasizing each sound as *c-a-p,* and so on. The child tries to distinguish the word from the separate sounds. She tries several other words in this way. If the child can figure them out, he has the ability to combine sounds, and it is safe to try the phonic approach.

The teacher reviews the sounds taught under Step One and then introduces a short vowel sound. For example, she prints the letter *a,* telling the pupil its name and short sound—"ă" as in *apple.* She then prints a suitable word, like *fat,* to demonstrate how the vowel can be blended with known consonant sounds to form words. Several different consonants are then substituted at the beginning of the word as in Step One. After the child practices them sufficiently, the teacher changes the final consonants, i.e., *fat* to *fan, mat* to *man, sat* to *sad,* and so on and asks the child to sound them out. If the pupil has difficulty, he is assisted in blending the sounds together. The teacher then proceeds to a more difficult step: interchanging initial and final consonants alternately. Finally, the teacher presents the most difficult step of all—reading words in mixed order: *mat, fan, sad, bat,* and so on. The degree to which the pupil is able to recognize the words in these progressive steps indicates the kind and amount of phonics work that he will need in remedial sessions.

Visual-Motor Method

To determine whether a child is able to recall nonphonetic words, the visual-motor method should be tried. The teacher chooses about three words with which the child is unfamiliar (about five to seven letters in length), such as *garage, night,* and *science.* She presents each word separately as follows:

She prints the word *garage* on a card and tells the child what the word is. She suggests that the pupil look at it carefully and then shut his eyes and try to see the word distinctly with his eyes closed because he will be asked to write it from memory. He opens his eyes and takes another look if necessary. The teacher asks him to name the word so as to remember it.

Sometimes it is necessary to show the card several times before he sees the word clearly enough to write it. The card is then removed and the child writes the word from memory. If he has much difficulty with one particular word, another should be tried. If he reproduces the word correctly, he writes it several times, covering up the words he has previously written so as to be sure he is recalling the word from memory rather than merely copying it. Other words are taught in a similar manner. After a period of time has elapsed, the words should be reviewed.

At the conclusion of the session, both pupil and teacher have a fairly clear picture of the methods which may be used successfully in teaching word recognition and which book or books he prefers to use for reading.

Reading Levels 4 through 6

For pupils reading at fourth through sixth grade levels and whose ages probably range from ten to seventeen years, trial lessons include investigation of advanced word-analysis techniques, comprehension skills, and reading material best suited to the pupil's reading level and interest. As already stated, it is especially important to have appealing reading material so that the pupil will become more involved in helping to improve his reading ability.

If the results of standardized tests indicate deficiency in phonics, he is shown how he will be taught any sounds or combinations that he does not know. If the pupil has difficulty with spelling, the visual-motor method is demonstrated to him as a means of studying troublesome words. In addition, the teacher evaluates the pupil's knowledge of specialized vocabulary (the technical words connected with the separate subject areas). She selects about ten words from the pupil's texts. Words from a social studies text might include *hemisphere, glacier, latex, primitive.* If the pupil is unfamiliar with them, the teacher shows him how they can be learned through various methods. The meaning is explained, if necessary, through graphic illustrations or vivid explanation. The pupil finds out how learning the specialized words connected with his different subjects can be a big boost in understanding his studies. He realizes that to some extent at least it was not the text he had so much difficulty with, but simply that the special vocabulary was unfamiliar to him.

The teacher has available a number of comprehension materials such as *Standard Test Lessons in Reading, New Practice Readers,* and *EDL Study Skills Library.*[13] The level of the material is determined by the pupil's per-

---

[13] See Appendix C for these and other suitable comprehension materials under "Materials for Vocabulary and Comprehension Skills."

formance on standardized tests. The pupil is told that such selections will help him understand his textbooks better, since they incorporate factual reading. As soon as he learns how to get information from the articles, he will be shown in future lessons how to transfer these skills to his textbooks. The teacher and the pupil glance through the materials so as to determine the pupil's preferences. It is important to discover which workbooks a pupil likes, which ones he may have already used in school, and if so, whether he has grown tired of them. Since there is a wide choice of appropriate materials, the pupil is encouraged to find those which he can readily accept.

In the same way the pupil samples recreational reading that has been carefully chosen. Stories can be selected from those listed at intermediate levels in Appendix B. The experienced teacher usually has a few excellent ones which she knows from past experience are apt to arouse the pupil's interest.

However, at times the pupil may not like any selections too well. He may have developed such intense distaste for reading that everything seems tiresome and uninteresting. In these cases, it is well that he receive some immediate reassurance so that future remedial sessions have a better chance of succeeding. The teacher might state that she has known other pupils who felt this way. To help him overcome his dislike, certain procedures will be tried. For example, very short selections will be used as a start. Secondly, many different topics will be chosen; sooner or later something will appeal to him.

In the end, the pupil should have a clear idea of any word-analysis or comprehension skills that he needs and the kinds of material that he will be using for remedial instruction. When he completes the session, he should have become fairly confident that, with such help, he can improve his reading and progress with less difficulty in school.

Reading Levels 7 through 9

Pupils with reading disability whose scores on reading tests range from seventh through ninth grade levels are probably between the ages of 13 and 18 years, with a wide range in intelligence, maturity, and interests.

A brief period might profitably be spent by answering the questions that must be uppermost in the student's mind. Even more than younger pupils, he wants to know the outcome of the examination, the meaning of his test scores, and above all, by what manner and means he can be helped.

The structure of the session and the procedures used are essentially the same as those described for pupils reading between fourth and sixth grade levels. However, the presentation is on a more mature level, and the materials selected are those designed for the pupil's level of functioning.

Reading Levels 10 through 12

As described above, this student is also very much interested in receiving an interpretation of his test results and finding out how he might be helped.

His major problems are likely to center around a slow rate of reading and lack of flexibility in handling different kinds of material. The teacher then describes what methods and materials might be used to good advantage. As the student looks over the workbooks, he finds that they contain articles which have been condensed from high school and college texts. He sees how practice with factual articles followed by pertinent questions will prove valuable in handling his own texts, as it will enable him to learn how to extract information quickly and efficiently.

The student is usually struck by the abundance of material available for high school and college students, specially designed to help university students in the many reading centers throughout the country. The effect is usually electric. He wants to know what has helped them and how he can proceed. Perhaps it has never before occurred to him that so many others have similar problems.

The teacher explains that articles with different formats, varying lengths, and many types of questions will help him shift his pace from one kind of reading matter to another. His rate of reading will be guided according to purpose, and he will thus develop flexibility.

If he reveals anxiety about working within time limits, he is assured that this is a fairly common concern. Even though most students are bothered at first by the use of a stop watch, after a while they get so accustomed to it they do not notice it. Finally, the teacher gives the student some idea of the methods he may adopt in order to speed up his reading. (These are discussed in Chapter 9.)

At the conclusion of the session, the teacher as well as the student has an overview of the program that will be devised on the basis of his particular needs. The student knows where to begin and how to go ahead. He is more aware of how much depends on his own efforts even though he will be given all the assistance possible. Having his problem interpreted and described in concrete fashion often offers him added incentive and encouragement.

In this way, trial lessons at all levels are extremely helpful in preparing the pupil for remedial instruction. Instead of leaving the examination with a vague feeling of "something's wrong with my reading," he knows what is wrong. He has been shown in which areas he needs help. It has been demonstrated that he can overcome his difficulties, and he has seen the specific methods and materials which are available. Gradually, as the pupil recognizes his problem and understands what he can do about it, he becomes more hopeful. His anxiety is lessened, and the foundation is laid for effective remedial treatment.

Suggestions for Further Reading

AUSTIN, MARY, BUSH, C., and HUEBNER, MILDRED, *Reading Evaluation*. New York: Ronald Press, 1961, Ch. 1.

BLAIR, G., *Diagnostic and Remedial Teaching*, rev. ed. New York: Macmillan, 1956, Ch. 2.

BRUECKNER, L., and BOND, G., *The Diagnosis and Treatment of Learning Difficulties*. New York: Appleton-Century-Crofts, 1955, Chs. 4, 6.

CHALL, JEANNE, "Ask Him to Try on the Book for Fit." *The Reading Teacher*, 7, (1953), pp. 83–8.

"Diagnosis of Reading Problems with Classroom Materials." *The Reading Teacher*, entire issue, *14* (1960), No. 1.

DOLCH, E., *A Manual for Remedial Reading*. Champaign, Ill.: Garrard Press, 1955, Ch. 4.

———, "How to Diagnose Children's Reading Difficulties by Informal Classroom Techniques." *The Reading Teacher*, 6 (1953), pp. 10–4.

DURRELL, D., *Improving Reading Instruction*. Tarrytown-on-Hudson, N.Y.: World Book, 1956, Ch. 5.

DYER, H., "Is Testing a Menace to Education?" *New York State Education*, 49 (1961), pp. 16–9.

"Evaluations of Reading Instruction." *The Reading Teacher*, 15, No. 5, entire issue (1962).

GATES, A., *The Improvement of Reading*. New York: Macmillan, 1947, Chs. 3, 6.

McCRACKEN, R., "Standardized Reading Tests and Informal Reading Inventories." *Education*, 82 (1962), pp. 366–9.

ROBINSON, HELEN M., ed., "Evaluation of Reading," *Proceedings of the Annual Conference on Reading*, Supplementary Monographs No. 88. Chicago: University of Chicago Press, 1958.

WOOLF, M., and WOOLF, J., *Remedial Reading*. New York: McGraw-Hill, 1955, Ch. 3.

𝒆 3

Diagnosis:
The Psychologist's Approach

𝒆 The reading disability cases which come to the attention of the psychologist are usually those which have not responded to educational procedures or who show deviant behavior. Thus the psychologist conducts a comprehensive diagnostic examination and investigates those factors which may be significant in the causation of the problem.

Since the examination presumably will be carried out by an experienced psychologist, the procedures and tests which are used routinely by psychologists will simply be mentioned here. Only those aspects of psychological testing which are especially pertinent to reading disability cases will be discussed at length. As recommendations for treatment add considerably to the usefulness of the findings, they are included in this chapter.

Areas of Investigation
Background Information

The psychologist gathers the pertinent background information required for a complete case history. To determine the possibility of neurological impairment, maturational lag, basic emotional disturbance, or poor educational training, he obtains as complete a developmental history as possible, paying special attention to (a) birth and early infancy, with special reference to the possibility of organic brain injury; (b) speech development; (c) early school experiences and attitudes; (d) present school experiences and attitudes; (e) attitude toward reading; (f) possibility of converted handedness; (g) attitude of the family toward the disability; (h) amount and kind of help that has been provided by the family and the school; (i) presence of similar or related difficulties in other members of the family; and (j) recreational and cultural interests and attitudes of the child and family.[1] For example, he asks the mother when the child cut his first tooth, sat up, stood, walked, said his first word, and put two or more words together. Is there any evidence of delayed speech or of any difficulty in articulation or enunciation? What childhood diseases, accidents, or unusually high temperatures did the child suffer? Is there evidence of awkwardness, clumsiness, or poor coordination? Which hand did and does the child prefer? Was any attempt made to convert him from left- to right-handedness? He makes sure that all possible visual defects have been or will be investigated at an eye clinic or by an individual specialist. The psychologist also asks whether the child was full term or premature, whether labor was prolonged or especially difficult, whether high or low forceps were used, whether there was any injury at birth, and whether there was any illness during pregnancy.[2] He is particularly interested in knowing whether there was any difficulty in establishing respiration at birth, because even short periods of oxygen deprivation can cause damage to the brain cells.[3] This can directly cause reading disability. He also looks for a history of difficulty in sucking and swallowing or of convulsive seizures.

School attitudes are important too, beginning with the child's reaction toward nursery school, kindergarten, first grade, and so forth, as well as his teachers' impressions and the child's attitudes toward his teachers. It is also useful to know the parents' attitude toward the child's disability, his teachers, and current educational methodology. Many parents are extremely critical of modern methods of teaching reading and of teachers, too. This information is frequently important, not only because it offers insight into parental attitudes, but also because it may reveal the ways in which the child was handled at school and at home. Even the distortions and misconceptions of parents may shed light on the problem.

Of course, evidence of severe emotional disturbance is investigated, particularly disturbance which developed before the child entered school. Such symptoms as enuresis, feeding problems, recurrent nightmares, stuttering, excessive fearfulness, and phobic reactions offer important diagnostic clues

[1] Albert J. Harris and Florence Roswell, "Clinical Diagnosis of Reading Disability," *Journal of Psychology, 36* (1953), pp. 323–40.

[2] A. Kawi and B. Pasamanick, "The Association of Factors of Pregnancy with the Development of Reading Disorders in Childhood," *Journal of the American Medical Association, 166* (1958), pp. 1420–3.

[3] A. Gesell and Catherine Amatruda, *Developmental Diagnosis* (New York: Hoeber, 1941), Ch. 2.

to the possible origin and degree of the emotional disturbance. As mentioned in Chapter 1, it is important to determine to the extent possible whether the reading problem was primarily affected by personality maladjustment or whether the emotional disturbance is a reaction to the reading failure itself.

Intelligence

It is important, first, to establish as valid a measure of intelligence as possible. Verbal and performance tests are usually selected at appropriate levels from the well-known *Wechsler Intelligence Scale for Children*,[4] the *Stanford-Binet, Wechsler-Bellevue, Wechsler Adult Intelligence Scale, Cornell-Coxe, Arthur Point Scales,* and other tests. In order to arrive at a rough approximation of the extent of the disability, a comparison must be made between the child's reading achievement and his potential, which indicates a measure known as his "reading expectancy" (see Chapter 2)—a score derived by subtracting five years from the child's mental age. (A child with a mental age of ten would be considered capable of reading at about fifth grade level.) As discussed more fully in Chapter 2, reading expectancy scores must always be interpreted broadly since they are influenced by the amount of schooling and the degree of experience of the child as well as the probable errors of measurements on the tests involved. For example, a seven-year-old child with a mental age of ten years can only in theory be expected to read as well as the average ten-year-old, because he has not had the same amount of schooling or comparable years of experience. He would, however, be expected to read considerably better than the average seven-year-old pupil.

Physical Factors

Physical problems may directly or indirectly influence a child's ability to focus his attention on learning. Therefore, a medical examination is always indicated to determine whether any physical condition may be causing or contributing to the learning problem.

The responsibility of the psychologist in these connections varies with the parent's ability to arrange for medical diagnosis and carry through on recommendations. The psychologist must decide the type of referral indicated, whether to a private physician or a medical clinic. It is important

---

[4] All tests mentioned in this chapter are listed in Appendix A.

in any case that relevant findings be reported to the psychologist so that he can integrate all the diagnostic information.

Assessing Neurophysiological Development

As described in Chapter 1, there can be varying irregularities in neuro-physiological growth. If a child shows extremely deviant development or where frank brain damage is suspected, naturally he should be referred for a neurological examination. If such an examination is not feasible, or if it is undertaken and reveals inconclusive results, the responsibility for evaluation often reverts back to the psychologist. Psychological tests have come to be used widely for diagnosis of cerebral functioning principally because the conventional neurological examination may fail to detect many aspects of the injury, particularly if it is minimal. Psychological instruments to measure the child's abilities in these areas are usually selected from certain verbal and performance items on individual intelligence scales and from other special tests. Some of those most helpful in this connection are certain items included on individual intelligence tests. Some of these tests are the *Block Design, Memory for Designs, Coding or Digit-Symbol, Object Assembly, Repetition of Digits,* and *Copying a Diamond.* Also, the *Rorschach, Human Figure Drawings, Bender Visual-Motor Gestalt, Benton Revised Visual Retention Tests, Ellis Visual Designs, Werner Marble-Board Test, Raven's Progressive Matrices, Archimedes Spiral After-Image Test, Harris Tests of Lateral Dominance,* and others according to the preference of the psychologist.

In observing the child's reactions on these tests, the psychologist pays particular attention to the child's perceptual functioning, analytic-synthetic ability, visual-motor coordination, grasp of spatial relationships, figure-ground differentiation, orientation problems, visual and other aspects of memory, attention span, abstract thinking, and associative learning. Impairment of ability in any of these functions may be diagnostically significant of neurological malfunctioning.[5]

Differential Diagnosis between Maturational Lag and Minimal Brain Damage

The psychologist is faced with a particularly delicate task when attempting to differentiate between minimal brain damage and maturational lag.

---

[5] N. Goldenberg, "Testing the Brain-injured Child with Normal I.Q.," in A. Strauss and N. Kephart, *Psychopathology and Education of the Brain-injured Child* (New York: Grune & Stratton, 1955), 2, pp. 144–64.

This is because maturational lag or delayed development is found in all gradations ranging from mild to severe, where it becomes indistinguishable from minimal brain injury. However, even without arriving at a differential diagnosis, the psychologist can still make a solid contribution toward understanding the nature of the child's learning problem by analyzing the degree to which he shows difficulty on those tests mentioned above that are commonly used to detect neurophysiological defects. It is imperative that he explore this area as thoroughly as possible, since his evaluation will be crucial in determining prognosis and treatment procedures. Thus, in considering performance on these tests, the psychologist tries to assess qualitatively in what way and to what extent any atypical reactions related to perception, analytic-synthetic ability, and the other factors mentioned will interfere with learning to read.[6] In addition to psychological tests, informal procedures to determine auditory blending ability furnish valuable clues regarding the child's integrative capacity. This would be reflected in his ability to synthesize sounds together to form whole words. This is discussed in detail in Chapter 5.

Extreme caution is always exercised with regard to diagnosis and prognosis in this area, because cases of irregular or delayed maturation or brain damage are unpredictable. Fortunately, developmental factors favor growth in the organism so that abilities that were lacking at the time of examination can emerge at a later time in the life of the child. (The case of Frank in Chapter 10 illustrates this point.)

Educational Factors

School has a major influence on the youngster's development, because he spends so great a portion of his life there. Such experiences as frequent moves from school to school, absences, or shifts in teachers have an obvious effect. In considering other school influences, it is advisable in some cases to observe the child while he is engaged in academic and free-time school activities with particular focus on his interpersonal relationships in the classroom. Does the teacher disparage him or tacitly insult him by ignoring him? Is she able to handle the pupil's deviant achievement or behavior within the group? Is the child affronted by being given babyish reading matter and, in addition, ashamed of bringing it home?

In school observations, the skilled psychologist is always aware of the role

---

[6] A. Harris and Florence Roswell, *op. cit.*; A. Silver and Rosa Hagin, "Specific Reading Disability: Delineation of the Syndrome and Relationship to Cerebral Dominance," *Comprehensive Psychiatry*, 1 (1961), pp. 126–34.

played by covert attitudes. Here his understanding of dynamic human relationships can prove invaluable. Observation also aids the psychologist in
gaining perspective as to the weight that each contributing factor may have.
Here he may see the child's characteristics as he is influenced by and
interacts with his classmates, the teacher, and the required schoolwork.
From the teacher, he may also acquire information regarding the parents'
attitudes toward the child's poor schoolwork and toward the child himself.
For example, consider twelve-year-old Ralph, who is repeating sixth grade.
His teacher keeps threatening to fail him this year, too, in order to "wake
him up." She has told the principal that she really does not expect to do so
but fears that if Ralph is sure he is being promoted he will stop working.
If the psychologist had been aware of this procedure, he might have worked
with the teacher toward a sounder method of motivating Ralph. If this
teacher's methods worked, what would be the implications from the stand-
point of the child and the teacher? Would the child have learned to work
only when a crisis was at hand? What is happening to his attitudes toward
learning and its ultimate values?

What part do parents play in all the interactions related to school? Are
they resentful of what they regard as the school's role in their youngster's
failure? As one mother complained, "It's a sad commentary on the schools
today that they cannot teach my child how to read." Are they indignant
about the fact that "none of the other children have this trouble?"

If the psychologist discovers that the parents are very authoritative and
that their attitudes distress the child, is the distress intensified by the school
situation? Or if the child is repressed, is this condition sufficient to make all
attempts to teach him futile?

In assessing school adjustment, the psychologist must also take into account any additional help the child may be obtaining. If he is receiving
remedial instruction, for example, what kind of help is it? Are sound procedures being used? What is the child's attitude toward the remedial
teacher? Is he profiting from the assistance? If not, does the problem lie in
the child, the teaching techniques, or the teacher? Is the teacher qualified
for remedial work? Has she been given adequate materials, or is the remedial
program a makeshift arrangement to satisfy a directive from the administration? How are the teacher's attitudes affecting the child? The answers to
these questions can explain why remedial treatment is or is not helpful.

Thus the psychologist observes the child in a variety of situations and
acquaints himself with as many aspects of the child's school life as possible.
Insights gained from such knowledge can aid him in working out with the

teacher ways to help the child in class, to provide additional treatment, or whatever else is needed.

Even where drastic change of procedure cannot be instituted, the psychologist can be of enormous help by explaining to the teacher, parents, and wherever appropriate to the child himself what is aggravating the problem and what might be done about it. Consider, for example, the case of Charles, a twelve-year-old boy in the seventh grade. With an I.Q. of 108, Charles barely reads at fifth grade level and is failing all his subjects. He was referred to a child guidance clinic for diagnosis. No gross physical defects were found, but there was some indication of immaturity, dependence, and fear of the father. Charles' parents were extremely concerned about the boy, who was an only child, and were willing to do everything possible to help him. However, the father became very anxious when he saw the child's failing reports and threatened to beat Charles if he did not improve. Investigation of his school behavior showed that Charles had been guilty of some forty minor infractions that year, such as sharpening pencils when he was not supposed to do so and not bringing in homework on time. He was the lowest achiever in the class. The only other seventh grade class to which he could be transferred consisted of boys with severe behavior problems, and it was felt that he might be influenced adversely by them. In Charles' case, circumstances did not permit the institution of major changes, but the situation was relieved to the extent that the child had a chance to make some progress in school. The result was better marks and fewer violations of the rules. The teacher was helped to find alternate ways of handling Charles in class. At a conference, the psychologist suggested that the reason for Charles' neglect of homework was that he just could not do it. He sharpened pencils because the work was so far above him that he became restless. Simpler books and materials were therefore supplied so that the teacher could give more realistic assignments to him.

In addition, the psychologist explained to Charles that he had probably had difficulty learning in the beginning because he had not been able to distinguish letters and sounds as well as many children of his age could. This caused him to fall farther and farther behind until he had become "lost." However, he could now profit from the kind of work the teacher would give him. This would help him to "catch up" in reading. Such explanations helped to lessen Charles' tendency to blame himself, made him grasp the problem better, decreased some of his apprehension, and made him more amenable to cooperation with the teacher.

Interpreting the boy's problems to his parents relieved some of their anxiety also. As Charles' marks improved, his parents became less and less apprehensive. Had the school situation not been investigated, few practical recommendations could have been offered and little could have been accomplished.

Emotional Factors

In assessing emotional factors in children with reading disability, it has often been assumed that such children suffer from an emotional disturbance which must be cleared up through some form of psychotherapy before they can benefit optimally from reading instruction.[7] This assumption is highly questionable not only because our theoretical framework is as yet on shaky foundations,[8] but because a great number of children with reading disability may be displaying emotional disturbance as a direct reaction to their poor schoolwork.[9] In addition, poor performance in school reinforces and intensifies any emotional disturbance that was already present. Illustrations of such developments have been implied throughout this chapter. Yet psychologists who have been trained in personality diagnosis, with little or no emphasis on educational problems, continue to investigate the behavior patterns, unconscious conflicts, and defenses of the child with reading disability in the same fashion as they do emotionally disturbed children who are free from academic problems. This sometimes has led to incomplete and distorted results because (1) a child who is not able to succeed in an area as crucial to his well-being as school is under a constant threat to his ego. The results of such threat can cause as great a constellation of personality disturbances as any other anxiety-provoking situation. (2) If poor schoolwork is the seat of the anxiety, psychotherapy alone, useful though it may be, may not be able to reach the crux of the problem. Furthermore, the longer the poor reading persists, the worse the personality disturbance is likely to become. (3) It is entirely possible that one set of factors in a child may cause the emotional disturbance, while quite another set may cause the reading disability.[10] Thus the most faithfully exe-

---

[7] Phyllis Blanchard, "Psychoanalytic Contributions to the Problem of Reading Disabilities." *The Psychoanalytic Study of the Child,* 2 (1946), pp. 169–74; Mary Kunst, "Psychological Treatment in Reading Disability," *Clinical Studies in Reading,* I. Supplementary Educational Monographs, No. 163 (Chicago: University of Chicago Press, 1949), pp. 133–40.

[8] G. Murphy, *Personality* (New York: Harper & Brothers, 1947), Ch. 41.

[9] G. Bond and M. Tinker, *Reading Difficulties: Their Diagnosis and Correction* (New York: Appleton-Century-Crofts, 1957), pp. 110–11.

[10] R. Challman, "Personality Maladjustments and Remedial Reading," *Journal of Exceptional Children,* 6 (1939), pp. 7–11; J. Whitehorn, "The Concepts of Meaning and Cause in Psychodynamics," *American Journal of Psychiatry,* 104 (1947), p. 289.

cuted personality descriptions, accurate though they may be, may have little or no relationship to the cause of the reading disability and be of no help in diagnosing or treating it. This can result in years of mismanagement of the problem.[11] (4) Doing nothing about the reading problem because psychotherapy is being inaugurated, or awaiting psychotherapy which is difficult to implement due to the well-known factors of lack of facilities, inability to pay, resistance on the part of the child or his parents, and the like, can waste years of valuable time. In the interim, schoolwork can become worse and worse.

Therefore, the psychologist's main concern is not merely to find out whether there is or is not evidence of emotional disturbance in the child with a reading disability; signs of emotional disturbance will be his most likely discovery. What has to be assessed is (1) the nature, degree, and complexity of the emotional problem itself; (2) the ways in which the emotional maladjustment is related to the reading disability or is reinforcing it; (3) how it may have arisen; whether it antedates the reading problem or is reactive to it; (4) whether it has arisen as a reaction to other causal factors such as physical immaturity, neurological impairment, or unfavorable environmental or educational circumstances; (5) how it may affect future school achievement. Results from such assessment can help to decide whether psychotherapy is or is not indicated; whether it should serve as one facet of treatment along with remediation and consideration of environmental adjustments in school and at home; or whether remedial treatment alone is sufficient.

The case of Paul, described below, may highlight the difficulty of making a diagnosis concerning the basic cause of failure to learn to read. It was eventually discovered that Paul's difficulty was neurological in nature. However, because of the unmistakable presence of psychogenic factors, Paul's reading disability was at first treated primarily as an emotional problem.

Paul was 8 years 11 months old when he was first referred for diagnosis. He was repeating second grade because of his extreme difficulty in learning to read. (Reading was at high first grade level.) His birth and developmental history were within the normal range. His speech had been somewhat immature until the age of seven. There was no indication of neurological impairment on any of the psychological tests. The reading tests revealed that he had marked difficulty in synthesizing sounds to form words, a strong tendency to reverse letters, such as *b* for *d*, and a tendency to confuse left and right. Tests of laterality showed consistent right-hand and right-eye

[11] R. Rabinovitch, A. Drew, R. DeJong, W. Ingram, and L. Witty, "A Research Approach to Reading Retardation," in R. McIntosh and C. Hare, eds., *Neurology and Psychiatry in Childhood* (Baltimore: Williams & Wilkins, 1954), pp. 363–96.

dominance. Projective tests revealed Paul to be very dependent and immature, with a great deal of anxiety and an extremely weak ego. In addition, it was learned that Paul's mother was overprotective and very controlling. Because the problem seemed to be primarily due to emotional factors, psychotherapy was instituted.

After one year, no appreciable improvement had taken place. Paul still read at a high first grade level, although he was scheduled to enter third grade the following fall. Diagnostic instruments that had not previously been used were administered to search further for possible causes. The *Kohs Block Design Test*, the *Knox Cube Test* from the *Arthur Point Scale*, and the *Benton Visual Retention Test* were administered. His poor performance on some of these tests strongly pointed to the possibility of neurologic impairment. Most revealing of all was Paul's continued inability to blend sounds, his faulty memory, and his tendency to confuse and reverse letters in reading and writing. He repeatedly transposed sequences in writing, such as *rnu* for *run*, *hwo* for *who*, and even *Plau* for *Paul*. Therefore, a complete neurological examination was undertaken. The findings of this examination, which included an electroencephalogram, were positive. The results of this investigation further suggested that Paul's emotional problems—his insecurity, immaturity, weak ego, and anxiety—were probably reactions to neurologic disorder. This is one example of many cases which "are treated as primary emotional disturbances where the neurological examination shows unequivocal evidence of central nervous system abnormalities."[12] Paul was subsequently placed in a class for brain-injured children where special educational techniques were employed. This example is but one of many which shows the advantage in using all the means at the psychologist's disposal to ensure an accurate estimate of emotional factors.

The tests for investigation of emotional factors in children with reading disability are the same as those customarily used. They include the *Rorschach*, the *Thematic Apperception Test*, the *Children's Apperception Test*, *Human Figure Drawings*, and *Sentence Completion* and informal methods according to the preference of the psychologist.

To complete the investigation of a child with reading disability, a reading diagnosis is conducted as described in Chapter 2. It consists of oral, silent, and diagnostic reading tests together with their quantitative and qualitative interpretation, as well as trial lessons. These are administered to find out in what way the child best learns, where his strengths lie, and how he can be helped to overcome his difficulties. From this information, recommendations can be formulated as to which methods are most suitable for the child. Such

---

[12] *Ibid.*, p. 377.

suggestions are particularly meaningful to the teacher, since they are directly connected with helping to overcome the reading difficulty.

Making Recommendations in Relation to the Diagnosis

Recommendations must be as inclusive as possible, consider all the causes of the reading disability, and emphasize the strengths that the child possesses.

Whether or not the diagnosis is definitively established, suggestions as to how to handle the child's difficulty in learning to read remain the responsibility of the diagnostician.

If the school is cooperative, a conference should be held with the parent, the teacher, the principal, and other school personnel concerned with the child in order to explain findings and discuss measures which might help to alleviate the child's problems.

A well-defined program for remedial work is of vital importance. If the psychologist is not professionally trained to make suggestions with regard to remedial work, the services of a reading specialist or remedial teacher should be sought. Ideally, the specialist maintains contact with the school.

If educational adjustment is needed, is it better for the child to be in a less competitive class or a more structured one? Is it more advantageous for him to be with a particular teacher regardless of the class composition or vice versa? Is there any other school the child might attend?

If remedial work is to be undertaken, is there an experienced teacher available or perhaps an appropriate group in the school for the child? Is the remedial work suited to the needs of the pupil?

If psychotherapy is advisable, is there a mental health clinic or family agency with facilities available? These agencies may have long waiting lists, whereas the schedules of private therapists are also crowded and their fees are beyond the reach of most people. Sometimes arrangements can be made for a child to attend a clinic once a week. If the child is deeply disturbed, however, being seen so infrequently may be insufficient for him. Thus too much reliance cannot be placed solely on such treatment.

However, in such cases even limited therapeutic treatment can be advantageous provided that the efforts of the therapist are coordinated with those of the school in planning for a more favorable school environment. This would include trying to keep anxiety-arousing situations in the classroom at a minimum and improving the child's functioning through effective remedial instruction. In addition, if help can be obtained for the parents, this might also add to the effectiveness of treatment.

Thus recommendations are made with regard to reality. Rarely are ideal solutions found. The psychologist tries to alleviate the difficulties to the extent possible.

When a plan is decided upon, all those involved—the parents, the teachers, and the specialist who is going to treat the child—share the responsibility for carrying out treatment. The treatment plan is interpreted to the parents, the child, and the teacher so that they all understand the problem, the ways in which it will be handled, and each one's part in the plan.

Many diagnoses must of necessity remain tentative. Children continue to grow and develop, and the present difficulty may gradually disappear due to a number of intervening factors. It has been found, for example, that many disturbed children who are given remedial instruction, but no psychotherapeutic treatment, make substantial progress in emotional adjustment as well as reading. Also, some children who have been diagnosed as brain-damaged, who showed extreme difficulty in learning, are eventually able to learn to read adequately despite their injury.

It is extremely rare to find a child so impaired that he cannot learn. There is little evidence in the literature to show, for example, that children with organic injury will never be able to perform the tasks in reading that are needed.[13] Also, where repression of intellectual drive exists, all avenues to learning need not be closed. Thus we cannot give up hope. We must find ways to teach the child, choosing the best possible alternatives from the resources available. Sometimes a change of educational milieu is the best solution; sometimes intensive remedial work with a skilled tutor is the best answer; sometimes a change to another teacher is reasonable; sometimes extensive therapy must be inaugurated; sometimes both remedial instruction and psychotherapy are advisable; but at all times, recommendations are made with a view to their practicability and feasibility.

---

[13] A. Strauss and N. Kephart, *Psychopathology and Education of the Brain-injured Child* (New York: Grune & Stratton, 1955), p. 177.

Suggestions for Further Reading

ANDERSON, I., and DEARBORN, W., *The Psychology of Teaching Reading.* New York: Ronald Press, 1952.

BENDER, LAURETTA, *Visual Motor Gestalt Test and Its Clinical Use.* Research Monographs, No. 3. New York: American Orthopsychiatric Association, 1938.

CAPLAN, H., "The Role of Deviant Maturation in the Pathogenesis of Anxiety." *American Journal of Orthopsychiatry, 26* (1956), pp. 103–4.

CHALL, JEANNE, ROSWELL, FLORENCE, and BLUMENTHAL, SUSAN, "Auditory Blending Ability: A Factor in Success in Beginning Reading." Paper presented at the Elementary School Session, February 19, 1962, American Educational Research Association.

"Clinical Problems." *The Reading Teacher, 15,* No. 6, entire issue (1962), pp. 409–54.

DE HIRSCH, KATRINA, "Specific Dyslexia." *Folia Phoniatrica, 4* (1952), pp. 231–48.

DELACATO, C. H., *The Treatment and Prevention of Reading Problems.* Springfield, Ill.: Charles C Thomas, 1959.

FROSTIG, M., *Developmental Test of Visual Perception.* Published by the author: 7257 Melrose Ave., Los Angeles 46, Calif., 1961.

GOLDSTEIN, K., and SCHEERER, M., *Abstract and Concrete Behavior: An Experimental Study with Special Tests.* Psychological Monographs, *239* (1941), pp. 158–62.

HALLGREN, B., "Specific Dyslexia ('Congenital Word-Blindness'): A Clinical and Genetic Study." *Acta Psychiatrica et Neurologica Scandinavica,* Suppl. 65 (1950), pp. 224–32.

KOPPITZ, ELIZABETH, *et al.,* "A Note on Screening School Beginners with the Bender Visual-Motor Gestalt." *Journal of Educational Psychology, 52* (1962), pp. 80–1.

LAWRENCE, MARGARET, "Minimal Brain Injury in Child Psychiatry." Presented to the *Academy of Psychoanalysis,* May 8, 1960, mimeographed, 14 pp.

LISS, E., "Motivations in Learning." *Psychoanalytic Study of the Child, 10* (1955), pp. 100–18.

McFIE, J., "Cerebral Dominance in Cases of Reading Disability." *Journal of Neurology, Neurosurgery & Psychiatry, 15* (1952), pp. 194–9.

ROSEN, V., "Strephosymbolia: An Intrasystemic Disturbance of the Synthetic Function of the Ego." *Psychoanalytic Study of the Child, 10* (1955), pp. 83–99.

VORHAUS, PAULINE, "Rorschach Configurations Associated with Reading Disability." *Journal of Projective Techniques, 16* (1952), pp. 3–19.

WEPMAN, J. M., *The Auditory Discrimination Test.* Chicago: Language Research Associates, 1958.

PART II &

ধ 4

Psychotherapeutic Principles in Remedial Reading Instruction

ধ Good teaching has far-reaching therapeutic results. Throughout the ages, teachers such as Plato, Rousseau, Moses, Confucius, and Dewey have had immeasurable influence on their students. As Henry Adams said, "A teacher affects eternity; he can never tell where his influence stops."[1] Teachers who work with children with reading disability also have effected remarkable changes in the lives of their pupils. Their influence is crucial and can make the difference between the success and failure of an entire life. It is not the techniques of instruction which are of such lasting influence. It is the attention and understanding that the children receive which help them overcome the massive frustration, despair, and resentment that they have stored for so long. Then positive feelings come to the fore, and they are finally able to use capacities which were formerly misdirected or lying dormant.

Children are born with curiosity and a craving to learn. The toddler is impatient to explore, to experiment, to search. When children begin formal education and are frustrated at every turn and scolded because they don't progress, they may develop anything from overt anger that results in explosive behavior to a dull passivity that ends in hopelessness and apathy. In considering frustration, Maslow has stated that there must be a distinction between a deprivation that is unimportant to the organism and one that is a threat to the personality, life goals, defensive system, and self-esteem of the individual.[2] Failure in school represents such a deprivation

---

[1] H. Adams, *The Education of Henry Adams* (New York: The Modern Library, 1931), p. 300.

[2] A. Maslow, *Motivation and Personality* (New York: Harper & Brothers, 1954), p. 156.

because it is the major work of the child. No wonder that improvement in school can have lasting therapeutic effects and fulfill some of the child's deepest desires. Like all psychotherapy, remedial treatment aims at reaching areas crucial to the child's emotional well-being. Let us consider further how this is brought about.

A child who does not succeed in school incurs the displeasure of his parents and teachers, to say nothing of losing status with his classmates. Not only are his parents and teachers displeased with him, but their anxiety often becomes uncontrollable. The parents wonder whether their child is retarded or just plain lazy. If they are assured that his intelligence is normal even the most loving parents can become so alarmed at their child's inability to learn that they tend to punish, scold and threaten, or even reward with the hope of producing the desired results. Teachers also feel frustrated by their inability to reach the child.

It is under such adverse conditions that the child tries his best to function. When he continues to fail, he can become overwhelmed and devastated. These feelings linger with him after school and on weekends. The notion that he does not measure up hangs over him relentlessly.

Even where psychotherapy for such children is secured (and the high cost of treatment and limited facilities often make it unobtainable), every effort must be made to improve school functioning by incorporating basic therapeutic principles with reading instruction. Few therapists treating neurotic adults would suggest that a patient forego working on a job and wait until major changes in his attitudes occurred. Yet one hears again and again, "There's no point in trying to teach him until his emotional problems are cured."

We do not mean that teaching is a substitute for intensive psychotherapy. Such therapy is indicated for any child whose problems are serious enough to warrant it. However, even where treatment at deeper levels is instituted, it may take many months or even years to effect changes. In the meantime, the child is still experiencing difficulty in school. This increases his problem in all directions, both academically and emotionally.

Therefore, learning to read in line with his ability is imperative for such a child. Self-realization, the goal of any type of psychotherapy, is impossible for him if he does not learn to read satisfactorily. Replacing his dreadful sense of failure and doubt with visible progress and increased confidence emphasizes the most forceful aspect of remedial treatment. This may account for its reaching down to the deepest levels of the child's personality. For very disturbed children, remedial treatment can be a vital auxiliary; for those who are less disturbed or whose maladjustment is directly caused by poor school performance, remedial treatment can effect positive personality changes that are fully restorative.

In considering how such effects have developed, we realize that those who work with children with reading disability apply many of the basic principles of psychotherapy, perhaps without being aware of them. In order to make the process more conscious and thereby perhaps more effective, we shall elaborate some of the fundamental principles that are inherent in any good teaching situation.

Establishing Relationship

One of the cardinal principles of psychotherapy is developing a good relationship. This is achieved through the total acceptance of the child as a human being worthy of respect, regardless of his failure in reading. It also encompasses a collaborative spirit within a planned structure, compassion without overinvolvement, understanding without indulgence, and, above all, a genuine concern for the child's development.

Teachers are troubled by pupils who do not learn satisfactorily. Not only do they consider it a burden to deal with the "slow" ones in their classes, but they feel that lack of progress is somehow their fault and a reflection on their teaching ability. It is understandable that teachers frown on problem cases because they require extra attention and their low test scores bring down the class average. Remedial teachers also share some of these feelings. Although they do not have to worry about lowered class averages, they are under pressure to have their pupils improve because they often need to justify their very existence to administrators by showing overall gains. Hence, concern over pupils' improvement can undermine a teacher's confidence.

When a teacher's confidence in her own ability is impaired, it is difficult for her to show approval toward the poor achiever. As a result, the child feels uncomfortable and fearful of the teacher. This can cause an even greater drop in his performance.

Anna Freud[3] has commented on children who equate receiving good grades in school with being loved and failure with being unloved and worthless. Even if such drastic comparisons are not made, certainly children who get poor report cards again and again lose status with all those on whom they depend for affection and approval. They may develop a

---

[3] Anna Freud, "Psychoanalysis and the Training of the Young Child," *Psychiatric Quarterly*, 4 (1935), pp. 15–24.

kind of free-floating anxiety toward schoolwork—always dreading it, always anticipating failure.

Since children with reading disability live in an atmosphere of rejection and disapproval, they often conclude that they have no ability or talent, that they are good for nothing, and that they rate no recognition whatsoever.

If children with reading disability feel so defeated and teachers feel so burdened by them, what can be done? A teacher needs to have confidence that she can help, but she needs to realize also that she is not personally responsible for lack of progress. She must understand that a child's weakness in reading is simply a reality that must be remedied. When a teacher realizes that her own status is not threatened, she is in a better position to accept her pupils. She can then recognize the child's ultimate potentialities, not his present achievement. To paraphrase Goethe, the child is treated not as he is, but as he can become.

Collaboration

Although the teacher knows the best methods and materials, she may not know which ones would be most suitable in planning a reading program for the child. Thus, she tries out many approaches, and as they work together, she can determine by the child's responses which work well and which do not.

For example, the teacher chooses the grade level of the materials, but the choice of subject matter may often be left to the child; e.g., would he prefer to read sport stories, science fiction, or folk tales? Where the child is reading at a low level, perhaps he may be permitted to make a selection from two or three readers at a suitable level. When this is not advisable (because the teacher wishes to use certain books for specific reasons), then the choice is up to her. But the pupil continues to participate actively even when the teacher assumes full leadership. Thus she does not foist her preconceived plans on him, and the child can feel the nature of the collaborative experience.

Treating his poor performance in a matter of fact way, as something that will eventually respond to one alternative or another, often relieves the pupil's anxiety considerably. His problems, which heretofore have been vague and mysterious, become evident and tangible. He may then be able to view his problem more objectively and accept a reasonable responsibility for it. The tone of the sessions, however, remains cooperative throughout, with both pupil and teacher entering into a give and take relationship.

Structure

Besides knowing what is expected of him, the child becomes aware of what is acceptable behavior and what is not. Although his reactions during the sessions are welcomed, he is not allowed to be destructive or totally unrestrained.

Structure as well as limits is even more important in teaching disturbed children, since it introduces order into their chaotic lives. Children who come from very unstable, inconsistent environments, where they do not know what to expect from one minute to the next, can be transformed from perverse, boisterous pupils to orderly, manageable ones as soon as they get accustomed to a routine that they understand and appreciate. When they finally become used to a routine, any change must be introduced carefully. If they are not adequately prepared for a shift in plan, they may revert to their former agitated behavior.

A planned program also eliminates discussion and disagreements over which activities should be performed and in what order. Children soon lose respect or become confused by being asked what they want to do next or which story they wish to read.[4] A child's natural reaction is, "If you don't know which book I should read, how am I expected to know?" Lack of direction and continued floundering of the teacher must be very disappointing to a child who comes for remedial instruction hoping that at last he will be helped. Moreover, where the child is given considerable leeway, too much time may be spent on unimportant activities. It also places unwarranted responsibility on the child. Furthermore, in an unstructured setting, the child's aggression might easily get out of hand, or he might decide to sit passively and do nothing.

The atmosphere should be neither too permissive nor too rigid. As a criterion, the teacher uses rational authority which has competence as its source.[5] The child is given freedom within reasonable limits.

After the sessions have been planned by the teacher in the best interests of the child, the question arises, "What happens if he does not abide by the plan?" In a good teaching program, where methods and materials are suited to the child and a collaborative spirit prevails, this difficulty rarely occurs. When it does, the teacher can shift to one of the child's favored activities. If this is insufficient, a frank discussion that reveals the teacher's acceptance of the child's occasional deviant behavior not

---

[4] C. Dahlberg, Florence Roswell, and Jeanne Chall, "Psychotherapeutic Principles as Applied to Remedial Reading," *The Elementary School Journal,* 53 (1952), p. 213.

[5] E. Fromm, *Man for Himself* (New York: Rinehart, 1947), p. 9.

only relieves his guilt, but enhances the human element in their relationship. Continued lack of cooperation, however, needs further investigation as to cause and treatment.

Sincerity

Children detect immediately whether a teacher has sincere and honest attitudes. In discussing this subject, one of our graduate students exclaimed that she knew one "must never display annoyance or disapproval." However, if such attitudes are present, the children soon catch the insincere undertones, no matter how much the teacher tries to conceal them.

Thus honest appraisal is necessary. If the child's work is poor, the teacher does not tell him that he is reading well. Instead, she tries to minimize his anxiety about errors and inconsistencies by telling him that many children have had similar difficulties and that they are unavoidable at his present stage. She might add that it is not his errors that are so important, but what matters is to find out how to overcome them. She assures him that ultimately he will improve as many others have.

Children often appear incredulous when they are treated this way, because they are so used to being conscientiously corrected, reprimanded, or given poor grades because they do not respond to instruction.

The teacher is also able to be more genuine if she encourages the child to work mainly for himself, not for anyone else. It is his life that will be affected if he does not learn. Particularly in reading disability cases, where motivation is so important, the child must be led to recognize the importance of work. He benefits from the support of a friendly, sincere ally with whom he shares his efforts and his difficulties. But in the long run, it is he who must become totally involved in the task.

Success

Obviously, achieving success in reading is paramount for the child in remedial treatment. But can a teacher provide experiences which engender these feelings merely by preparing a suitable program and proper materials? With reading disability, it is not that simple. Although all competent teachers know that materials must be within the range of the child's ability, they know too that they dare not risk permitting him to fail. Does that mean that the books he is given must be so easy that he will never miss a word? Does it mean that the child should never be permitted to falter? Many teachers reflect commonly accepted pedagogy when they answer, "A child with reading difficulty should be given a book at least one year below his reading level or even two; he must succeed!" A feeling of success is not always achieved through giving the child easy materials which he can read without error. Building up feelings of success in these defeated children is a very complex problem, which has long been oversimplified by reading specialists and educators. Teddy, for instance, is ten years old, in the fifth grade, of average intelligence, and is reading at third grade level. A book one year below his reading level means we must give him a second grade book. Will this make Teddy feel successful? It will be hard enough to find a book at third grade level which will be sufficiently mature without going lower. More important than finding books which he can read without error is to show Teddy that reading words incorrectly is not fatal, that a certain amount of unevenness is to be expected, and that he will not be reprimanded for his mistakes. As long as the teacher supplies unknown words while he reads aloud, Teddy could use third or possibly fourth grade books. (This does not apply to independent reading. In this instance, it would be advisable to suggest books at third grade level, which he can read with little or no assistance.)

Children need stimulation. Their curiosity and interest must be constantly aroused and furthered. Reading very easy material perfectly is less rewarding than making errors in more stimulating stories, provided, of course, that the child is receiving instruction in developing the necessary reading skills.

Are there cases where offering more difficult material may be harmful? Yes, very definitely. As in all remedial work, nothing is ever absolutely right or wrong. Everything depends on the needs and the vulnerability of the child. One must assess the child's capacity for making mistakes without his becoming extremely upset over them. There are some children who have suffered so drastically because of their failure that misreading words arouses the dread of failing again. Nonreaders, let us say, who are fourteen, fifteen, or older cannot possibly be given materials sufficiently challenging for them. In these cases, the teacher explains that the simple books will be discarded as soon as possible.

Interests

The chances of success are increased through providing reading materials based on the child's interests. However, determining true interests is not as easy as it seems. Actually, many children with reading disability have only transitory interests or no interests at all. Sometimes the teacher uses an interest inventory or asks the child what activities he especially enjoys—sports, tropical fish, snakes, stamp collecting, and so on. In order to please her, he may name one at random. Unsuspecting teachers may attempt to find materials based on this false response. They try hard to find articles about the topic that are exciting. But to get information within the desired reading level is almost impossible. Probably these children's knowledge, based on television and other visual media, so far surpasses what they can read that they are utterly bored with the selections finally presented. We have observed teachers, in their attempts to coordinate material with interests, exhaust all available resources, only to end up exhausting themselves and, no doubt, the child.

Even when appealing selections on a specific interest are discovered, they are useful only for a short while or as an introduction. If pursued, they become too narrow and confining. Reading competency cannot be built up merely on sports, mystery stories, or any other single category. Gradually, the child must be weaned away from a restricted field.

To discover true interests, the teacher cannot depend on what the child may originally report. She provides a variety of stimulating material and evaluates his responsiveness to it. Careful observation of the child's reactions offers the best and safest clues as to his true interests.

Bibliotherapy

For many years, the authors have been closely observing children's reactions to the themes of stories. They have noted their sheer delight and excitement with particular material. They have been impressed, too, with the opportunity for personality development and pupil-teacher relationship which these stories afford.

Certain themes seem to have universal appeal for children as well as grownups. For instance, the Cinderella story has been woven into adult and children's plays, novels, and movies throughout the years. It has maintained its appeal because so many of us can identify with ill treatment, and our wishes are fulfilled in the happy ending.

In children's books, there are various versions of the mistreated, pathetic figure who is victorious in the end. One story especially satisfying to boys is "Boots and His Brothers," in which Boots is always the underdog—the child rejected by his brothers as well as his parents. The king is faced with an impossible situation. He becomes so desperate that he offers half his kingdom and the princess in marriage to the one who solves his problem. Boots inevitably performs the difficult tasks and conquers all obstacles in the end. The boys are very intrigued with this story. Frequently they ask to read more like it. Then their resistance to books begins to lessen.

Humorous stories tend to cause children to relax. When the teacher and pupil share genuine laughter, it encourages a free and easy situation conducive to learning. Biographical sketches are apt to stimulate dramatic reactions, particularly those that show the hero who rises above disaster. These and other moving themes have a profound effect on children with reading disability because they identify so strongly with those who suffer misfortune.

The term *bibliotherapy* is sometimes used in this connection, referring to reading as a means for promoting personality development. Shrodes[6] has described the "shock of recognition" that comes when the reader beholds himself or those close to him in a piece of literature. At times, the shock is so great that dramatic changes take place. The following cases of Claude and Barry illustrate this process.

Claude, aged 12, with average intelligence, was in seventh grade. He was the youngest of four children. All the others did well in school. Claude had difficulty with spelling as well as reading. His mother reported, "Everybody feels sorry for him. He tries hard but he gets nowhere. He has no friends and spends his time all alone. During the past three years he has been annoying his classmates and teachers by acting like a clown in class."

Claude was most resistive during the diagnostic examination and presented a façade of not caring about his poor achievement in most of his school subjects. In fact, it seemed that establishing a good relationship in this case would be a long and arduous task. Test results were as follows:

Stanford-Binet I.Q.	109
Gray Oral Paragraphs	4.7
Metropolitan Intermediate	
Reading	5.8
Vocabulary	6.1
Spelling	5.6

It seemed advisable to use materials no higher than fourth grade level at the beginning because of his severe fear of failure. He came to the first remedial session under strong protest. During this session he was given *Greek and Roman Myths* in the hope that the mythical characters might appeal to him, but he remained unmoved. Because of Claude's marked rebelliousness, it was impossible to get even an inkling of any interest he might have. The author who worked with him could not reach him at all at this point. (See Appendix B for a complete bibliography of reading materials listed according to grade level.)

During the second session, she tried another type of story, Hans Chris-

---

6 Caroline Shrodes, "Bibliotherapy," *The Reading Teacher*, 9 (1955), pp. 24–9.

tian Andersen's life in *Stories to Remember*. (This is the Classmate Edition of the sixth grade book; readability level is high fourth grade.) This time Claude perked up a bit. During the remainder of the session he even became more cooperative in spelling and other activities.

In trying to analyze why Claude's attitude changed, it seemed likely that he was relating to the serious problems in Hans Christian Andersen's life that were similar to his own. He seemed to share Andersen's anxieties, his quality of oddness, and his feelings of rejection. Claude was probably able to develop hope about himself as he read of Andersen's final triumphs. He was astounded when he heard that the story, "The Ugly Duckling," was about Andersen's own life.

In succeeding sessions, we continued in the same book reading the stories of Stephen Foster and William Tell. These did not have too much personal significance for Claude, but he enjoyed them and continued to be cooperative. Soon humorous stories were introduced, and these definitely made Claude more relaxed. As he and the author shared their enjoyment, the first sign of a closer relationship became apparent.

The next story which seemed to have special meaning for Claude was that of Thomas Edison in *Teen-Age Tales,* Book I, about high fifth grade level. He identified with the "Edison boy" who was looked upon as "queer" by his neighbors. As a child, he didn't play much with other children; he was always asking questions, and he was thought to be dull and stupid. He lasted only three months in first grade; the teacher saw no hope for him. These three months were all he ever had of formal schooling. After that his mother took him out of school and taught him herself. The story described Edison's struggles, working many hours alone in the basement, revising his experiments and laboring assiduously. His attempts at selling his gadgets frequently ended in failure. He was often penniless and hungry and had many ups and downs before his eventual success.

Claude seemed to identify closely with Tom Edison. Not that he for a moment thought he was another great inventor, but he could see the similarity between himself and Edison who was given up by his teacher, had no friends, and was considered stupid and queer.

Much later Claude read about Dr. Fleming and Madame Curie in *Doorways to Discovery*, a seventh grade book. Claude, like many adolescent boys, was very intrigued with the account of how Dr. Fleming happened to discover penicillin. According to the story, Dr. Fleming worked for ten years trying to find something that would kill diseased bacteria in a person's bloodstream. He accidentally discovered a green mold which later became the base for penicillin. He wrote two papers which were published in a scientific journal in Great Britain in 1929. Apparently he received little if any recognition from them. Yet he kept on with his research. It was not until World War II that penicillin was produced on a large scale, and Dr. Fleming was at last given a measure of recognition. Claude was astonished that Fleming "didn't give up even though it took all those years before he finally made it!"

The story of Madame Curie in the same book is similarly vivid, appealing, and inspiring. In addition, it offers a fascinating discussion about the discovery of radium and the nature of radiation.

Besides identifying with these characters, Claude was fascinated by the factual content. It happened that related topics were being covered in class, and he took great pride in contributing his share to the discussion. The author seized upon this sudden spurt of interest, and through judicious choice of exercises in comprehension materials from SRA *Laboratory* and *Practice Readers*, it was possible to open new vistas that were coordinated with school topics. As he became familiar with different fields, he continued to contribute to class discussions. His parents reported that he also had lively dinner conversations with them on diverse topics.

Claude's growing fund of information enabled him not only to do better in school, but to relate more easily to people as well. Instead of feeling sorry for him, his parents and teachers were suddenly aware that he really knew his subject matter and, even more important, was genuinely interested in it. As people around him began to pay attention to what he had to say, Claude was slowly able to develop positive feelings about himself. Gradually his self-image changed from a person who felt worthless to one who at last had something to offer. His need to act as a clown in order to gain his classmates' attention disappeared entirely.

Claude had a total of 39 weekly 45-minute sessions in one year. Besides training in comprehension of stories and subject matter, he received help in spelling and in advanced word recognition techniques. Scores on comparable tests at the beginning and end of remedial instruction were as follows:

METROPOLITAN ACHIEVEMENT TEST

	Grade Scores (Intermediate)	Grade Scores (Advanced)
Reading	5.8	9.4
Vocabulary	6.1	8.5
Spelling	5.6	8.3

Claude's responsiveness to the stories had engendered positive attitudes toward the other aspects of the reading instruction. It also motivated him to improve in his school subjects. Learning about the trials of people who had surmounted their troubles seemed to strike home. This inspiration spurred him forward, while the author's guidance sustained him along the way. After he had reached this stage, remedial treatment was discontinued. Claude was able to keep up with his class and function on his own. At the last follow-up, he was in the tenth grade in high school and still functioning well.

What are the therapeutic effects of such articles and stories? There is ability to identify on an emotional level. The child finds he is not alone in having failed. He finds that others were able to surmount their shortcomings. He finds out that factual material can be interesting and useful. He learns that school can be worth while and rewarding rather than senseless and painful. Since he has been continually admonished and prodded with such commands as "Do your homework," "Work harder," "Apply yourself," "You can do it if you want to," he is astonished to discover that intellectual endeavor can be rewarding.

Claude, like most children who have failed, divided his classmates into two distinct categories: "the brains," those who did well consistently, and "the stupid ones," those who did poorly. He believed that only those people who manifest superiority in their early years ever succeed. To achieve success after failure he did not consider possible.

The stories of Edison, Fleming, and Madame Curie pointed to the need for perseverance in the face of failure. He saw that even people who had been ridiculed and rejected and who had failed in school had eventually become loved, respected, and even famous.

These insights seemed to be the impetus for improvement in every area. He became ambitious even in subjects in which he was still doing poorly. He wished so earnestly to succeed that he began to develop stronger inner resources. From a resistive, indifferent youngster, he grew resolute, determined, and enterprising.

The next case is more complex. Barry, the son of a well-known writer, was a bright eleven-year-old in sixth grade. He was an extremely disturbed child. After a long period of intensive psychotherapy, his psychiatrist felt that Barry's progress was being impeded by his failure in school and recommended remedial instruction. Shortly after this, therapy was discontinued. The following account of remedial treatment covers a period of two years.

Barry had considerable difficulty in interpersonal relationships. He had no friends and barely spoke to adults. He daydreamed a great deal and enjoyed a world of fantasy. Rapport was difficult to establish and was developed only gradually. Because of Barry's very unfavorable attitude toward school, the usual remedial program was greatly modified. There was almost exclusive reading aloud, with the author reading one page, Barry the next.

Barry showed a strong leaning toward tales of the jungle and primitive modes of living. He sought them out wherever he could find them. They all revolved around the son of a tribal chief who never was as brave as his father. The son in each story worried about how he would eventually take his father's place as head of the tribe. Barry loved the descriptions of primitive dwellings made of mud and straw or baked clay. There was never any furniture, so everyone usually sat on the dirt floor. The children played with birds and animals. Their toys were of the simplest kinds, which they made themselves. The children learned how to climb a tree as fast as a monkey. The stories to which Barry returned over and over again were "Kintu" in *Roads to Everywhere*, fourth year level; "Simba" in *Days and Deeds*, fifth year level; "Child of the Jungle," in *Let's Travel On*, fifth year level; and "Mafatu" in *Doorways to Discovery*, seventh year level.

A summary of one of the stories is offered as an example. Mafatu had been christened "Stout Heart" by his proud father, but he was afraid of the sea. How could Mafatu provide the fish that were a part of every family's food? Kana, the one boy who had been friendly to Mafatu, called him a coward and so voiced the feeling of the whole tribe. Mafatu found the skeleton of a whale. He wanted to make tools from it, but his "hands were all thumbs." Mafatu's feelings as he reflects on life were described; he felt cowardly, inferior, frightened, and worried about his status in his family. At last, with a knife made from the skeleton he had found, Mafatu stabs a shark. The struggle with the shark and his eventual victory were extremely meaningful to Barry. He understood his icy fear, his trembling, his torment. Other reading material was covered, but he never seemed to tire of these selections and went back to them periodically. Barry's singular identification with Mafatu was apparent from his facial expression and his bodily movements.

It might be interpreted that Barry was reacting against his overcivilized world, where everything was handed to him ready-made. Perhaps his life seemed exceedingly complex. There was no recognized role in which he could find his own strength. He rarely had the opportunity to explore or contribute to his family's affairs. In Mafatu's primitive world, he seemed vicariously to get to the element of living. Primitiveness might have meant freedom to move and to create. If he could start out at this simple level, perhaps he too could accomplish something worth while and finally find himself.

But even more important consequences seemed to result from Barry's fascination with the stories. Slowly he was able to express his astonishment that anyone else could feel so helpless, terrified, and isolated. From this beginning he talked more and more readily and formed a closer relationship with the author. His parents reported that he now played with children more easily, too, and got along better in the family. As time went on, these changes became more and more marked.

It may be conjectured that when Barry read about others who had the same problems as he, he felt less alone. They had conquered their terror; he might overcome his, too. From Mafatu's struggle, Barry derived hope. Perhaps this lent him the courage to change as he did, to reach out to others, and to move forward slowly toward the world.

Thus reading can foster vital changes in a child's life. Shrodes[7] has presented a rationale in this connection, which is paraphrased here. Bibliotherapy, drawing upon the novelist's and playwright's ability to plumb the depths of man's nature, is founded on the relationship between personality dynamics and vicarious experience. It is a process of interaction between imaginative literature and the perceptions of the reader which stirs his emotions and frees them for more conscious use. The reader, of course, perceives according to his own wishes, desires, needs, and background experiences. Thus a character may become particularly arresting to him. The identification may be positive and enhance the individual. Or it may be negative, and then he may project his feelings onto the character. In this way bibliotherapy resembles psychotherapy—promoting insight, identification, and release.

From this point of view, stories can be extremely vital in a child's life. Adults are moved, influenced, and enriched through literature because it represents the world. Inspiration from stories has compelled many of us to an unaccustomed course of action and startled us into seeing our problems from a new perspective. With children who have reading difficulty, themes in stories can serve several additional purposes. Relating to a story can lead the way for enjoyment in reading never before possible. Reading can fill in background, extend knowledge, and widen horizons that have been closed for so long. Finally, learning about the experiences of others, particularly people who failed, can foster release and insight as well as personal hope and encouragement. When children identify with

---

[7] *Ibid.*, p. 24.

others who are downtrodden, estranged, ridiculed, or unloved, or in contrast, noble, brave, and courageous, they get a glimpse into the lives of other people and other families. They can vicariously share some of their inspirations and some of their regrets. Relating in this way to characters and themes often diminishes the heavy sense of loneliness and isolation so common, not only to these children, but to all individuals.

Thus the psychotherapeutic principles in remedial reading are not something diffuse and intangible. Developing contact with others, achieving academic success, and inducing constructive attitudes toward work for its own sake causes feelings of failure, discomfort, and misery to diminish. It is then that dormant attitudes such as perseverance, hope, and application can come to the surface. This type of remedial treatment can be one of the most provocative, stirring experiences in the child's life.

Suggestions for Further Reading

BRUNER, J., *The Process of Education*. Cambridge, Mass.: Harvard University Press, 1961, Chs. 2, 5.

ERIKSON, E., *Childhood and Society*. New York: Norton, 1950, Chs. 7, 11.

HUNT, J., ed., *Personality and the Behavior Disorders*. New York: Ronald Press, 1944, Vol. I, Part III.

KRUGMAN, M., "Reading Failure and Mental Health." *Journal of the National Association of Women Deans and Counselors, 22* (1956), p. 10.

MURPHY, G., *Human Potentialities*. New York: Basic Books, 1958, Ch. 7.

PELLER, LILI, "Daydreams and Children's Favorite Books." *Psychoanalytic Study of the Child, 14* (1959), pp. 414–36.

WHITAKER, C., and MALONE, T., *The Roots of Psychotherapy*. New York: Blakiston, 1953, Chs. 7, 8.

ટ~ 5

Methods of Teaching
Word Recognition to Children
with Reading Disability

ટ~ The current controversy over the best method of teaching word recognition techniques has little relevance to children who have
reading disability, since the method or methods used with such children
must be chosen on the basis of suitability for each individual. Most children who have difficulty with reading can and do learn. It is the teacher's
responsibility to find out where each child's weaknesses in word recognition lie and to be sufficiently acquainted with the various approaches to
choose and use those most appropriate. If none of the usual methods is effective, the teacher must undertake more extensive investigation or refer
the child for further diagnosis.

The ultimate objective in teaching word-analysis techniques is to help
the child learn to read and derive meaning from what he reads. This chapter describes the basic word-analysis skills necessary for pupils of any
age and grade in order to develop competence in reading. Chapter 6 shows
how these skills may be adapted for pupils of varying ages, both individually and in a classroom. Although word recognition is never separated
from understanding, for purposes of clarification comprehension techniques
are elaborated in Chapter 7.

Sequence of Word Recognition Instruction in Remedial Reading

Although many of the word recognition skills that are taught in remedial
reading are the same as those in a regular program, there are certain
major differences. In the usual program, sometimes known as the develop-

mental reading program, there are a large number of skills that are presented according to a systematic plan. In remedial reading, however, instruction is simplified. The number of skills are cut to a bare minimum to make it easier for children with reading disability who have already been exposed to them unsuccessfully for one or more years.

Reading authorities differ as to which skills in remedial reading are most important and which sequence is most effective. The authors favor the sequence of skills that is listed below. Of this sequence only those skills are taught that the pupils do not already know. Thus the authors first identify the gaps in the pupils' word recognition skills and adapt the program accordingly. This streamlined procedure serves to keep the pupils' discouragement at a minimum at the same time that it promotes rapid and effective progress in reading. Instead of spending an undue number of lessons on numerous rules and techniques, the additional time is spent in reading as many stories and books as possible. The pride of continued accomplishment—even though the reading may remain somewhat uneven —often spurs their acceptance of the reading process until they are able to develop more proficiency.

The word-analysis skills for remedial reading listed below form a basis for figuring out many unknown words.

Total nonreaders who do not know 50 to 100 sight words, such as *want, anyone, same,* learn those that are introduced in the easy materials they are using. More advanced readers learn any of the basic sight words that they do not already know—perhaps five to ten at a time. In addition, the teacher introduces sounds that need practice. She presents one vowel sound simultaneously with the sounds of four or five consonants (or consonant combinations if all the consonants are known). This allows practice with the phonic approach as soon as possible. Once the children learn the additional skills listed and apply them in their reading, they seem to learn more readily any other word recognition skills that they may need.

WORD-ANALYSIS SKILLS FOR REMEDIAL READING
(In Suggested Sequence for Teaching)

1. *Sight words*
   (a) The 95 most common nouns (see Appendix D)
   (b) The basic sight vocabulary of 220 words (see Appendix D)
2. *Initial consonants—s, d, m, t, h, p, f, c, r, b, l, n, g, w, j, k, v, y, z*
   (4 or 5 initial consonant sounds are taught at a time, along with one vowel sound.)
3. *Short vowel sounds—a, i, o, u, e*

4. *Consonant combinations*—*sh, ch, wh, th, st, tr, gr, br, fr, dr, cl, pl, fl, sm, sw, sp*

5. *Long vowel sounds,* taught in conjunction with the two vowel rules:
   (a) *The silent* e: When *e* is added at the end of a one-syllable word, it usually is silent and makes the first vowel long, e.g., *at, ate; bit, bite.*
   (b) *The double vowel:* When two vowels come together, the first is usually long and the second silent, e.g., *paid, seat.*

6. *Syllabication*—The two major rules are:
   (a) In case of two adjacent consonants, the syllables are divided between them.
   (b) When two consonants are not found together, the word is divided after the first vowel.

Teaching Word Recognition

In introducing word-analysis skills, sight words are usually taught first. These words make up a large part of the material that children meet in their books—for example, *this, their, what, whose, come, many.* They are called "sight words" because the pupil must learn to recognize them at a glance. They occur so frequently that inability to recognize them prevents fluency. Many of them cannot be figured out phonetically; many are similar in configuration; many are abstract and elusive in meaning. Often they are difficult to learn. Pupils are encouraged to recognize such words in their entirety rather than sound them out. The teacher can refer to any one of the several published lists of sight words to decide which words warrant special study. Dolch's list of the 220 words that comprise the basic sight vocabulary and his list of most common nouns are reproduced in Appendix D.

There are several ways of teaching sight words: the visual, the visual-motor, and the kinesthetic methods.

The Visual Method

The visual method consists of exposing words again and again until the pupil learns to identify them by their general configuration. Children with reading disability tend to have difficulty perceiving accurately and are likely to confuse words of similar shape. Many pupils with disability can learn words in isolation and yet be unable to recognize them in context. They may know the words one day and forget them the next; they may recognize them in one sentence and mispronounce them a few lines later in a different context. Adults often show similar difficulty in associating faces and names. For example, one may know the face and name of one's bank teller, yet be unable to recall his name or to identify him if we see him sitting in a restaurant. Pupils need to see sight words in a variety of contexts until the word is firmly fixed in their minds. For this reason, sight words are presented in as many different ways as possible—in picture cards, stories, games, workbooks, and worksheets.

LEARNING SIGHT WORDS THROUGH PICTURE CARDS. In presenting sight words, the teacher might use commercially prepared or homemade picture-word cards.[1] She chooses nouns unfamiliar to the children but representing well-known objects. Each word is printed under a picture. (If the teacher makes her own cards, she might mount pictures cut from magazines.) Identical cards contain the word alone. The children look at the picture cards first, pronouncing the appropriate words. Then they match the non-illustrated card to its illustrated counterpart. The picture card is then removed, and the children try to say the printed word. This is repeated several times.

Each child can keep his own pack of picture-word cards and practice them by himself until they are learned. The illustration thus serves as a self-checking device. He can also compile an individual picture dictionary, drawing or cutting out pictures corresponding to the words.

LEARNING SIGHT WORDS IN STORIES. To improve carry-over from isolated word practice to recognition of the same words in context, emphasis is placed on sentences and stories that use these words. The children are given the most interesting books that can be found at their level[2] and asked to read aloud. The teacher should supply unknown words as quickly and as unobtrusively as possible so that the reading proceeds smoothly. Often the child can remember these words if they appear again. If not, the teacher supplies them as often as necessary until they are recognized. Appropriate support during reading plus constant repetition of the same words apparently helps the children to learn as they read. The joy of completing story after story adds immeasurably to the child's positive feelings toward reading as well as reinforcing recognition of sight words.

---

[1] E. W. Dolch, *Picture-Word Cards* (Champaign, Ill.: Garrard Press), presents the "Ninety-Five Commonest Nouns." Cp. Appendix D.

[2] A selected list of books at the primary level is offered in Appendix B.

The Visual-Motor Method

Words that the children have not been able to learn by the simple visual approach or sight method can sometimes be mastered by the visual-motor method.[3] This method is particularly useful in learning nonphonetic words. Some children have considerable difficulty in visualizing words either because of poor visual discrimination or poor memory. In such cases, the use of the method should be discontinued.

The teacher chooses three words, each about five to eight letters long, that are unfamiliar to the pupils. The words are clearly printed on cards or chalk board and presented one at a time. The teacher says, "This is the word *fruit*. Look at it carefully. What is the word? Now close your eyes. Can you see it with your eyes closed? Look again. What is the word?" The word is covered and the children write it. They then compare their written word with the model. If the written word is incorrect, the procedure is repeated. No erasures are permitted. If a child makes a mistake, he starts over again. Sometimes it is necessary to show the word several times before the children are able to write it correctly. When the word is reproduced accurately, the children write it several more times, covering up each previous sample to make sure that they are recalling the word from memory rather than merely copying it. The teacher checks carefully to see that it is written correctly each time. Another word is then introduced, and the procedure is repeated. After a period of time has elapsed, the words are reviewed.

The Kinesthetic Method

The kinesthetic approach, developed by Fernald,[4] is relatively laborious and time-consuming and is most effective for individual cases under careful supervision. It is recommended when all other methods have failed. In this method, the teacher writes or prints unfamiliar words on unlined paper in letters approximately two inches high. The child is told that he will be taught by an entirely new method—through his fingers.

The child then looks at one word, is told what it is, and traces it with his index finger, simultaneously pronouncing each sound of the word. If he makes an error or is uncertain of the word, he retraces it, again saying

---

[3] This method was originally suggested by Durrell. See D. Durrell, *Improving Reading Instruction* (Tarrytown-on-Hudson, N.Y.: World Book, 1956).

[4] Grace Fernald, *Remedial Techniques in Basic School Subjects* (New York: McGraw-Hill, 1943), Part II.

each part of the word aloud. Then he tries to reproduce the word without reference to the model. Erasure is not permitted. He continues to trace and say it over and over until he can write the word easily without consulting the original sample.

As soon as the child can write these words adequately, he begins to make up his own stories, asking for the words he does not know. Each of these words is written for him and taught as just described. Whatever he writes is typed out for him quickly so that he can read it while it is still fresh in his mind. Each pupil keeps an alphabetical file of the words he has requested so that he can practice them at his leisure and refer to them if necessary in writing additional stories.

After the teacher introduces sight words, systematic practice is afforded by games and devices based on reliable word lists and by workbooks or made-up materials which use these words in different contexts. The teacher can make up her own games, use those that can be obtained commercially, or refer to compilations of classroom games such as are found in "Reading Aids through the Grades."⁵

Here are a few word games and how they are played. (A list of these games and their sources will be found in Appendix C—Games and Devices for Teaching Sight Vocabulary.)

"PANTOMIME GAME." In the Pantomime Game the teacher writes on the board the words to be reinforced. Nouns, verbs, or other words that can be acted out are suitable (e.g., *jump, walk, cold, sat, bird*). She selects a child to be "it." "It" picks a word, writes it on a slip of paper, and gives the slip to the teacher. He then acts out the word while the other children try to guess it. The one who succeeds becomes "it," and the game continues. Any number can play.

"GRAB." Grab is a card game played like rummy. It involves a child calling out a particular word on a card and asking the other player or players for desired word cards. Three like cards form a "set." The one who gets the most "sets" wins. Two to four individuals can play. Grab comes in six levels, containing words of increasing difficulty. Each level has 15 words in "books" of three. The game is extremely popular even with older children.

"GROUP WORD TEACHING GAME." The Group Word Teaching Game utilizes the basic sight vocabulary. It consists of nine sets of cards, each con-

---

⁵ D. Russell and Etta Karp, *Reading Aids through the Grades* (New York: Bureau of Publications, Teachers College, Columbia University, 1951).

taining six cards. Each card includes 25 words. The words are the same in each set, but the order in which they are placed on each card varies. The first set has the 25 most common words; the other sets have words of gradually decreasing frequency of use. The game is played like bingo. Each child has a card. The teacher calls out the words from a master sheet, and the children look for it. Two to six children can play with one box.

"THE ROLLING READER." The Rolling Reader consists of several dice with sight words printed on each side. Blank dice are also provided for writing individual words that need practice. No matter how the dice fall when they are rolled out on the table, they can always be formed into a complete sentence.

HAND TACHISTOSCOPES. The teacher can make a hand tachistoscope or use a commercial one such as the one put out by the Reading Institute of Boston. This tachistoscope, called Pocket-Tac, consists of a small case with a mechanically operated shutter that flashes sight words or numbers. Several sets of material are available for practice at elementary through high school levels. For other available hand tachistoscopes, see Appendix C—Games and Devices for Teaching Sight Vocabulary.

WORKBOOKS Workbooks must be used with caution since they often do not fulfill the pupil's needs. Few workbooks are designed just for teaching sight words. Therefore the teacher selects exercises carefully. The most useful ones for teaching sight words include such features as picture dictionaries for ready reference, simple riddles, or sentences using the words to be practiced. Suitable exercises for beginners are included in workbooks such as *Let's See* by Clarence Stone (St. Louis: Webster Publishers, 1949). Others may be selected from any of the standard workbooks that are used in connection with primary reading or from those listed in Appendix C.

The Phonic Method

The learning of sight words must be supplemented as soon as possible with phonics so that the child gains greater independence in word analysis. This knowledge is then used immediately in sentences and reading matter. Many children with reading disability, however, have difficulty in blending sounds together to form whole words. In most cases, this difficulty is overcome at about nine years of age, at which time a systematic phonic approach may be used. In rare cases the child is ten or eleven or older before he can synthesize sounds together. If, despite all the teacher's ingenuity, the child is still unsuccessful with the phonic method, it must be discontinued and the alternate methods discussed in this chapter used until such time as the child is able to profit from phonic instruction. However, the teacher does not merely wait without trying to demonstrate from time to time how sounds can be combined to form words. Sometimes a little assistance in this direction can help the child use the procedure. For instance, the teacher might encourage him to fit sounds together the way links of a chain are combined. Also, she can pronounce the separate sounds simultaneously with him to help him capture the sensation. This procedure is known as choral blending.

In the phonics procedure the pupil first learns the sounds of the letters, then how to substitute initial consonants in known words in order to figure out new ones, and finally how to blend separate sounds together in words. When using the phonic method with reading disability cases, the teacher must remember that most of these children have been exposed to similar procedures many times before. Therefore, she seeks to minimize embarrassment by choosing material and techniques suitable for older pupils.

TEACHING SOUNDS OF CONSONANTS AND CONSONANT COMBINATIONS.[6] The teacher introduces the selected sounds by presenting them in upper and lower case with pictures whose content is mature in format. Some children can learn as many as four or five sounds in a single lesson. The consonants listed below have suggestions for illustrations that the writers have found appropriate.

s—sun	b—button
d—door	l—ladder
m—matches	n—nest
t—televison	w—window
h—house	j—jacks
p—pencil	k—key
f—fish	v—vest
c—cake	y—yellow
g—gate	z—zebra
r—radio	

[6] For further suggestions on teaching sounds see D. Durrell, Helen Sullivan, and Helen Murphy, *Building Word Power* (Tarrytown-on-Hudson, N.Y.: World Book, 1945).

The teacher should have the children name each object pictured to avoid possible confusion—e.g., "fence" for "gate," "radio" for "television," "blouse" for "vest."

When teaching several sounds in succession, the teacher is careful to use those which differ markedly in appearance and sound. (For example, *b* and *d* are easily reversed and hence confusing.) The order in which the letters are listed on page 79 follows this principle, but the teacher always chooses the order most suitable to her pupils' needs.[7]

Auditory Discrimination

The children are told the name and sound of one letter at a time. Vivid associations are given wherever possible. In teaching *h*, for example, the teacher might say, "You can make steam on a window pane or mirror when you go 'hhhhh.' "[8] The children listen to words beginning with *h* and then are asked to distinguish a word that begins with a different letter sound. The teacher shows them a picture of a house with *h* printed in upper and lower case alongside it. At the same time the children pronounce the name of the letter and its sound. The teacher then pronounces other words that begin with *h*, such as *hat, hit, hose*, asking the children to listen carefully to the beginning sound. She then asks them to volunteer additional words beginning with the same sound. (They often have difficulty thinking of examples.) The teacher might then ask riddles:

Here are some riddles that give you hints of the words that I am thinking of that begin with *hhhh*.

1. You have two of them. You use one to write with. (hand)
2. You climb it. (hill)
3. A musical instrument. (harp)
4. You do it when you go up and down on one foot. (hop)

---

[7] For the letters *g* and *c*, the hard sounds are introduced first (*g* as in *good*, *c* as in *cup*.) The soft sounds (*g* as in *gem*, *c* as in *circle*) are best delayed until later as they occur less frequently. The letters *q* and *x* have not been listed because they do not have single sounds (*q* in words is always followed by *u*, sounding as *kw*; *x* usually sounds like *ks*). Pupils are less confused if they are taught these sounds when they meet them during their reading.

[8] The authors have found it effective with reading disability cases to isolate the sound at the beginning. Of course, extraneous vowel sounds at the end of a consonant, such as *huh* for *h*, should be avoided.

The teacher might develop the children's auditory discrimination further by pronouncing groups of four words, three of which begin with *h*.

1. hat	hit	miss	hope
2. fake	hose	here	him
3. have	card	help	hero
4. hot	hall	head	bear

The children are asked to listen carefully as she says the words and to indicate the one that does not begin with the sound being taught by clapping or raising their hands. The teacher does not go on to a new group of four words until the children have identified the word that begins differently. This is continued until sufficient auditory discrimination has been attained. Other letters are then taught in the same way. Where children learn letter sounds easily, the teacher can dispense with training in auditory discrimination.

When the children have learned several consonants and one short vowel sound, they are shown how to blend them together into words. The picture cues for the separate sounds are left in evidence for ready reference as long as necessary.

Consonant combinations are taught in the same way as single consonants. The teacher points out how two consonants already learned are combined to form blends. There is no need to dwell on teaching a large number of blends because many of them tend to fall into similar patterns such as *tr, gr, br*. However, the consonant combinations which represent a single sound do have to be taught as entirely new sounds as *sh, ch, wh, th* (as in *thimble*), *th* (as in *those*), and *ph*.

Games are usually more satisfactory than workbooks in helping children learn the sounds of consonants and consonant combinations. Many are listed in Appendix C. Two of the most useful are:

"CONSONANT LOTTO." The rules of Consonant Lotto resemble those of the long-time favorite, lotto. Each player has a master card. Separate picture cards are placed face down in a pile and drawn one at a time. Each player tries to keep the card he draws by saying the word and finding a picture on the master card that begins with the same initial sound.

"GO FISH." The rules of Go Fish are similar to those of regular rummy. Players take turns asking for sounds of the letters. Three identical letter sounds make a "book." Set I affords practice with single letters, Set II with consonant combinations.

Rudimentary Blending of Sounds

If the child can grasp a visual procedure readily and shows some knowledge of letter sounds, a rudimentary phonics, or "word-family," method may be tried. This technique of word analysis is especially useful for children who are not yet able to blend sounds letter by letter. However, it affords only limited independence in word analysis. This approach consists of changing a known word into many new words by substituting for the first letter other letters whose sounds are being taught or reviewed. Thus the known word *cold* is changed to *gold, hold, sold,* and so forth.

A variation of this method is to substitute the same initial consonant in several words that the pupils already recognize, thus changing them to entirely different words. For example, if the pupil knows the words *sat, fill, Sam, like,* and *day,* the teacher tells him to read the list aloud substituting the letter *h* for the initial consonant in each word and to pronounce the new word that has been formed. (The words in which the substitution is made must be chosen carefully, so that the pupil has only the new sound to deal with and need not struggle with anything additional.)

Practice in word families is presented to children in context instead of isolated lists wherever possible. For instance, the child is shown how he can extend his sight vocabulary as he reads by noting similarities in words and applying his knowledge of sounds accordingly. That is, if the pupil comes across the word *hike* in his reading he is encouraged to figure it out from those elements which he knows—the sight word *like* and the sound of *h*.

Teaching Vowel Sounds

Vowel sounds are taught in the same way as consonant sounds, but they are much more difficult to distinguish and hence usually take longer for the pupils to master. Although there are many different sounds for each vowel (*Webster's Dictionary*[9] lists twelve separate sounds for *a*), only the short and long sounds are taught at the outset to children with read-

---

[9] W. Neilson *et al., Webster's New International Dictionary of the English Language,* 2nd ed., unabridged (Springfield, Mass.: G. & C. Merriam, 1951), p. xxxix.

ing disability. The authors recommend that the short vowel sound be taught first because words of one syllable, as *tag, mat,* and so on, are readily sounded out and written from dictation. As the pupils' mastery of reading and writing increases, diphthongs and other vowel combinations are taught. The pupils can begin to draw their own generalizations as they go along, from their growing familiarity with the construction of words.

In learning the vowel sounds, many children have considerable difficulty distinguishing between the short sounds of *a* and *e.* Therefore, it is advisable to postpone teaching the short *e* until the other vowels are learned. Whatever sequence is followed, however, vowel sounds are presented one at a time, interspersed among the teaching of consonants. All the while the sounds are used in words, sentences, and stories. As for *y,* the children learn that sometimes it is a vowel, sometimes a consonant. Its use as a vowel is given little emphasis; instead, the children discover its function in connection with words that they encounter in reading.

The vowels might be illustrated by the following words:

Aa	Ii	Oo	Uu	Ee
Apple	Indian	Octopus	Umbrella	Elephant

AUDITORY DISCRIMINATION OF SHORT VOWEL SOUNDS. In introducing vowels for the first time, the teacher shows the children the five vowels and explains that every word in the English language has at least one vowel in it. They might then be challenged to suggest a word without a vowel. The teacher then presents the vowel sound. The procedure is similar to that of consonants except that only one vowel is taught at a time. (As already stated, it may be taught simultaneously with four or five consonants in one lesson.)

For example, the teacher presents the letter *a* and says, "This is *a,* and the sound is ă as in *apple.*" The use of an accompanying picture may serve as a cue for remembering the sound. The children learn to hear it at the beginning of other words (*absent, answer, after*). Then they listen to groups of words, one of which has a different sound at the beginning (*act, ill, am, add*) and try to distinguish the one word in the group that begins differently. After the pupils have distinguished the sounds satisfactorily, one-syllable words are presented with the short *a* in the middle (*fat, can, lap, pat*). Then one word in each group is changed to a different medial sound, and the pupils indicate the word that does not have the ă sound in the middle (*fan, but, tag, had*).

After the pupil has learned the short vowel sounds and has shown ability to apply them in figuring out phonetic words, the long vowel sounds are taught. This is discussed on pages 91–92.

BLENDING SEPARATE SOUNDS. To determine whether blending sounds can be used successfully with children who have reading disability, an informal test of auditory blending is given. The teacher pronounces a word, e.g., *set*, first quickly, then slowly, *s-e-t*. Similarly, the word *fat* is pronounced naturally and then slowly as *f-a-t*. The pupils are then asked to identify other words that are said only slowly (*s-i-t, p-e-t, t-o-p*). If they can learn to recognize words from hearing the separate sounds, the phonic approach can be introduced. It should be remembered, however, that these children often need encouragement and help in understanding what they are expected to do.

In introducing blending, the pupils are shown several letters that they have learned. For example, the consonant sounds of *s, d, m, t, h,* and *p* are reviewed along with the short vowel sound of *a*. The letters might be printed on the chalkboard, or on a sheet of paper, or selected from a set of lower-case letter cards.

A word such as *hat* is printed for the child. The teacher illustrates how the separate sounds *h-a-t* may be blended together to form the word *hat*. She gives as much assistance as necessary in helping the child synthesize the individual sounds into a whole word. She then illustrates how *hat* may be changed to *mat, sat, pat* in word families as described in rudimentary blending. This makes the introduction to synthesizing separate sounds fairly easy. The next step, which involves substituting final consonants, is much more difficult for children to learn, such as changing *hat* to *had, mat* to *map*. The hardest step of all is reading words in mixed order, as *sap, pan, had, mat*. Frequently much practice is needed before children master the last two steps. To reinforce learning of letters and their associated sounds, the teacher may dictate words which the children sound out and write simultaneously.

DICTATION. The dictation of simple phonetic words can help the pupils connect letters with the corresponding sounds. This usually helps their reading as well as their spelling ability. The teacher dictates word families first since they are easier. If the pupils know the consonants *h, t, n, f, l, d,* and *s* and the vowels *i* and *a*, for example, the teacher dictates *fit, hit, lit,* and *sit;* then *sin, tin, fin;* and finally *fat, hat, sat* and *tan, fan*. During the next stage, she dictates the words in mixed order: *lit, tin, sit,* and *fin*.

Later still, she might try more difficult dictation such as *fin, fan, sat, had, lit,* and so on, interchanging initial and final consonants and middle vowels. The pace, of course, depends on the pupils' progress.

FURTHER PRACTICE WITH BLENDING. The teacher presents additional vowel sounds as soon as she considers the pupils ready. The children read words containing the added vowel. Sufficient practice is given throughout so that when all the consonants and vowels are learned, the children can write or sound out accurately any phonetic words in whatever order they appear as: *pet, map, hid, rug,* and *job.*

In presenting phonics exercises, the teacher avoids using nonsense syllables and words which children rarely meet. Exercises are not used merely as isolated drills, but are applied immediately in sentences, poems, limericks, or stories. A collection of poems and limericks may be gradually developed as the teacher comes across them in books and anthologies of children's literature. Words of some folk songs and certain stories which have rhyming in them, such as those by Dr. Seuss, may provide additional sources for practice. Phonics exercises are presented systematically at each session, but the presentation remains brief lest the children become resistant or satiated.

TEACHING LONG VOWEL SOUNDS. Once short vowels have been mastered, the sounds of the long vowels are introduced. These are simple to learn since the long sounds just make the vowels "say their names." Nevertheless, the rules governing their usage are more complex and depend to a large extent on knowledge of the short vowel sounds. It is unnecessary to go through auditory discrimination training as described with regard to short vowels. Long vowels are taught in connection with the two major rules governing their use.

RULE OF THE SILENT *e.* In one-syllable words ending in a consonant with the vowel in the middle, the vowel is usually short—e.g., *mat, bit, cut.* However, when *e* comes at the end of such a word, it can make the first vowel say its own name. The pupils are then shown familiar words that change vowel sounds because of the silent *e*—e.g., *can, hid, mat,* which change to *cane, hide,* and *mate,* respectively. The children should be encouraged to formulate the rule for themselves.

RULE OF THE DOUBLE VOWEL. When two vowels come together in a word, the first one is usually long and the second one silent, as in *paid, coat,* and *seat.* It is always good practice to present words and encourage the children to figure out the rule for themselves. A rule stated in their own words is frequently more meaningful. However, children should be told the rule if they do not see it for themselves. The important point is that they understand how it works and how to use it.

DIPHTHONGS. It is usually sufficient for children with reading disability to be taught the short and long sounds of the single vowels. However, if pupils have difficulty with vowel combinations, these must be taught as well. Vowel variations are taught in the same ways as are single vowel sounds. The teacher need not waste time teaching rare combinations. The most common diphthongs are listed below.[10]

$\bar{oo}$ as in *moon*	*ay* as in *say*	*ow* as in *how*
$\breve{oo}$ as in *good*	*y* as in *my*	$\bar{ow}$ as in *slow*
oi as in *spoil*		*au* as in *fault*

Games help to lighten the tedium in learning phonics and can be a supplementary device for practice. As already stated, phonics must be applied and used in reading as much as possible after any isolated practice is completed. Several commercial phonics games are available. A few are listed below; a complete listing with sources will be found in Appendix C.

"PHONIC RUMMY." Phonic Rummy is a game of word cards. The words are constructed to help the pupil practice blending vowel sounds with consonants. It is played like rummy. Three words containing the same vowel or vowel combination make a "book." There are several different sets. Set A reviews the short vowel sounds; set B reviews long vowel sounds; sets C and D review various vowel combinations.

"VOWEL LOTTO." Vowel Lotto reviews short and long vowel sounds and vowel combinations. It is played like regular lotto. A card containing six illustrations is given to each player. Separate picture cards are placed face down in a pile. A player draws a single picture card and tries to match it with the same sound represented by another picture on his master card.

"TAKE." Take consists of a number of cards, each containing a word and a corresponding picture. The players take tricks by matching sounds in var-

---

[10] W. Kottmeyer, *Teacher's Guide for Remedial Reading* (St. Louis: Webster, 1959), pp. 138, 139.

ious positions in the words. Thus tricks might include words such as, *mule—mine, jam—hat, top—ship*, which have identical sounds at the beginning, middle, and end, respectively.

The workbooks that are used in teaching phonics skills at primary levels are numerous. Some are listed below; others are found in Appendix C, under "Workbooks for Practice in Word Analysis."

Building Reading Skills, Books 1, 2, 3, by Rowena Hargrave and Leila Armstrong. Wichita, Kansas: McCormick Mathers.

Conquests in Reading, by William Kottmeyer and Kay Ware. St. Louis, Mo.: Webster.

Eye and Ear Fun, Books 1, 2, 3, by Clarence Stone. St. Louis, Mo.: Webster.

Happy Times with Sounds, Books 1, 2, 3, by Lola Thompson. California: Allyn & Bacon.

My Own Reading Exercises, Book 2, by Robert Bedwell and Mary Hutchinson. Auburn, Ala.: Prather.

Phonics We Use, Books A, B, C, by Mary Meighan, Marjorie Pratt, and Mabel Halvorsen. Chicago: Lyons & Carnahan.

Additional Word-Analysis Skills

STRUCTURAL ANALYSIS. Structural analysis, according to Gray,[11] is ". . . the means by which we identify the parts of a word which form meaning units or pronunciation units within a word." It therefore supplements the methods described previously in this chapter and includes the teaching of such word endings as plurals, compound words, syllabication, and roots, prefixes, and suffixes.

WORD ENDINGS. For children with reading disability, it is generally sufficient to point out the various endings of words; overemphasis should be avoided; time should not be spent on endings that occur rarely. The children are shown the base word and add several endings to see how the word changes. The most common endings are *s, ed, ing, er, est, y,* and *ly.*[12]

COMPOUND WORDS. Compound words are also fairly easy for children with reading disability to master. In most cases they need only be shown that

---

[11] W. Gray, *On Their Own in Reading* (Chicago: Scott, Foresman, 1948), p. 76.

[12] Once in a while children become confused because *ed* sometimes sounds like *t* as in *liked,* at other times like *ed* as in *parted,* and at others like *d* as in *roared.* If the pupil does not grasp the sound from reading the word in context, the teacher must take time to explain the differences.

some words are made up of two separate words, as *up stairs, blue bird, pea nut.*[13]

SYLLABICATION. Stressing too many rules of syllabication can diminish rather than promote reading fluency. Pupils need to know the major rules of syllabication so that they can recognize words. Syllables are presented most effectively at first by exaggerating the pronunciation of words so that the separate syllables are easily distinguished. Until the pupils learn to recognize the number of syllables in a word and understand that each syllable always contains one vowel sound, they cannot determine how to divide words into syllables. Oral work must be undertaken with the teacher until it is established that the children know where the separations come.

The main concept in syllabication is that long words are made up of shorter elements, each containing a single vowel sound. Parts of words usually follow the same rules which have been previously learned as part of the basic word-analysis skills. For example, rules of the double vowel sound and silent *e* continue to control the vowel sounds in most syllables just as they do in one-syllable words (eg., *fif-teen, e-ven, ro-tate*).

When possible, the teacher should give the children enough experience in dividing words so that they can evolve the two major rules for syllabication, formulating them in their own words. If they cannot do so, she gives them the two rules that have been found most useful in this connection:

When two consonants come together in a word, we usually divide them between two syllables. This rule can be taught by starting with two-syllable words that have double consonants to simplify the demonstration: *lad-der, pret-ty, muf-fin, hap-py.* Once the concept is clear, words with two unlike consonants may be divided: *him-self, pic-nic, prob-lem.*

When two consonants do not come together, the word is usually divided after the first vowel. Two-syllable words beginning with a consonant provide the best illustrations of this rule: *po-lite, de-cide, de-mand.* Words that begin with a vowel sometimes present difficulty. Pointing out that the first vowel can constitute a syllable all by itself usually clears up the problem: *o-pen, e-vil, a-corn.*

ROOT WORDS, PREFIXES, AND SUFFIXES. Knowing that certain base words can be combined with prefixes and suffixes may be an aid to word recogni-

---

[13] Authorities sometimes recommend that the child "find little words in big words." If this technique is used, it is advisable to conduct it orally because finding the short word can actually hinder recognition. For example, focusing on *get* in *together* or *cat* in *locate* is very confusing.

tion. However, for the child with reading disability, this concept must be simplified in order to eliminate confusion.

In teaching base words and suffixes, the teacher might point out that whenever a standard ending appears in a word, a suffix has been added. She then shows the pupils how to distinguish between the root and the suffix, as in *jump-ing, fast-er, quick-ly.* Prefixes are taught in the same way. The base words used in teaching should be complete in themselves. For example, pupils quickly grasp that the prefix *dis* (meaning *not*) placed before the word *believe* results in *disbelieve,* and its changed meaning is clear. Obviously it would be confusing to use such words as *disdain* and *revoke,* for which there is no independent base word in English. Finally, the relationship between the prefix, the root word, and the suffix is demonstrated, as in *re-wind-ing, re-work-ing,* and so on. From their knowledge of the base words, the pupils may be able to discover that *re* means *again,* and so on.

The suffixes and prefixes that are taught should be chosen on the basis of consistency of meaning and frequency of occurence. According to a study made by Stauffer,[14] the following prefixes fulfill these criteria:

com	dis	ex	pre	re	sub

Lazar[15] and Kottmeyer[16] suggest the following suffixes, using these same criteria:

tion	ment	ful	less

As the foregoing discussion implies, extensive practice with root words, prefixes, and suffixes is more suitable for pupils at upper levels. Further discussion of methods for older pupils is presented in Chapter 8, pages 142–148.

DICTIONARY SKILLS. Children must learn to use a dictionary efficiently for pronunciations, meanings, and word usage. Dictionaries are now available at all levels starting with the very easiest picture dictionaries and ranging on

---

[14] R. Stauffer, "A Study of Prefixes in the Thorndike List to Establish a List of Prefixes that Should Be Taught in the Elementary School," *Journal of Educational Research,* 35 (1942), pp. 453–8.

[15] May Lazar, "Ten Years of Progress in Remedial Reading: A Summary," *Elementary School Journal,* 59 (1959), pp. 386–7.

[16] *Op. cit.,* p. 152.

up through various levels. The teacher gives practice in any skills the pupils lack, such as finding entries, identifying word meanings, and using the pronunciation system. Two excellent simple dictionaries published by Scott, Foresman are the *Thorndike-Barnhart Beginning Dictionary*, at fourth grade level; and one slightly more difficult, the *Thorndike-Barnhart Junior Dictionary*. They both include instructions for their use. Guides and workbooks for the teaching of dictionary skills are available from publishers such as Scott, Foresman, G. & C. Merriam, Holt, Rinehart and Winston, and Wordcrafters Guild.[17] Similar exercises are incorporated in many other workbooks that accompany basal readers.

CONTEXT. Usually children with reading disability have previously learned how to figure out a word from context. Too often, time that might profitably be spent on foundation skills is wasted on teaching the use of context. Many children, in fact, overemphasize this skill, with the result that they tend to rely on indiscriminate guessing. Their eyes flit back and forth from the word to the picture; they use the initial consonant, general configuration, or other means to help them. For example, if the child does not know the last word in the sentence "The book is on the *table*" the teacher might suggest that he look at the picture and the initial consonant to guess the word. If the picture is clear, the child is likely to guess correctly. Many times, however, the illustration is ambiguous, and if the child continues to rely on this means, his guessing may become wild and his reading more inaccurate than ever. If children are not familiar with the use of context, merely pointing out that words can sometimes be ascertained from the rest of the sentence or other clues is usually sufficient.

OVERCOMING REVERSAL ERRORS AND INACCURACY IN READING. The group of skills described in this chapter constitute the minimal word-analysis techniques that are needed by reading disability cases. There are certain special problems, however, that frequently occur in children with reading disability. They may tend to reverse letters, words, or phrases. They may add, omit, or substitute words when reading a paragraph aloud. They often phrase poorly and have little expression in their oral reading.

Reversing such letters as *d* and *b*, *p* and *q*, is common in reading disability cases. In the first instance, it is sometimes helpful to show the pupil that he can change small *b* to capital *B* by adding another loop in the same direction. (See illustration, Page 103.)

---

[17] Wordcrafters Guild, St. Albans School, Washington 16, D.C.

Another technique has also been found useful. Children never reverse the *d* or *b* in cursive writing. Therefore, when they are puzzled as to which letter a word begins with, they might be told to trace the letter with their forefingers. A cursive letter *d* can be traced over a printed *d*, since it "goes" in the same direction. The same thing can be accomplished with the letter *b*. (See illustrations, Page 103.)

With the letter *q*, it can be pointed out that *q* is always found with *u*.

Reversing letters in such words as *was* (*saw*) is also common. Sounding out the first letter of the word should act as a correct clue for the whole word. For example, sounding *n* at the beginning of the word *no* should help to distinguish it from *on*.

A large arrow drawn at the top of the page may remind the children to read words and sentences from left to right.

Placing a zipper over a line of print and letting the child open it from left to right is another useful method. Young children especially enjoy unzipping it and seeing the letters or words appear.

Beyond these simple devices, reversals must be corrected by practice in reading and strengthening of all word recognition techniques.

Finally, two additional characteristics of children with reading disability —inaccuracy and lack of fluency in oral reading—may become habitual patterns of performance due to the insecurity and anxiety inherent in the situation. Developing rapport with a competent teacher, improvement in word recognition, and experience in reading suitable material usually alleviate these difficulties.

Encouraging the Use of Word-Analysis Skills

The skills outlined in this chapter can be incorporated in regular class work, as is described in Chapter 6. The teacher's relationship with pupils who have reading difficulty is of the utmost importance. Spending even a short time with an individual or small group can make an enormous difference in their progress. According to a study made by the New York City Board of Education, "Even five minutes a day of . . . individual contact which engrossed the child's real attention was worth much more to him than one-half hour a day in a group reading situation which merely tapped his surface attention. Moreover, the teacher's concern and efforts in his behalf seemed to convince the child that she understood his difficulties and meant to help him."[18] Children with disability need the

---

[18] Board of Education, *Teaching Guides*, Language Arts, No. 2 (New York: Board of Education of the City of New York, 1955).

satisfaction of being singled out as individuals in positive ways, since too often they have been singled out only for ridicule or reprimanding. In addition, it is helpful to use a multisensory approach wherever indicated. All methods must be explored until reading becomes more fluent and proficient.

Spelling

Most children with reading disability have just as much trouble with spelling as with word analysis. Teaching spelling along with the teaching of letter sounds acts as an effective reinforcement for using phonics.

Before beginning instruction with children who have spelling disability, the teacher administers a standardized spelling test. Spelling subtests are included in most standardized achievement batteries. Some of these are listed in Appendix A.

The basis of spelling is the knowledge of sounds. Pupils must be aware of the connection between hearing a sound and reproducing it accurately in writing. In teaching word analysis by the phonic method, for example, the instructor points out the visual symbols for every sound. For non-phonetic words, the visual-motor method (refer to Page 82) is effective because it makes use of both kinesthetic and visual clues in recall. For particularly troublesome words, the kinesthetic method alone might be used.

Spelling lists, to which the teacher and the children can refer, have been compiled from the words most frequently used in children's compositions. Excellent examples are the lists published by the New York City Board of Education,[19] in which the words are arranged according to their frequency of use by children. Dolch[20] has compiled a similar list, as has Johnson.[21] Pupils can use the latter booklet, designed for junior high school students, as both a reference and a personal dictionary, because there are both a dictionary of frequently misspelled words and blank pages on which the student can write any other words he wants to learn.

Such lists are much easier for children with reading disability to use than dictionaries, for they contain far fewer words and are much less confusing. Although dictionary skills are important, they frequently prove

---

[19] Board of Education, *Spelling Words* (New York: Board of Education of the City of New York, 1954).

[20] E. Dolch, *The Modern Teaching of Spelling* (Champaign, Ill.: Garrard Press, 1950), p. 4.

[21] E. Johnson, *Improve Your Own Spelling* (New York: McGraw-Hill, 1958).

discouraging for these children. For example, a pupil once asked the author, "How on earth do you spell *pearl?*—and don't ask me to look it up in the dictionary because I've already looked under 'pir,' 'pur,' and 'per' without finding it."

Pupils may also be taught spelling in connection with written compositions. However, the teacher should not correct misspellings in written work by underlining the mistakes, for that calls attention to the incorrect spelling. Instead, misspelled words should be crossed out and the correct spelling written above each error. The child keeps a record of these words and tries to learn them. Many high school and college students with spelling disability have found it useful to keep an alphabetized notebook of troublesome words to which they can refer when necessary. This simplifies their looking up words, gives them an additional individualized reference, and encourages correct spelling. Students who wish to become better spellers must continue to improve their basic knowledge of sounds, rules, and spelling principles, but despite conscientious effort, some of them have extreme difficulty in this area for many years. Whether this is due to a general language disorder or other factors is not known. Students and teachers, however, who realize how long spelling and reading disability sometimes persist, can at least view the difficulty constructively by using every means of compensation for it rather than feeling apprehensive and guilty if practice and application are not entirely successful.

Suggestions for Further Reading

ARTLEY, STERL, A., *Your Child Learns to Read.* New York: Scott, Foresman, 1953.

DAWSON, MILDRED, and BAMMAN, H., *Fundamentals of Basic Reading Instruction.* New York: Longmans, Green, 1959, Ch. 6.

DURRELL, D., NICHOLSON, ALICE, OLSON, A., GAVEL, SYLVIA, and LINEHAM, ELEANOR, "Success in First Grade Reading." *Journal of Education,* 140 (1958), pp. 1–8.

HARRIS, A., *Effective Teaching of Reading.* New York: McKay, 1962, Chs. 4, 5, 8, 9.

KELLY, BARBARA, "The Economy Method vs. the Scott, Foresman Method in Teaching Second-Grade Reading in the Murphysboro Public Schools." *Journal of Educational Research,* 51 (1958), pp. 465–9.

McCullough, Constance, "What Does Research Reveal about Practices in Teaching Reading?" *English Journal, 46* (1957), pp. 475–90.

McKee, P., *The Teaching of Reading in the Elementary School.* Boston: Houghton Mifflin, 1948, Part 2.

Roswell, Florence, and Chall, Jeanne, "Helping Poor Readers with Word Recognition Skills." *The Reading Teacher, 10* (1957), pp. 200–4.

Sartain, H., "Do Reading Workbooks Increase Achievement?" *Elementary School Journal,* 62 (1961), pp. 157–62.

Tinker, M., and McCullough, Constance, *Teaching Elementary Reading.* New York: Appleton-Century-Crofts, 1962.

Toop, D., "An Analysis of the Points of View, Practices, and Procedures Related to the Programs of Helping Children with their Reading Problems in Selected Elementary Schools in Indiana." *Studies in Education,* 1955, pp. 345–48. Thesis Abstract Series, School of Education, Indiana University, No. 7, 1956.

Traxler, A., "What Does Research Suggest about Ways to Improve Reading Instruction?" *Improving Reading in the Junior High School,* 5–15. U.S. Department of Health, Education and Welfare, Office of Education, Bulletin No. 10, 1957.

Selected Research on Phonics Instruction

Austin, Mary C., "Phonetic Elements and Principles Basic to Reading." *Supplementary Educational Monographs, 82* (1955), pp. 51–5.

Betts, E., "Phonics: Practical Considerations Based on Research." *Elementary English, 33* (1956), pp. 357–71.

Burrows, Alvina T., *What About Phonics?* Bulletin No. 57, Association for Childhood Education International, Washington, D.C., 1951.

Clymer T., *The Utility of Forty-four Phonic Generalizations.* Presented at the IRA–NCTE Conference, St. Louis, May, 1961.

Dolch, E., and Bloomster, M., "Phonic Readiness." *Elementary School Journal,* 38 (1937), pp. 201–5.

Durkin, Dolores, *Phonics and the Teaching of Reading.* New York: Bureau of Publications, Teachers College, Columbia University, 1962.

Figurel, J., "What Research Says About Phonics." *A Report of Twelfth Annual Conference and Course on Reading* (June, 1956), pp. 106–24, University of Pittsburgh.

Gates, A., *A Review of Rudolf Flesch, Why Johnny Can't Read.* New York: Macmillan, 1955.

Gates, A., and Russell, D., "Types of Material, Vocabulary Burden, Word Analysis and Other Factors in Beginning Reading." *Elementary School Journal,* 39 (1938), pp. 27–35, 119–28.

Gray, W., "Reading: IV: The Teaching of Reading," in C. W. Harris, ed., *Encyclopedia of Educational Research,* 3d ed. New York: Macmillan, 1960.

HILDRETH, GERTRUDE, "The Role of Pronouncing and Sounding in Learning to Read." *Elementary School Journal, 55* (1954), pp. 141–7.

LICHTENSTEIN, A., "The Letter-sounds: A Reading Problem." *Elementary English Review, 17* (1940), pp. 23–7.

McDOWELL, J., "A Report on the Phonetic Method of Teaching Children to Read." *Catholic Educational Review, 51* (1953), pp. 506–19.

MILLS, R., "An Evaluation of Techniques for Teaching Word Recognition." *Elementary School Journal 56* (1956), pp. 221–5.

MORRIS, JOYCE M., "The Relative Effectiveness of Different Methods of Teaching," *Educational Research* (Nov. 1958, Feb. 1959), pp. 38–49, 61–75.

"Phonics in Reading Instruction." *The Reading Teacher, 9* (1955), entire issue.

RAMSEY, Z., "Will Tomorrow's Teachers Know and Teach Phonics?" *The Reading Teacher, 4,* No. 15 (1962), pp. 241–4.

SMITH, NILA B., "What Research Says about Phonics Instruction." *Journal of Educational Research, 51* (1957), pp. 1–9.

————, "What Research Tells Us about Word Recognition." *Elementary School Journal, 55* (1955), pp. 440–6.

SPARKS, P., and FAY L., "An Evaluation of Two Methods of Teaching Reading." *Elementary School Journal 57* (1957), pp. 386–90.

STAIGER, R., "Your Child Learns Phonics." *The Reading Teacher, 9* (1955), pp. 95–9.

WITTY, P., and SIZEMORE, R., "Phonics in the Reading Program: A Review and an Evaluation." *Elementary English, 32* (1955), pp. 355–71.

Some Phonic Programs and Readers
Based on Phonic Instruction

Phonic Programs

BLOOMFIELD, L., and BARNHARDT, C., *Let's Read: A Linguistic Approach.* Detroit: Wayne State University Press, 1961.

CARDEN, MAE, *The Carden Method.* 619 S. Maple Ave., Glen Rock, N.Y.

HAY, JULIE, and WINGO, C., *Reading with Phonics.* Philadelphia: Lippincott, 1960.

GILLINGHAM, ANNA, and STILLMAN, B., *Remedial Training for Children with Specific Reading Disability in Reading, Spelling, and Penmanship,* 5th ed. 25 Parkview Ave. Bronxville, N.Y.

SCHOOLFIELD, LUCILLE, and TIMBERLAKE, JOSEPHINE, *Phonovisual Method.* Phonovisual Products, Inc., P.O. Box 5625, Washington, D.C.

SLOOP, CORNELIA, et al., *A Teacher's Manual for the First Grade, Phonetic Keys to Reading.* Oklahoma City: The Economy Co., 1958.

SPAULDING, ROMALDA, and SPAULDING, W., *The Writing Road to Reading.* New York: Whiteside & Morrow, 1957.

Readers

DANIELS, J., and DIACK, H., *The Royal Road Readers*. London: Chatto & Windus, 1957.

EATON, WINIFRED, and JAMES, BERTHA, *The Iroquois Phonics Series*. Columbus, Ohio: Iroquois, 1960.

WENKART, A., *Wenkart Phonic Readers*. 4 Shady Hill Square, Cambridge, Mass., 1960.

Selected Research on Individualized Reading

BARBE, W., *Educator's Guide to Personalized Reading Instruction*. Englewood Cliffs, N.J.: Prentice-Hall, 1960.

———, *Personalized Reading Instruction*. Englewood Cliffs, N.J.: Prentice-Hall, 1961.

BETTS, E. A., "Meeting the Needs of Individual Children." *The Reading Teacher*, 6 (1952), pp. 4–11.

BRAIDFORD, MARGARET, *A Comparison of Two Teaching Methods, Individual and Group, in the Teaching of Comprehension in Beginning Reading to Selected First Grade Children in the Public Schools of Great Neck, New York*. Unpublished doctoral dissertation. New York University, 1960.

BURROWS, ALVINA, "Individualizing the Teaching of Reading," in *Teaching Children in the Middle Grades*. New York: Heath, 1952, Ch. 10.

CARLINE, D., *An Investigation of Individualized Reading and Basal Text Reading through Pupil Achievement and Teacher Performance*. Unpublished doctoral dissertation. Pennsylvania State University, 1961.

DICKENSON, MARIE, et al., "Through Self-selection to Individualized Teaching Procedures." *California Journal of Elementary Education*, 27 (1959), pp. 150–77.

DOLCH, E., *Individualized vs. Group Reading*. Free booklet. Champaign, Ill.: Garrard Press, 1962.

DRAPER, MARCELLA, and SCHWIETERT, LOUISE, *A Practical Guide to Individualized Reading*. New York: Board of Education, Pub. No. 40, 1960.

FOX, LORENE, and McCULLOUGH, C., "Individualized Reading." *NEA Journal*, 162 (1958), p. 3.

GRAY, W., "The Role of Group and Individual Instruction in Reading." *Third Annual Reading Conference Proceedings*. Sacramento, Calif.: Sacramento State College Council International Reading Association, 1 (March 1, 1958), p. 5.

"Individualizing Reading Instruction." *Proceedings of the 39th Annual Education Conference*, Vol. VI, Russell Stauffer, ed. Newark, Del.: The Reading Study Center, School of Education, University of Delaware, 1959.

ISAACS, ALICE, "Individualized Reading Instruction." *The Educational Journal*, 1 (1958), pp. 13–14.

Izzo, Ruth K., *A Comparison of Two Teaching Methods, Individual and Group, in the Teaching of Word Identification in Beginning Reading to Selected First Grade Children in the Public Schools of Great Neck, New York,* Unpublished doctoral dissertation. New York University, 1960.

Jacobs, L., "Reading on Their Own Means Reading at Their Growing Edges." *The Reading Teacher, 6* (1953), pp. 27–32.

Jenkins, Marion, "Self-selection in Reading." *The Reading Teacher, 11* (1957), pp. 84–90.

Lazar, May, "Individualized Reading: A Dynamic Approach." *The Reading Teacher, 11* (1957), pp. 84–90.

Meil, Alice, ed., "Individualizing Reading Practices." *Practical Suggestions for Teaching,* No. 14. New York: Bureau of Publications, Teachers College, Columbia University, 1958.

"News and Comment." *Educational School Journal,* (1960), pp. 411–28.

Sartain, H., "The Roseville Experiment with Individualized Reading." *The Reading Teacher, 13* (1960), pp. 277–81.

Smith, Nila, "Something Old, Something New in Primary Reading." *Elementary English,* (1960), pp. 371–5.

Stauffer, R., "Individualized and Group Type Directed Reading Instruction." *Elementary English,* (1960), pp. 375–85.

———, "Individualized Reading Instructon—A Backward Look." *Elementary English, 36* (1959), pp. 335–41.

Veatch, Jeanette, *Individualizing Your Reading Program.* New York: G. P. Putnam & Sons, 1959.

———, "In Defense of Individualized Reading." *Elementary English, 37* (1960), pp. 277–84.

Witty, P., "Individualized Reading—A Summary and Evaluation." *Elementary English, 36* (1959), pp. 401–12.

Zirbes, Laura, "The Experience Approach in Reading." *The Reading Teacher, 5* (1951), pp. 1–2.

Supplementary illustrations; see pages 96–97.

⅌ 6

Application of Word
Recognition Techniques

⅌ Chapter 5 has described the major word recognition techniques for children with reading disability. It was suggested briefly that these techniques be incorporated in reading material wherever possible rather than taught in isolation. In this chapter we will describe some of the general approaches that may be used in the actual teaching of word recognition to a group and to individuals in or outside the classroom.

Oral Reading

While oral and round robin reading may have some disadvantages in developmental reading instruction, it is useful in working with children who have reading disability, particularly when their reading level is low. Although rarely considered a method, oral reading is one of the best means for practicing word recognition. Many words, especially sight words, are repeated again and again. The teacher can supply those that the child does not know. He repeats them in the course of reading and, in this way, gradually learns to recognize them. Although this is sometimes called "incidental" teaching, it is a sound and valid way for reinforcing words. Where indicated, the teacher can also help the pupil to sound the words out and use structural analysis and context while reading. In this way, the pupil learns the words he does not know not just as an entity, but he sees them embedded in many different contexts. For example, a child may know the word *there* in isolation, but it seems to be less recognizable when interwoven in different sentences where the individual *Gestalt* appears altered. Therefore, as long as the oral reading is not allowed to become laborious, the pupil has a better chance of strengthening his word recognition ability in this natural and less taxing setting than he has through meaningless drill. Also, the teacher can determine from the oral reading the pupil's progress in word recognition and what skills he still may need.

Round robin reading has other advantages for children with reading disability. They frequently tend to be either very passive and dependent or disruptive and disorderly. If they are not involved in a task every second, the first group resorts to daydreaming, the second to aggressive behavior. It is desirable, therefore, to have them all keep the place together, reading alternately, with the teacher joining in also. This means that all the children finish the story at the same time, while the teacher's rendition adds interest, expression, phrasing, and understanding. Children who tend to lose the page and daydream need to be prodded every once in a while by pointing to the place in their book. This keeps them alert and prevents embarrassment when it is their turn to read. For restless children, reading suitable material aloud often has a soothing effect. Furthermore, the joy of the poor reader who is at last able to perform adequately far surpasses any negative aspects that may be present. For all these reasons, oral reading plays an important part in the remedial sessions.

Phrasing and Expression

Before any attempt is made to practice phrasing or improve expression, the child should be reading within the scope of his ability and have mastered all the needed word recognition techniques. Otherwise there are too many skills for him to consider at once. In any beginning foreign language class, for example, it takes a high degree of mastery before the pupils—regardless of their age—can read the text fluently or with expression.

To improve children's performance in reading, several procedures can be tried. The teacher might alternate with the pupil in reading paragraphs or pages, or she might try choral reading (reading simultaneously with the pupil). Thus the pupil may be able to imitate her example. She might use a tape recorder so that the child can hear how he sounds. For many pupils, tape recordings provide added incentive for improvement. For others, however, tape recording renditions are a threat, particularly those whose performance is very poor.

The most effective means of all is to encourage as much supplementary reading by themselves as possible. Most children with reading disability shy away from independent reading and therefore rarely gain the practice needed for a fluent performance. They should be guided toward exciting stories at a level that they can handle. More and more high interest, low vocabulary books with mature content are becoming available. Several of them are listed in Appendix B.

Comprehension in Oral Reading

For children with reading disability who are functioning on a primary level, the authors do not treat comprehension in connection with their reading in the manner recommended by the standard manuals for developmental reading. Since these pupils are usually reading material containing concepts designed for much younger children, they rarely have trouble with the meaning unless they have a language problem or an extremely limited experiential background. Their major problem stems from difficulty in recognizing words.[1] Therefore, to follow the widespread practice of answering questions about the content, looking back to substantiate answers, finding explanatory phrases or paragraphs to elaborate specific points, is not only inappropriate, but it smothers any spark of interest that may have been aroused. In fact, some of the deep resistance to reading that the authors have encountered with such children has been due to the endless questions they were asked which ruined any delight in the story itself. Imagine how a child feels who is struggling with word recognition, feeling clumsy in reading aloud, and worrying lest he sound utterly absurd. Then at the end of this wretched experience he must think up answers to comprehension questions! Instead of concern over understanding the material at this stage, the teacher seizes every opportunity to promote pleasure in completing the story. Wherever there are strong reactions to the ideas themselves, she of course encourages spontaneous discussion. More often than not on the lower reading levels, however, the teacher and children finish the story with brief comments and go on to the next procedure. (Comprehension at higher levels is discussed in Chapter 7.)

The Place of Word Analysis in the Remedial Program

After oral reading and discussion have been completed, some extra practice on the separate skills may still be needed. The children learn consonant sounds, vowel sounds, consonant combinations, and so on by

---

[1] Florence Roswell and Jeanne Chall, "Helping Poor Readers with Word Recognition Skills," *The Reading Teacher, 10* (1957), p. 200.

the methods described in Chapter 5. The visual-motor and most other special methods can also be used easily in group instruction.

As we have noted, only those word-analysis techniques that are most essential are emphasized with children who have reading disability. Because they usually have become discouraged as a result of previous failures and tend to carry over these negative attitudes, the teacher attempts to show them that certain basic skills will increase their reading ability quickly and effectively. She names the skills to be learned and explains how they are used. This encourages a collaborative spirit and sets concrete and realistic goals. Rather than plowing through endless lists and countless exercises, the pupils can learn a streamlined version of word analysis and proceed as rapidly as possible.

In working with such children, the teacher should not expect 100-percent accuracy. She knows their prolonged tendency to mistake sight words and confuse letter sounds. Whether this is due to perceptual difficulties, anxiety, or other factors related to reading disability is not known. What we do know is that many children with reading disability experience difficulty over a long period before they are able to achieve accuracy in word recognition. Instead of expecting perfection, the experienced teacher strives for steady improvement. If the teacher shows understanding and acceptance of the fluctuations in the child's progress, the child's anxiety about making mistakes usually lessens. This in turn tends to decrease his errors and gradually results in smoother and more proficient reading.

The Classroom Library

The ultimate objective of teaching word recognition is to develop the pupil's reading ability. To promote this aim, the teacher should have a large selection of appropriate reading materials on hand in the form of a classroom library. A selected list of such material is offered in Appendix B.

Although many classrooms have libraries, children with reading disability usually are reluctant to use them. They have been discouraged long ago by their unsuccessful attempts to read any of the volumes. When these children are assigned outside reading, their major criterion is the slenderness of the book. In order to try again, they need a great deal of encouragement.

The teacher can foster more positive attitudes toward reading by providing a wide variety of materials with controlled vocabulary but high interest. If only a limited amount of money is available, books can sometimes be borrowed in quantity from the public library. Another possibility is to purchase a number of short-story collections at varying levels. These can sometimes be cut up into their separate selections.[2] The children can help to prepare the material and to make suitable covers for each story. The result is hundreds of attractive booklets that offer pleasurable reading to many children at different stages of reading competency.

To facilitate the pupils' choice of suitable reading matter, the teacher might code the books according to level, marking them conspicuously on the back binding or cover with an appropriate symbol. For example, she might use the letters S, T, U, V, and so on, S representing preprimer; T, primer; U, first grade; V, second grade; and so forth. The pupils are then told which "letter" books are most sensible for them to read at present. A similar system can be used having different colors to represent the different levels. If such a procedure is used, the children should be told the reason for it: it is good to find books that are enjoyable; they cannot be appreciated if they are too difficult;[3] therefore, they are coded for convenience just as in regular libraries.

The teacher might check on the pupils' reading by asking them to tell what part of a story they liked best or found funniest. If a story seems suitable for other children as well, she might ask them to share it with the class. This practice is accepted enthusiastically by most children. It seems to effect an improvement in the attitude of the poorer readers in particular. Disheartened readers often become interested in exploring the possibilities of the library when they find out that they can really read and derive pleasure from books.

Teaching Pupils of Disparate Ages Reading at Primary Level

A teacher who knows how to teach word recognition to six- and seven-year-olds may be totally at a loss in dealing with older pupils because the techniques must be carefully modified. To illustrate the possible approaches, three pupils will be described who were eight, eleven, and sixteen years old respectively, yet who all read at first grade level. They were taught basic word recognition techniques by their own teachers in their regular classes with the authors serving as consultants. They all learned sufficient word-analysis skills so that they were able to read at third grade level at the end of the term. Although the procedures were used individually for the most part, they can be adapted easily to group work.

---

[2] Florence Roswell, "When Children's Textbooks Are Too Difficult," *Elementary School Journal*, 60 (1959), pp. 146–57.

[3] Jeanne Chall, "Let Them Try the Book On for Fit," *The Reading Teacher*, 7 (1953), pp. 83–88.

A description of background information in all the cases in this chapter has been omitted because the purpose is to point up ways of integrating word recognition techniques into the total reading program. Also, in many cases full background data is unavailable to the teacher. (Omission of background description here is in contrast to the cases discussed in Chapter 10, where fuller information on each case is included.)

A Third Grader Reading at First Grade Level

Jim, aged 8 years 9 months, was in third grade. He presented the least complicated problem because a third grader reading at first grade level is still fairly receptive to stories and books on a first grade level. Also it is likely that he can be brought up to grade level in a relatively short period of time.

Jim's I.Q. was 99. He could handle a book at low first grade level. His sight vocabulary was limited, and he showed poor ability to blend sounds together into whole words.

Jim was seen individually for ten minutes a day by his teacher. At the first session he read *Sailor Jack*,[4] which is at primer level. As he read, the teacher supplied unfamiliar words quickly. The frequent repetition helped Jim remember the words, and he soon handled this reader quite easily. She also helped him to utilize context and phonics wherever it would help him figure out a word. Success spurred his incentive, and he became more confident.

At each oral reading session, the teacher selected words that she considered worthy of practice. She explained that many of them were sight words and made up about three quarters of the material in the books he would be reading in and out of school.[5] To help him recognize them more quickly, she showed Jim how he could practice them by himself. She gave him the Dolch "Picture-Word Cards" and the workbook *Let's See*. (See the appendices for a complete bibliography listed according to reading level.) Jim studied the words on the cards a few at a time, then tested himself. Sometimes he worked with another child. The workbook provided additional experience with the sight vocabulary, for it gave clues for many of the words through illustrations and repeated them in many different contexts.

After he read several books in the *Sailor Jack* series with his teacher or

---

[4] Full reference for all books and materials cited in this chapter can be found in Appendices B and C.

[5] E. Dolch, *A Manual for Remedial Reading* (Champaign, Ill.: Garrard Press, 1955), p. 29.

by himself, the *Cowboy Sam* books were introduced. This series is generally popular with children, and correlated workbooks are available. (Any graded series with corresponding workbooks is suitable as long as the child has not already been exposed to it.) Such material is easy for the teacher to handle and even permits her to work with several children simultaneously if they are reading at about the same level.

Jim was also encouraged to read short stories and books independently. The *Beginning Reading* series, published by Random House, and the *I Can Read* books, published by Harper and Row, were helpful. If such material had not been available, however, alternate graded readers could have been used.

In Jim's case, the teacher continued to supply words in oral reading for a long period. In addition to the vocabulary cards and the workbook, sight words were reinforced through games such as Grab and the Group Word Teaching Game, in which other children in his class participated. He was taught any additional word-analysis techniques that he needed. He was told that there were other ways to figure out words, because after all no one can memorize all the words in the English language by sight. For example, when he knew the word *went*, he was shown that by substituting initial consonants, the words *tent* and *sent* are produced. The sounds of any consonants which he did not know were taught as quickly as he could master them. He was encouraged to use these sounds as much as possible in reading. Also, rhymes, limericks, folk songs, and workbook exercises were adapted for such practice. Jim also received help in distinguishing endings and other suitable structural analysis skills that he needed.

Even though Jim became adept at figuring out new words by a word-family approach, it was several months before he could blend sounds together into whole words.[6] During this time, the teacher helped him as much as possible to develop blending ability. For instance, she talked about how we mix separate ingredients to make a cake or blend flour and water to make paste. The blending gives us a different product. Similarly we blend sounds to form words. She pronounced words slowly to help him understand the process somewhat. She had him pronounce words slowly, too. Also, she pronounced separate sounds simultaneously with him to help him capture the sensation of blending.

---

[6] This inability to synthesize sounds into meaningful wholes is encountered in many children with reading disability, and we believe it is frequently due to delayed maturation, though sometimes to other factors as well. In most cases, this difficulty is overcome between the ages of 9 and 11, at which time a systematic phonic approach may be used. When children who cannot blend sounds together are pressed excessively to learn by the phonic method, the result is failure, complicated by anxiety and resistance.

Since there were other children in his third grade class who had not yet mastered phonics, he was included in a group of pupils who received systematic phonics instruction almost daily. Whenever Jim and the other children encountered nonphonetic words which were troublesome, the visual-motor method was used. This method was also helpful in spelling lessons.

Thus Jim was given a well-rounded word-analysis program including practice in sight words, phonics, and structural analysis. He learned how to apply them in his reading, starting with simple materials and gradually reading books which were on third grade level.

A Fifth Grader Reading at First Grade Level

Eleven-year-old Cary, I.Q. 105, was in the fifth grade but read at high first grade level. His problem was more serious than Jim's because of the marked discrepancy between his functioning and that of most of the children in his class.

Even though one would proceed along the same lines as those just described, techniques and materials must be geared to the special needs of an eleven-year-old boy who is still reading at such a low level. Thus, more mature reading material with simple vocabulary was carefully selected. The pace at which word-analysis skills were developed was more rapid, and more emphasis was placed on finding simple material connected with the subject matter, such as social studies and science.

The teacher started with oral reading from selected issues of *My Weekly Reader,* levels one and two. She used only those which covered timely news and informational matter that seemed interesting. She also used such books as the *Jim Forest* readers and the *Dan Frontier* series. These books provide a somewhat higher level of format. Although some of them are a little less mature than desirable, they were the best available. The teacher explained that more interesting material would be used as soon as Cary was able to figure out words more effectively. The procedure used for oral reading was the same as that described previously, with the teacher supplying unknown words and helping Cary figure out those that he could through phonics. The more proficient Cary's reading became, the more hopeful he grew and the better he read. He came in proudly one day, announcing that he had finished *Jim Forest and the Bandits* at home. This signified that the first big hurdle had been surmounted. Cary continued to do supplementary reading of material with which he could cope, and he progressed quite rapidly.

With regard to word-analysis skills, Cary, like many other pupils of his age, showed ability to learn by the visual, visual-motor, and the phonic methods. They were all used concurrently according to the words being analyzed. Sight words were practiced as a whole, phonic words were figured out by separate sounds, and nonphonetic words were learned by the visual-motor method. This helped him to understand which techniques he should use for different words and lent flexibility to his approach.

At the same time, Cary reviewed the Dolch Basic Sight Vocabulary with the aid of another pupil. Mastery of this vocabulary, together with word-analysis skills, enabled him to read second grade material within a short period. He then read such books as *Sea Hunt, Treasure under the Sea,* and *Pueblo Stories.* These are all true stories on second grade level. Later still, *Robin Hood Stories* and *Chief Black Hawk,* on high third grade level, were read.

Although oral reading and training in word recognition were extremely important for Cary, integrating his reading with classroom requirements in arithmetic, social studies, and science was even more imperative. Therefore, he was taught the special terms needed in each subject starting with second grade textbooks. Cary required a good deal of help in this area. He also complained very often to his teacher that he could not take part in classroom activities or discussion because there was nothing he could read for his project. Therefore, as soon as he was reading at mid-second-grade level, the teacher tried to find material related to the topic being discussed in class. Although there is a dearth of such material at low levels, the teacher started by using the *SRA Reading Laboratory,* elementary edition, at high second grade level. By learning new vocabulary and making use of context clues, Cary was able to read the articles before too long. The shorter articles were used because they are less formidable than longer ones and offer a sense of accomplishment. In addition, Cary read the articles entitled "Rockets Away" and "Let's Ride in a Jet Plane" in the *Reader's Digest Skill Builder,* Book II, Part 1. He prepared these articles during his ten-minute sessions alone with the teacher and soon was able to join in class discussions. He could also participate by reading articles to his classmates and by posting news clippings from the *Weekly Reader* on the bulletin board.

In this case it can be seen that whereas developing independence in word recognition forms the basis of all reading, isolated teaching of skills is only a temporary measure. Reading material which is as mature as possible is chosen. Emphasis is also placed on selecting informational reading matter in connection with the separate subject areas.

A High School Student Reading at First Grade Level

Fred, aged 16 with average I.Q., in tenth grade, presented an even greater problem than Cary. By the time a pupil has reached this age and is still virtually a nonreader, he feels extremely discouraged and defeated. However, any method which will demonstrate to him that he can read may engender hope and create the impetus for renewed learning.

Material devised for teaching English to adults or any other reading matter which is mature in format is usually acceptable. Thus, *First Steps in Reading English* and selected exercises from *The Veteran's Reader* were used for Fred. These books provided him with a sight vocabulary pertaining to things with which he was generally familiar. In addition, he was taught to read labels on foods and drugs, safety signs, subway signs, and want ads. (All of these procedures are elaborated upon in the cases of Matthew in Chapter 8 and Lloyd in Chapter 10.) As Fred learned about things connected with his everyday life, he became more responsive and was willing to assume a greater responsibility for his work. He worked diligently with the sight word cards; he took home pictures which would help him recall letter sounds and words. He accepted material at low readability level regardless of the content because he recognized the need for doing supplementary reading.

Fred's new optimism led him to ask for help with spelling and letter writing. He confided to his teacher that he hoped to enlist in the service when he was eighteen, and he wanted to be able to write letters home. Because of the deep interest Fred showed in continuing to learn, he soon was reading between second and third grade level. Then the teacher was able to broaden the scope of his reading through simple books such as *Greek Stories, Daniel Boone, Stories from Mexico,* and the like. This beginning provided sufficient basis for Fred to continue learning. He would gradually be able, in all probability, to read well enough to join the service and later to obtain a suitable job. Even though he might never attain ability in line with his potential, at least he might function fairly adequately.

Not all pupils with similar difficulties would show the same persistence and ambition as Fred. In dealing with the older pupil, (as is explained in more detail in Chapter 8) much would depend on his occupational goals, how long he is likely to remain in school, how often he could receive remedial help, how responsive he would be to such instruction, the skill of the teacher, and many other factors. However, acquisition of even minimum reading ability is extremely important, because if illiteracy continues, it may have a totally disabling effect on an individual's adjustment.

The cases of Jim, Cary, and Fred illustrate how three children of varying ages, all reading at approximately the same level, required different treatment even though the same basic principles of remedial reading were followed in each case. They illustrate also the different expectations that must be kept in mind. The more severe the disability, the more difficult it is to overcome completely. It also can be seen how word recognition skills are first presented according to the child's ability to grasp them, but are gradually expanded to incorporate all the major methods discussed in Chapter 5.

Word Recognition Techniques for Pupils Reading above Fourth Grade Level

In dealing with children who are reading at fourth grade level or above, the teacher is often perplexed by those whose basic foundation in word recognition is fairly satisfactory, but who still do not read as well as they are able. This may be due to many factors, such as insufficient development of comprehension and study skills; these are discussed in Chapter 7. Very often, however, it is due to inability to utilize word recognition skills properly. The cases of Roy and Tina, both eleven years of age, describe how difficulties in this area were handled.

Roy, aged 11, in sixth grade, I.Q. 114, obtained a score of 4.6 on the paragraph reading section of the *Stanford Achievement Test*. His teacher reported that he was very alert in class and contributed much to group discussions. However, she could not identify the nature of his reading problem. She tested his word-analysis ability and found only a few gaps in his knowledge of phonics. She knew also that his comprehension of subject matter was satisfactory. Why, then, did Roy fall so far below grade level in this test and find his homework in geography and history so difficult?

The teacher consulted the writer regarding a program of remedial instruction for Roy which she could implement during brief sessions with him several times weekly.

In the course of informal testing with the writer, Roy read some passages from a textbook which he claimed just did not make sense. As he read aloud, his problem became quite clear. Some typical errors were *scoring* for *securing* and *revolution* for *resolution*. When he came to words such as *ancient, foreign,* and *alien,* he tried to figure them out phonetically, grappled with them for a few seconds, and then continued reading. No wonder he lost the trend of thought so easily.

An analysis of the types of errors he made indicated that although his word recognition skills were fairly satisfactory, he needed strengthening in the four major areas in word analysis: phonics, syllabication, specialized vocabulary in school subjects, and dictionary skills.

Even though Roy needed this type of remedial work, the way in which instruction was presented was most important so as to gain his cooperation. For example, merely using a series of exercises in each of these four areas would not have encouraged active involvement on his part, nor would there be any assurance of carry-over in his actual reading. The program had to be well balanced with some teaching of specific skills and some supportive help so as to prevent the work from becoming too tedious. Also, all the skills had to be interwoven into a total plan.

The writer and Roy's teacher set up a program with these goals in mind. First Roy was taught only the few phonic elements which he did not know. These he grasped quickly, as most bright pupils do who are reading above fourth grade level. Next, he was shown how to divide words into syllables according to the two major rules described on Page 94. Practice in applying these principles was given through a device such as the Syllabascope and the game of Grab (Advanced Level). Roy, like many other children of this kind, enjoyed both of these techniques. The teacher then checked briefly to determine whether he was able to utilize these skills in handling class assignments. If he read *invitation* for *invention,* he was merely reminded that he now knew various means of figuring out this word correctly and was given additional help if he needed it.

Although Roy was taught dictionary skills through the use first of a glossary and then a dictionary, he was not expected to look up every word he did not know. This would have been too irksome. The teacher consulted the *Handbook of Technical Vocabulary* and his texts. The words which occurred most frequently were identified and taught. Roy was well oriented as to how mastery of the arithmetic, geography, and history lists in this book would facilitate his reading. He was intrigued with the idea that someone had gone to the trouble to compile such lists.

In going over the words, Roy was helped to use many approaches. Words like *insurrection* and *emancipation* could be figured out through syllabication, whereas *geyser, plateau,* and *drought* had to be looked up in the dictionary. He was not overburdened with such work. Instead, he was frequently told the pronunciation of unfamiliar words and given vivid descriptions of their meanings.

It took some time before Roy overcame his habitual manner of skimming over difficult words and guessing from their general shapes and from context. However, because he knew that absolute accuracy was not expected immediately, and because the work was pared down to its essentials rather than remaining overwhelming, he was gradually able to incorporate his newly learned skills into his reading. Homework became less of a chore, and satisfactory gains were evidenced on achievement tests.

Tina's problem was very different from Roy's. Yet their oral and silent reading test results were at about the same level.

Tina, 11 years of age, in sixth grade, with an I.Q. of 109, read at fourth grade level. Diagnostic tests and other qualitative evaluation revealed an excellent background in phonics and complete mastery of a basic sight vocabulary. Yet when she read aloud, she made innumerable errors. She misread words, read haltingly, repeated words, or showed marked hesitation. However, when her errors were pointed out, she was able to correct them at once. Where such characteristics appear, two major causes seem likely: (1) Dealing with words in isolation is a simpler task than reading. It allows the pupil to take more time with less familiar words and does not interfere with the rendition or with the thought processes that are necessary for understanding connected reading material. (2) Added tension due to many factors may interfere with the pupil's ability to read aloud smoothly.

In Tina's case, both these areas were considered. First, suitable words were presented in isolation. She knew them instantly. Even when they were presented in a hand-operated tachistoscope, Flash X,[7] which exposes words at the rapid rate of $\frac{1}{25}$ of a second, she had no trouble. She saw, without question, that she knew the words very well indeed. Thus, the first assumption was ruled out.

The second possibility relating to anxiety in the reading situation is an extremely complex area to explore, particularly if one desires the child to develop a certain amount of insight. This can sometimes be imparted in terms the child can understand.

In talking with Tina, the writer indicated that perhaps they might try to discover the sources of her difficulty. She pointed out how Tina was able to read words correctly with merely the briefest glimpse. Her problem was certainly not due to inability to recognize words. There must be other reasons. They discussed how she must have been embarrassed in front of her classmates when she read so poorly. She must also have been

---

[7] Hand-operated tachistoscopes are listed in Appendix C and also in Chapter 9. However, teachers may obtain similar results by flashing words quickly on cards.

afraid of getting low marks on her report card and was probably very concerned about what her teachers and parents thought of her. Perhaps as she reads aloud now, some of these worries are still present. And, since she wants so much to do well but is still uncertain about her ability, she reads hesitantly and cautiously. Also, her fear of exposing herself in front of classmates, teachers, and her family might still upset her. This happens to many children with similar difficulties.

Tina brightened up as the discussion progressed. Perhaps she was relieved to find an explanation of her stumblings and repetitions. Perhaps she now felt that they were not altogether her fault. When she found out, too, that the writer was accustomed to uneven reading in many other children like her and that a perfect performance was not expected, she seemed to relax visibly.

As sessions continued, Tina's reactions were even more dramatic. Instead of mobilizing her forces to try harder and thereby intensifying her anxiety, she no longer had to pretend to be what she was not. Her tension decreased even more noticeably, and she began showing marked improvement in her oral reading. Since the writer knew that such a high level could not in all probability be maintained, she wished to prevent the possibility of future discouragement. Also, she did not want Tina to be frightened at having to sustain a standard so high it might prove unrealistic. Hence, she rejoiced with Tina over her improvement, but told her, too, that everyone's performance varies; some days she would undoubtedly do better than on others.

In addition to oral reading, Tina practiced answering questions on silent reading exercises. These were carefully selected on the appropriate interest and ability level. She was able to do well on them, and her high scores gave her concrete evidence that she really could do creditable work. Success during remedial sessions in oral and silent reading bolstered her courage sufficiently so that Tina was able to contribute to class discussions. In fact, she reached the point after about ten sessions where she volunteered to read answers to specific questions aloud in class and finally managed satisfactorily without extra help.

Tina's case cannot be considered strictly one of word recognition difficulty. Yet, this is one of the ways in which her anxiety, due to unfavorable past experiences with reading, was manifested. Tina's problem is typical of that of many pupils who are considered by teachers to have serious word recognition problems. In most cases, the remedial treatment consists of plying these pupils with exercises in all aspects of word analysis in the hope that a firmer foundation will improve their reading. However, such emphasis tends to intensify the child's problem. As one older pupil hopelessly recounted, "I went voluntarily to corrective reading classes, but all they did was drill me on sounds, prefixes, suffixes, and roots. Now I just can't stand to read anything."

Thus, the various aspects of the child's problem must be identified and appropriate treatment planned. Where word recognition is the difficulty, it must be skillfully interwoven not only with reading activities, but with understanding the child himself.

Suggestions for Further Reading

ADAMS, FAY, GRAY, LILLIAN, and REESE, DORA, *Teaching Children to Read*, 2nd ed. New York: Ronald Press, 1957, Part III.

ARTLEY, S., "Progress Report on the Champaign Reading Study, 1952–5: A Review and Discussion." *Elementary English*, 34 (1957), pp. 102–5.

AUSTIN, MARY, "Retarded Readers Speak." *The Reading Teacher*, 12 (1958), pp. 24–8.

BETTS, E., *Foundations of Reading Instruction*. New York: American Book, 1946, Ch. 24.

BLAND, PHYLLIS, "Helping Bright Students Who Read Poorly." *The Reading Teacher*, 9 (1956), pp. 209–14.

BLIESMER, E., "Some Notes on Helping Children with Reading Difficulties." *Education*, 77 (1957), pp. 551–4.

DAWSON, MILDRED, and BAMMAN, H., *Fundamentals of Basic Reading Instruction*. New York: McKay, 1963, Chs. 5, 6, 7.

DEBOER, J., and DALLMAN, MARTHA, *The Teaching of Reading*. New York: Henry Holt, 1960, Chs. 6A, 6B.

JACOBS, L., "Reading on Their Own Means Reading at Their Growing Edges." *The Reading Teacher*, 6 (1953), pp. 27–32.

McCRACKEN, G., "The New Castle Reading Experiment: A Terminal Report." *Elementary English*, 30 (1953), pp. 13–21.

McCULLOUGH, CONSTANCE, "Changing Concepts of Reading Instruction," in *International Reading Association Conference Proceedings*, Vol. 6. New York: Scholastic Magazines, 1961, pp. 13–22.

ROBINSON, HELEN, "Corrective and Remedial Instruction," in *National Society for the Study of Education Yearbook*. Chicago: University of Chicago Press, 1961, pp. 357–75.

ఏ 7

Basic Comprehension,
Study Skills, and Vocabulary

ఏ Comprehension is applying thought processes to read-
ing; there are as many ways to teach it as there are variations in the pupils
and their teachers. The main difficulty of pupils with reading disability
who are reading at high third grade level or above usually lies in the
manner of handling textbooks and the understanding of information found
in reference books, newspapers, and magazines. They are less likely to have
trouble comprehending simple narrative material. Thus at this stage, the
focus of instruction shifts. Instead of dealing with story-type material and
word analysis, the remedial program is concerned mainly with comprehension and study skills. Work on word recognition continues where necessary, but greater stress is placed on reading to gain information. There is
also more emphasis on silent reading than on oral, since eventually most
reading is done silently.

In teaching comprehension and study skills, two broad aspects are kept
in mind. One is helping pupils to apply the basic comprehension and
study techniques wherever they are needed; the other is to overcome the
distaste and aversion for schoolwork that most of them have developed over
the years.

Of course adequate diagnosis, as described in Chapters 2 and 3, should be
undertaken as early as possible, since it determines ultimate expectations
and suggests the areas which need special attention.

This chapter will discuss basic components and remedial techniques connected with developing comprehension and study skills in pupils of all
ages. Because of the particular needs of junior and senior high school
pupils who are severely behind in their reading (where the achievement
might range from nonreader through fifth grade levels) Chapter 8 is

chiefly concerned with remedial programs for them. On the other hand, there is the problem of the bright high school students whose reading scores are about average for their grade placement, but far below expectancy for their intellectual capacity. These students pose other special problems, which are discussed in Chapter 9.

Teaching Comprehension and Study Skills to Pupils with Reading Disability

The most important factors interfering with comprehension are limited intelligence, insufficient familiarity with the basic concepts of the subject matter, lack of interest in the material, and meager vocabulary.

Pupils who have such difficulties should be placed in a class where the level of achievement is fairly close to their own. The experienced teacher is aware of the nature of their problems, so that the reading program is geared toward remedying their deficiencies. Furthermore, the program is streamlined so that the essential comprehension techniques are taught effectively, while the many subtle and complex ones are omitted until the pupils' competency is more advanced.

Comprehension should be taught in its entirety according to the demands of the topic. However, for purposes of clarification and emphasis, it is often discussed in terms of separate processes. Therefore, it is convenient to consider that the most important components of comprehension center around: (1) finding the main idea and important details, (2) following directions, (3) adjusting rate of reading to multiple purposes, and (4) vocabulary development. If the pupils have sufficient foundation in these four basic areas, the special subject teacher can develop others that may be needed in a particular course of study, such as finding inferences, critical reading, and interrelationships of ideas.

Thus teachers can develop comprehension in many ways. Simple stories usually present no problem. It is with texts and informational matter that the difficulty manifests itself. When comprehension techniques are focused on acquiring specific information in the subject areas, they are usually called study skills. In teaching such skills, the pupils need systematic guidance.

Use of Textbooks

In dealing with a text, the teacher might begin by familiarizing the pupils with the organization of the textbook. They might examine the table of contents, chapter headings, illustrations, and index to develop an over-all conception of the major information that is offered in the book. Then the pupils might begin to practice using these aids to locate specific information.

In introducing a particular topic the teacher builds up understanding through extensive discussion. She explains unfamiliar concepts and vocabulary that appear in the selection. Then the pupils turn to the portion of the book under consideration. They are encouraged to use any aids the author supplies in the form of heading arrangements in different type, italicized words, charts, maps, and so forth.[1] It is sometimes useful to consider each subheading as a main idea and have the pupils turn it into a question. The heading indicated below becomes, for example, "What are the products of Texas?" and the answer includes the chief details of the section. The teacher might write the relevant material on the blackboard so that pupils can copy it into their notebooks.

Products of Texas
A. Oil
B. Cattle
C. Cotton
D. Lumber

Such a practice obviously helps the pupils learn outlining as well.

The teacher is specific in her assignments. That is, she asks questions, the answers to which she knows can be easily found in or deduced from the text. This sets the purpose for reading and helps pupils work more efficiently. The more success the pupils gain and the more adept they become, the more advanced can be the materials they use and the skills they can learn.

Sometimes the textbook is too difficult and substitute material must be found. For example, a group of twelve seventh graders had difficulty with social studies. They worked as a group with the remedial teacher[2] at the school three times a week. After a conference with their teacher, the remedial specialist knew that they were currently taking up early explorers in North America. She substituted *The Story of Our Country* by Barker *et al.*, which is at fifth grade level, for their regular text. She found that by showing the pupils how to use this book in ways similar to those described previously, she could develop the skills they needed. For instance, the pupils read to find the main idea and relevant details. As she helped

[1] Florence Roswell and Ruth Adams, "Teaching Social Studies in a Remedial Program," *Intercom, a Publication of the Junior High Schools of New York City,* 6 (1962), No. 1, pp. 14–19.
[2] Ruth Adams, Junior High School 104, New York, N.Y.

them organize their work in notebook form, they soon had a rough outline of each chapter. This information paralleled the work being done in their regular classroom. It could be used for review purposes or even for test preparation. Such outlines were also used for teaching sequential reading. Thus not only did the pupils learn how to study, they were able to apply the content in their social studies period. This heightened morale and accelerated their learning. Eventually they were able to use the seventh grade text along with the rest of the pupils and did not need the extra remedial work.

Thus comprehension and study skills cannot be taught in a vacuum. When the text is difficult, the teacher must offer help by way of building background and demonstrating efficient methods for finding meaning from the text. When material in the regular classroom is beyond the pupils, then special arrangements must be made to give added assistance in whatever way is possible.

Use of Workbooks

Even though comprehension and study skills are best taught through using the actual material in connection with a topic under consideration, this is not always feasible. When dealing with pupils who have difficulty in comprehension, the teacher or reading specialist does not always have sufficient time to use the regular text, which may be broad in scope and coverage. Workbooks which contain a variety of interesting selections offer a convenient shortcut in developing comprehension and study skills. Also, they simulate other types of informational matter that the students will use. They are available at all levels of reading ability, from second grade level through college. The wide range of subject matter covered by these workbooks makes them especially valuable for pupils with reading disability, for it helps them to build up, in a relatively brief period, the foundation that so many of them lack because of their history of sparse reading. Also, the brevity of workbook selections is inviting to pupils who shrink from more lengthy works. In addition, they provide a basis for a systematic, periodic record from which the student can gauge his progress.

For example, workbooks were used as the initial source for developing comprehension skills in a sixth grade class supervised by members of the staff of the City College Educational Clinic.[3] The children in the class varied in cultural, racial, and socioeconomic background. There was a wide

---

[3] The project refers to one carried out by Professors Florence Roswell and Jeanne Chall under the sponsorship of the City College Educational Clinic in New York City, Professor Herbert Nechin, Director.

range in intelligence and in reading levels. The class was divided into two groups: those reading between high third and high fifth and those reading above sixth grade level. They spent three hourly sessions a week reading the workbooks *Practice Readers*.[4] For the lower reading group, each pupil had the *Practice Readers*, Book I, which is at high third grade level. The children read two selections at each session. Before reading them the teacher presented any new vocabulary and concepts that were necessary.

At the same time, the more competent readers were doing similar exercises in *Practice Readers*, Book III, which is at about fifth to sixth grade readability level. This group needed only a little direction from the teacher. They finished the exercises more quickly than the other group, at which point they read library books. For this group it was not necessary to purchase a workbook for each child. Instead, two copies of the *Practice Readers*, Book III, were cut up into individual exercises, thereby providing 81 selections. The exercises were mounted on oaktag, with answers recorded on the reverse side. The pupils prepared the material under the direction of the teacher, and they themselves took charge of distributing it. At every session each pupil chose two selections he had not read before. He then checked his answers with the key on the back and kept a record of which exercises he had read.

Whenever workbook exercises are employed, a plan is followed similar to the one described under "Use of Textbooks," i.e., the teacher builds up background, explains unfamiliar concepts and vocabulary, and so on. However, since the teacher has wide latitude in choosing selections, she is careful to preread articles in order to select those most appropriate in content and format. After the selection is read, the pupils can answer the questions orally or silently. If the work is written, however, the teacher must be sure to look it over so that the pupil has the benefit of her comments and suggestions to guide him in subsequent exercises. It is important at this time to make certain that the pupil understands the type of error he makes and is shown ways in which he might avoid it in the future. Also the answer key supplied with the workbook need not be regarded as sacrosanct; sometimes questions are ambiguous no matter how carefully they are selected, and more than one answer may apply. Therefore, if a pupil can sufficiently substantiate his answer, even though in disagreement with the key, the teacher should make allowances for it and explain the ramifications of the topic.

With very severe cases of comprehension difficulty, the teacher may

---

[4] All workbooks mentioned in this chapter may be found in Appendix C, under "Materials for Vocabulary and Comprehension Skills."

need to participate more actively and introduce silent reading in gradual stages. For example, she might start out by reading an article to the pupils and have them answer the questions orally, so that she can see where they are confused and can clarify meanings immediately. In subsequent sessions, she can guide them to read the selection silently, but still have them answer questions orally with her so that she may keep a close check on their progress in comprehension skills. Finally, they can be encouraged to work more independently and be given help only as needed.

Throughout the period that workbooks are used, the teacher makes sure that the pupils know why they are working with them and how they may help them. Nothing is more unproductive for pupils than reading articles and answering questions mechanically without direction or purpose. The effective teacher does not expect workbooks to supplant instruction. By themselves, they never impart all that is needed. After they have served their purpose, the pupils must be guided toward transferring their skills to texts and other material.

A list of material for developing comprehension and study skills follows. All the workbooks contain a variety of exercises for developing these skills at the levels indicated. Teachers' manuals and answer keys are available in all cases unless otherwise noted. Any additional features of particular material are described.

MATERIALS FOR DEVELOPING VOCABULARY AND COMPREHENSION SKILLS

		Readability Level
Be a Better Reader by Nila Smith, Prentice-Hall.	Books I–VI	5–12
Developing Reading Skills by Elma Neal and Inez Foster, Laidlaw.	Books A–C	4–6
Driving the Reading Road by Paul Spencer and Thomas Robinson, Lyons & Carnahan. A hard-cover book for junior high school use.		7–9
EDL Study Skills Library by H. Allan Robinson *et al.* Educational Developmental Laboratories, Huntington, New York. The material provides separate boxes of study skills lessons in science and social studies with individual worksheets. There are three boxes at each grade level for each content area covering grades 4 through 9.		4–9

New Practice Readers by Clarence Stone *et al.*, Webster.	Books A–G	2–8
	Books I–III	3–6
Practice Readers by Clarence Stone *et al.*, Webster.	Book IV	7–10
Practice Exercises in Reading by Arthur Gates and Celeste Peardon, Bureau of Publications, Teachers College, Columbia University. There are 16 booklets in all, four different books at every level; each booklet is designed to develop a different skill:	Books III–VI	3–6

    Type A—Reading for General Significance

    Type B—Reading to Predict Outcomes

    Type C—Reading to Follow Directions

    Type D—Reading for Details.

For example, Book III, Type A, at third grade level, contains exercises to develop the general significance of each article; Book VI, Type D, at sixth grade level, consists of selections offering practice on finding the important details, and so on.

Reader's Digest Reading Skill Builders, Guy Wagner *et al.*, *Reader's Digest* Educational Service. There are two booklets available at each level, one easy and one more difficult, designated as Part One and Part Two.	Books II–VI	2–6
	Advanced Books	7–8
SRA Reading Laboratory, Elementary Edition by Don Parker, Science Research Associates. Comprehension and rate exercises are printed on cards and encased in box form. The selections are mature in format. Other laboratory boxes available; see Appendix C.		2–9
Standard Test Lessons in Reading by William McCall and Lelah Crabbs, Bureau of Publications, Teachers College, Columbia University. There are five books. A, B, C, D, E. Books A through D are for grades 3 through 6, respectively. Book E is for pupils in junior and senior high school.	Books A–D	3–6
	Book E	7–12

If the teacher finds that her pupils are particularly weak in one of the comprehension skills, she may wish to teach it separately as a temporary measure. She then selects suitable material which lends itself to practice in a specific area from texts or workbooks such as those listed in the preceding section. Once sufficient practice on an isolated technique is accomplished, however, the teacher makes sure that it is integrated properly in a variety of materials used in regular classwork. Suggestions for practice in finding the main idea and important details, following directions, adjusting reading rate, and vocabulary development all follow.

Finding the Main Idea and Important Details

In discussing a main idea and its supporting details, the teacher might start by showing the pupils a picture or even by having them look out the window or around the room and then describe what they see. The teacher tries to get them to condense their thoughts into a few words or a sentence such as: "I see a country scene." This is the main idea. Then she asks them to list more specific aspects of this concept which form the details. For example: "Two boys and two girls are going on a picnic. They have a Thermos jug and picnic basket with them." These are the details. The pupils are helped to distinguish between the general concept and the details which they described by identifying the essential differences in the statements. Then the teacher explains that authors of paragraphs and selections have written down the main ideas and details that they wish to convey. Selections are then taken for illustration. Short paragraphs are best for purposes of clarity. For instance, the teacher might make up a paragraph similar to the following:

> Termites are destructive insects. They chew up almost anything to get where they wish to go. They can chew through firewood or houses. Termites look like ants.

The teacher would first explain any words that might be unfamiliar, in this case perhaps *termite* and *destructive*. She might ask if the pupils ever had experience with termites doing damage in their homes, and so on. After the pupils have read the paragraph, she asks them to state the main idea and supporting details. The teacher can then introduce short selections in workbooks in similar fashion and later show how to utilize this technique with books and reference materials.

It should be noted here that another way to practice the main idea and details is to explain the use of the topic sentence and its relation to the rest of the paragraph. As is well known, however, the topic sentence may be the first or last sentence in a paragraph or come somewhere in between. This variability often confuses pupils with reading disability who are not fluent readers to begin with. Hence if taught at all, it should be delayed until they show evidence that they can profit from such practice.

Following Directions

Those who correct children's examination papers are well aware of the many points lost because the children made mistakes in following the directions. Pointing out this fact, plus other such dramatic examples as mistaking sugar for salt in a recipe, usually alerts the children to their problem. A variety of practice materials can be read from cookbooks, magic books, card trick instructions, mathematics problems, science experiments, and so on. An example of how an experiment might be used follows:

> Stir a few drops of ordinary writing ink into half a glass of water, making a fairly dark mixture. Add two or three drops of household bleach and stir again. The liquid will rapidly lose its dark color, becoming almost colorless as the dye in the ink is oxidized.[5]

The teacher can have the materials for the experiment on hand and have one pupil come to the front of the room for demonstration purposes. Words such as *ordinary, liquid,* and *oxidized* are explained and pronounced if necessary. The pupils then read the experiment silently. The teacher asks them to watch the pupil who will demonstrate the experiment and check to see whether he is following the directions correctly. Discussion as to the necessity for following directions can then ensue.

Each subject has its own characteristics with regard to following directions, and the pupils must be taught the specific approach suitable to a particular field.[6] The pupils can then be given experiences in the thought processes necessary for the particular subject at hand. As they

---

[5] From Mae Freeman and I. Freeman, *Fun with Chemistry* (New York: Random House, 1944).

[6] Bureau of Secondary Curriculum Development, *The Road to Better Reading* (Albany: New York State Education Department, 1953), Ch. 5.

practice different approaches they gain facility in handling each specialized area of knowledge.

Adjusting Reading Rate

Adjusting the rate of reading to the material being read is usually one of the last skills to be taught. It is important to delay this skill until all problems in word recognition and fluency have virtually disappeared. After children have relatively little difficulty in these areas, one can consider how to utilize their reading skills most effectively. Rate is not stressed per se but rather flexibility in reading that is adjusted to purpose. For example, even a "fast" reader does not read a technical report at the same rate or in the same way that he reads a mystery story. Nor should he. We consider, even if not consciously, what we want to get out of a selection and then read it accordingly. The one rate which the child may have used previously in stories will be inefficient for handling more mature types of reading matter. Thus pupils may have to be cautioned to read carefully and slowly just as much as they need to be taught to read more rapidly.

At every opportunity the teacher points out and gives practice in reading for a variety of purposes. When the class is studying social studies, for example, the teacher can ask for particular information and guide the children in deciding where and how to look for it, as well as how to approach the subject matter. For instance, finding the number of people living in Russia and where most of them live will require skimming, whereas discovering the major changes from feudalism to communism requires careful, concentrated reading. Such contrast in different types of reading dramatizes the flexibility that must be developed for efficient reading. In one junior high school, for example, the teachers complained that the students did not know how to use library references in connection with writing reports. The pupils not only were having difficulty finding information, but when they did come across relevant material, they tended to copy it indiscriminately. Although they had all been introduced to the use of the library, it was apparent that they could benefit from further guidance and the practical application which is necessary in research.

The remedial teacher[7] and the librarian[8] undertook a joint venture to teach research skills to these pupils. They formed several groups,

---

[7] Ruth Gottesman, Greenburgh Junior High School.
[8] Urania Fuller, Greenburgh Junior High School.

each one differing in level of ability. (The minimum reading level for the lowest group was 5.0. Below this level the program would have been too difficult. More advanced groups ranged up to eighth and ninth grade reading achievement.) The groups met for approximately seven lessons; the slower groups had more, and the faster groups fewer, sessions. Some lessons emphasized where to find particular information, others how to keep notes of information obtained, still others how to use particular reference material. All the lessons were given in conjunction with regular reports that the children were required to write. After reports were submitted, the remedial teacher and the classroom teacher evaluated them and looked for possible weaknesses in specific skills. These skills were then taught later on.

Some lessons emphasized how to use a "skimming" technique to gather information quickly and accurately. The *World Book Encyclopedia* was used for these lessons. Two sets of encyclopedias, fourteen volumes each, were available in the school. Every pupil received a volume of the encyclopedia at random. A skimming quiz was available for each volume. After an orientation period in which "skimming" was explained and illustrated, the pupils worked individually on their quizzes. Assistance was available when needed. An example of one quiz follows:

Skimming Quiz for Volume A of the *World Book Encyclopedia*

NAME: DATE:

GRADE:

1. Who was the wife of John Adams? When did she live?
2. What does air pollution cost the United States in damages each year?
3. What are the chief kinds of alfalfa grown in the United States?
4. How old are the oldest existing copies of almanacs?
5. What color does arsenic turn when it is combined with copper?
6. What are two kinds of asbestos?

After such practice, the pupils reported that they were better able to handle their research and homework assignments in their varied classes.

Teaching Comprehension in a Classroom

When teachers are faced with a class whose pupils show a wide variation in ability to utilize and master comprehension techniques, they often do not know how to provide for those whose foundation skills are weak.

Sometimes a method suggested by Chase[9] is effective. Teams of two or three pupils are formed, each team with one good reader, to read the material that has been assigned. After discussion in class, the pupils are given questions for which they must find the answers. The good reader serves as a resource to help with words or passages that present difficulty. According to Preston,[10] who has used this method successfully, "Every child gains security as he is put through the paces of a disciplined study procedure." Of course the teacher uses her ingenuity in forming teams so that the more proficient member remains helpful and does not become domineering.

Other teachers handle the problem by having a collection of books, texts, and other material at different levels. Through the years they have developed a resource file on the main topics in the course of study. It includes sufficient variety to provide reading matter for both good and poor readers. Often teachers ask, "Doesn't this take a great deal of preparation?" It does. But, as one teacher said, "I'd rather spend one hour a day preparing materials and reap the sense of satisfaction of a happy, responsive class than be miserable five hours a day, five days a week."

One teacher,[11] whose sixth grade class was studying the American Revolution, used such a file to good advantage. He first discussed the lives of the people and government of that time. Then he raised the questions: "Do you think the American people treated England so unfairly that they were responsible for the events that followed? If you had been in the English Parliament would you have supported King George?" This led to research in which the more able pupils consulted English as well as American texts and had the startling experience of discovering that reputable English authors presented a strong case against the colonists. The less able pupils, in the meantime, read material at fourth and fifth grade levels, such as *The Golden Book of the American Revolution*,[12] *The First Book of the American Revolution, Exploring Our World*, and numerous simple pamphlets and articles that the teacher had collected in the past. Later, when the pupils decided on the unusual procedure of having a trial in the classroom to investigate whether King George and

---

9 W. Chase, "Individual Differences in Classroom Learning," in *Social Studies in the Elementary School*, Fifty-sixth Yearbook of the National Society for the Study of Education (Chicago: University of Chicago Press, 1957), Part II, Ch. 7.

10 R. Preston, *Teaching Study Habits and Skills*, Rinehart Education Pamphlets (New York: Rinehart, 1959), p. 30.

11 Donald Lonergan, Bellows School, Mamaroneck, N.Y.

12 All material referred to in this chapter can be found in Appendixes B and C.

his government should have been held responsible for the American Revolution, all the pupils were able to acquire sufficient information to participate and contribute according to their ability. Thus comprehension skills were developed at different levels according to the stage at which each pupil was at the time. Since materials were also coordinated, poor readers could gain in knowledge and skill to the same degree as the others.

Thus there are many ways to teach comprehension and study skills. The teacher must use her ingenuity and her interest in the subject to instill curiosity and excitement in the pupil. Once this kind of reaction is aroused, it is relatively simple to teach how to find the main idea and details, how to follow directions, how to draw inferences, summarize, or whatever else might be required in the course of study. The most important source for strengthening comprehension is reading books, but the difficulty in getting pupils with reading disability to read voluntarily is obvious. There are certain books, however, that are more tempting and have a better possibility for sustaining interest than others. Many have been listed in Appendix B, but the major sources from which informative, interesting, and less taxing books can be chosen have not been specifically listed there. The following publishers are among those that have developed series of biographical, historical, scientific, and other material written on a simplified level. Such material can be coordinated with specific subject matter or serve as an over-all means for developing background. For a complete listing of the hundreds of available titles, the individual publishers' catalogues should be consulted.

BIOGRAPHY, HISTORY, AND SCIENCE SERIES

	Readability Level
American Adventure Series, Wheeler. This is a series of 16 biographies of American heroes, describing their lives and times. Representative titles are:	2–6
Anderson—*Pilot Jack Knight*	3
Beals—*Davy Crockett*	5
Childhood of Famous Americans, Bobbs-Merrill. These are the childhood stories of people who helped America grow. The achievements of their adult life are summarized in the end. There are over 100 titles, two of which are:	3–5
Wilson—*Ernie Pyle*	4
Wagoner—*Louisa Alcott*	4

Readability Level

Discovery Books, Garrard. This is a series of true to life   3
biographies of famous men. Some titles are:

   Dolch, ed.—*Leif the Lucky*   3
   Dolch, ed.—*Abraham Lincoln*   3

First Book Series, Watts. There are over 60 titles in the   3–5
series covering topics on science, the world and its work,
nature, hobbies, the arts, and America. Sample titles are:

   Bendick—*The First Book of Airplanes*   3
   Commager—*The First Book of American History*   4

Golden Book Series, Simon & Schuster. Many subjects are   5
included in this series, such as science, history, hobbies.
Some titles are:

   Cook—*Golden Book of the American Revolution*   5
   Parker—*Golden Treasury of Natural History*   5

Junior Science Books, Garrard. These books contain pro-   4
lific illustrations and are informative. Representative titles
are:

   Larrick, ed.—*Junior Science Book of Electricity*   4
   Larrick, ed.—*Junior Science Book of Flying*   4

Landmark Books, Random House. The series includes   5
dozens of books about people, places, and events in American history. Some titles are:

   Pinkerton—*The First Overland Mail*   5
   Stewart—*To California by Covered Wagon*   5

Signal Books, Doubleday. Each book describes adventures   4
of individuals in different situations and careers of particular interest to junior and senior high school pupils. Titles
include:

   Parker—*Carol Heiss: Olympic Queen*   4
   Orbaan—*Civil War Sailor*   4
   Gelman—*Football Fury*   4
   Bjorklund—*Rodeo Roundup*   4

Signature Books, Grosset. A great quantity of biographies   4–6
on historical figures are available. Some titles are:

   Leighton—*The Story of Florence Nightingale*   6
   Malkus—*The Story of Winston Churchill*   6

World Landmark Books, Random House. This series con-   4–6
tains dozens of books describing events and people who
are prominent in world history. Selected titles are:

   Winwar—*Napoleon and the Battle of Waterloo*   6
   Bliven—*The Story of D-Day*   6

SIMPLIFIED CLASSICS

Many publishers offer famous stories and classic novels rewritten at different reading levels. A representative listing of such publishers with a sampling of the titles they offer follows. For a complete listing the publishers' catalogues should be consulted.

GARRARD PRESS

Dolch, ed.—*Greek Stories* (Hercules, Jason, and other Greek heroes)   3

Dolch, ed.—*Ivanhoe*   3

GLOBE

(Shakespeare)—*Julius Caesar*   6

(Twain)—*The Prince and the Pauper*   6

(Stevenson)—*Treasure Island*   7

(Dumas)—*Count of Monte Cristo*   8

(Eliot)—*The Mill on the Floss*   8

SANBORN

Beals and Bernadine, eds.—*The Story of Lemuel Gulliver in Lilliput Land*   6

Beals and Bernadine, eds.—*The Story of the Three Musketeers*   5

SCOTT, FORESMAN

Moderow, ed.—*Eight Treasured Stories* (adapted versions of "A Christmas Carol," "The Lady and the Tiger," "The Golden Touch," "The Necklace," "The Jumping Frog," "Ulysses and Cyclops," "Rip Van Winkle," and "The Legend of Sleepy Hollow")   5

Moderow, ed.—*Six Great Stories* (adapted versions of *As You Like It*, "The Legend of Sleepy Hollow," "Gureth and Lynette," "The Golden Touch," "Rip Van Winkle," and *Treasure Island*)   4

(Twain)—*Tom Sawyer*   5

(Kipling)—*Captains Courageous*   6

WEBSTER

Kottmeyer, ed.—*Ben Hur*   5

Kottmeyer, ed.—*King Arthur and His Knights*   4

Helping Pupils to Extend Their Vocabulary

It is well known that one of the ways of acquiring a large vocabulary is through wide reading. As we have pointed out, this avenue has usually been closed to pupils with reading disability. Thus the teacher continues to encourage them to read suitable supplementary material, although she recognizes that their reading difficulty may retard their vocabulary development for an extensive period. Books that usually appeal to such pupils have been offered in the preceding section. Others may be found in Appendix B. Also all the workbooks listed in this chapter, Page 124, and in Chapter 9, pages 168–169, have exercises for vocabulary development.

To aid in vocabulary development, the teacher can try several techniques. She can encourage the pupils to use a more varied vocabulary in speaking and in writing. She can encourage using the dictionary. (But caution should be exercised in dictionary practice as it can become tedious for children who have to look up a great number of words and have not developed facility with using diacritical marks and accents or blending sounds together easily.) Sometimes pupils need to be reminded to use the context in figuring out unfamiliar words. Also, in explaining new words, the teacher can make them more vivid and alive by using related audiovisual aids and connecting words with their own experiences wherever possible. Finally, she can extract words for practice that they will meet in connection with the subject matter that they read. These are referred to as technical vocabulary.

In deciding which words are used often enough to warrant special practice, the teacher can refer to the following:

> E. Thorndike and I. Lorge, *The Teacher Word Book of 30,000 Words.* New York: Bureau of Publications, Teachers College, Columbia University, 1944.
>
> Luella Cole, *Handbook of Technical Vocabulary.* Bloomington, Ill.: Public School Publishing Co., 1940.

The first book lists the words most commonly used in popular reading; the second includes representative words from subject matter texts, although the frequency of words listed by Cole varies somewhat since the time that they were published, and modern scientific terminology often is not included. For this reason, the teacher may wish to compile lists of words from the pupils' own texts and materials. In this way, vocabulary practice is based on the words directly useful to them. If, in addition, the teacher encourages the pupils to use the words in a variety of contexts, it is more likely that they will remember them.

Origins of Words

Children can become more interested in extending their vocabulary by learning the origins of words. An enthusiastic teacher can communicate her interest in words and capitalize on dramatic examples. For instance, the word *Herculean,* of course, is derived from the name *Hercules.* Most children know the feats that Hercules accomplished, involving strength and prowess. Therefore, they can easily understand the meaning of *Herculean.* This and other interesting word derivations may be found in *Picturesque Word Origins.*[13] Other interesting books for children on the same subject are *The First Book of Words*[14] and *Words.*[15]

Words with Multiple Meanings

Every subject employs its own vocabulary with special meaning. Therefore, words and concepts used in special ways must be explained. For example, *company* used as an economic term is very different from *company* meaning guests.

Children must also learn that even common words have more than one meaning. For the simple word *run,* which most young children think of as meaning "moving very rapidly," the *Thorndike-Barnhart Beginning Dictionary* lists about forty different meanings. In one instance, the authors, while reading a story with a child, came across the word *bluff* used in the sense of a high, steep place, or cliff, whereupon the child seemed very confused and seemed to lose the sense of what he was reading. The child said, "I don't understand this. The word *bluff* means 'to fool somebody.' How could somebody fall off a bluff?" The fact that words may have many different meanings had to be explained to him.

These examples dramatize how experience is related to interpretation. They also point up the necessity for the teacher to develop multiple meanings of words and give considerable attention to extending them as an important aspect of vocabulary development.

Keeping Lists of Words

Asking children to memorize long lists of words with their meanings is usually ineffectual. Sometimes children remember the definitions for a short period of time. More often they confuse the definitions. Further, the rote method of learning gives the pupil no idea what the words really mean.

Instead it is better to have him keep a notebook in which he writes

---

[13] *Picturesque Word Origins* (Springfield, Mass.: G. & C. Merriam, 1933).

[14] S. Epstein and B. Epstein, *The First Book of Words* (New York: Franklin Watts, 1954).

[15] Marguerite Ernst, *Words* (New York: Alfred A. Knopf, 1951).

in sentences the words he does not know. When reviewing, he can use context aids in recalling their meaning. Care must be taken that this exercise makes sense to him and that he understands why he is doing it. Sometimes the ingenious teacher can develop sufficient curiosity in words or instill pride in acquiring a richer vocabulary. It is helpful also to ask the pupils to incorporate new words into their class recitations and into their written assignments as often as possible. Unfortunately intrinsic interest in vocabulary development is rare, particularly for pupils with reading disability. Often they become interested in improvement only when they become aware of the importance placed on vocabulary scores on achievement tests. In any case they must have a clear-cut purpose for learning words before isolated vocabulary practice is at all effective.

Prefixes, Suffixes, and Roots

It has long been advised to extend vocabulary through the study of prefixes, suffixes, and roots, but this would seem to apply mainly to the brighter students free from reading handicaps. The writers have found, along with others,[16] that this kind of word study is not very suited to pupils with reading disability. Therefore we rarely stress it.

When the occasion does arise for its use, we have found it best to teach only those prefixes and suffixes that are consistent in their meaning and occur often enough to make it worth while. Stauffer[17] made a study of the most commonly used prefixes. We have adapted this list to eliminate the more ambiguous ones, as follows:

Prefixes: com, dis, ex, pre, re, sub

Some of the suffixes that authorities[18] consider merit special attention are:

Suffixes: tion, ment, ful, less

With pupils who suffer from reading disability, the writers rarely teach Latin and Greek roots. Instead we explain that certain main or base words can add prefixes and suffixes which alter their meaning. Attention

---

[16] May Lazar *et al., The Retarded Reader in the Junior High School.* New York: Board of Education, Bureau of Educational Research, J. Wayne Wrightstone, Director, Publication No. 31, 1952, p. 86; A. Harris, *How to Increase Reading Ability,* 4th ed. (New York: Longmans, Green, 1961), p. 418.

[17] R. Stauffer, "A Study of Prefixes in the Thorndike List to Establish a List of Prefixes that Should Be Taught in the Elementary School." *Journal of Educational Research,* 35 (1942), pp. 453–8.

[18] Lazar, *op. cit.,* p. 86.

is then called to the way in which words change. In the following examples, the meanings of the parts are mentioned; then the words are listed and gone over with the children.

way	subway
marine	submarine
do	redo
make	remake
wonder	wonderful
help	helpful
fear	fearless
point	pointless
care	careless

Games and Devices to Increase Vocabulary

The best plan in extending vocabulary is to use words in a variety of ways. Learning them in connection with subject matter, using them in written and oral expression, and getting the pupils interested in their own vocabulary improvement as an aid in reading and expression, as well as in higher test scores, are the most effective ways to enlarge both general and technical vocabulary.

Games can be used from time to time to enliven the program and arouse enjoyment in using words. In Act in the Manner of the Adverb, for example, the teacher writes a list of adverbs on the blackboard:

curiously	dangerously
delicately	courageously
cheerfully	rapidly
nimbly	frankly

She first explains the words and uses them in sentences until the pupils clearly understand them. One child then chooses a word on the blackboard without divulging its identity and is "It." Next, one pupil at a time requests "It" to act so that a hint of the word is given. For instance, let us say that the word the pupil thought of was *rapidly*. A member of the class might say, "Please walk in the manner of the adverb." "It" then would stride across the room. Other pupils similarly take turns commanding him to "Talk in the manner of the adverb"; "Eat in the manner of the adverb"; or whatever. "It" responds by acting as closely to the chosen word as he can.

Another way of developing word meanings is to organize words into categories. Exercises can be made up by the teacher using synonyms and antonyms or whatever. Also published devices can be used. For example, Durrell[19] has sets of cards to help with practice of words. By classifying them into specific categories, the child is aided in vocabulary growth, word analysis, and spelling. The cards are self-administering and self-scoring and are available at fourth, fifth, and sixth grade levels. *Word Clues* is a programmed instruction workbook published by Educational Developmental Laboratories, Huntington, New York. It is suitable for junior and senior high school levels. These and additional workbooks that have provision for vocabulary development along with other comprehension skills are listed in Appendix C.

Supplementary Reading to Develop Comprehension and Vocabulary

It is obvious that the more books that the pupils read, the more competent their reading, the wider their vocabulary, the broader their background, and the more they will understand concepts in varied fields. Since pupils with reading difficulty find it laborious, they rarely engage in recreational reading. Teachers and parents sometimes become annoyed that students will not even attempt to go to a library or pick up a book in their leisure. Or if they do, they will not finish it. Exhorting them to read, urging them to get a book, nagging them continually all prove fruitless. Instead the teacher might carefully select two or three books that she knows from past experience are likely to interest a particular pupil. Reading a few pages with him to help him choose among them sometimes turns the trick. Once the first few books are enjoyable he will be less reluctant to try others.

Also, a teacher is in a better position to help poor readers select books successfully if she becomes familiar with a large body of material appropriate for them. As she gets to know more and more such books, she has a better idea which ones are long-time favorites, which ones are likely to be accepted, what the readability levels are, and which pupils might appreciate them. Such familiarity also allows her to seize every opportunity to help a pupil select a book that he truly likes. Once a child has experienced pleasure from a book, she can encourage him to discuss it with the other pupils or in front of the class. Then others may be more willing to read it, since they often value their classmates' opinion above any other. Once the ice has been broken, the teacher can encourage the pupil to

---

[19] D. Durrell *et al.*, *Word Analysis Practice* (Tarrytown-on-Hudson, N.Y.: World Book, 1960).

read additional books by the same author. This may lead, in turn, to looking up information about the author in the *Biographical Dictionary* and often initiates genuine interest in books and authors.

Sometimes even enjoyment of a brief article read in class can evoke interest in outside reading. For instance, after one pupil had read a short selection about Thomas Edison's life,[20] he became so enthusiastic that one of the authors under whose supervision he was introduced him to a longer story, "The Wizard of Menlo Park," in *Teen-Age Tales*, Book I. He read it avidly. This evoked further interest in other biographies. He then took home books about the lives of scientists, such as *Robert Fulton: Boy Craftsman* and *The Wright Brothers*. In this way he was started on the road toward reading for his own pleasure. Without some guidance, however, he might have chosen a book so difficult or so inappropriate for him that his small spurt of curiosity would have been smothered.

Even though enticing those pupils with reading disability to read for pleasure is a dubious venture, it can be done. Once the initial hurdle is surmounted the task becomes less and less difficult. As the teacher knows more about her pupils and the type of material that is available, she will find that many of them are able to read a book or an article with satisfaction and a feeling of accomplishment.

More and more books with strong appeal for older pupils but with ease of readability are becoming available. Some of the books and material that the authors have found most suitable for pleasure reading as well as to round out background and bring depth of understanding regarding general information and vocabulary are listed in this chapter and in Appendix B.

Suggestions for Further Reading

BURTON, W., BAKER, CLARA, and KEMP, GRACE, *Reading in Child Development*. New York: Bobbs-Merrill, 1956, pp. 277–303.

CARNER, R., and SHELDON, W., "Problems in the Development of Concepts through Reading." *Elementary School Journal*, 55 (1954), pp. 226–9.

DEBOER, J., and DALLMAN, MARTHA, *The Teaching of Reading*. New York: Henry Holt, 1960, pp. 117–51.

---

[20] A. Gates and Celeste Peardon, *Practice Exercises in Reading*, Book V, Type A, Selection 28 (New York: Bureau of Publications, Teachers College, Columbia University, 1944).

HARRIS, A., *Effective Teaching of Reading*. New York: McKay, 1962, Ch. 11.

McCALLISTER, J., "Reading—Study Skills: Evaluation of Reading," ed., Helen Robinson, *Supplementary Educational Monographs*, No. 88. Chicago: University of Chicago Press, 1958, pp. 106–10.

McCULLOUGH, CONSTANCE, "Implications of Research on Children's Concepts." *The Reading Teacher*, 13 (1959), pp. 100–7.

PRESTON, R., and BOTEL, M., *How to Study*. Chicago: Science Research Associates, 1956.

ROBINSON, HELEN, "Development of Reading Skills." *Elementary School Journal*, 58 (1958), pp. 268–74.

———, "Sequential Development of Reading Abilities." *Supplementary Educational Monographs*, No. 90, Chicago: University of Chicago Press, 1960, Part 5.

ROSWELL, FLORENCE, "When Children's Textbooks Are Too Difficult." *Elementary School Journal*, 60 (1959), pp. 146–57.

SMITH, NILA, "Teaching Study Skills in Reading." *Elementary School Journal*, 60 (1959), pp. 158–62.

STRANG, RUTH, and BRACKEN, DOROTHY, *Making Better Readers*. Boston: D. C. Heath, 1957.

8

Remedial Techniques
for Older Pupils with
Severe Reading Disability

The severest cases of reading disability are the cases of those pupils in junior and senior high school who may be nonreaders or who may read anywhere up to fifth grade level. Although the method of handling these pupils is similar to the one used with others, they present certain special problems. First of all, attitudes ranging from apathy to antagonism are extremely pronounced. The older the pupils and the lower the achievement, the more defeated, frustrated, angry, or fearful they become; finally they are unwilling to try, or pretend not to care whether they learn to read or not. They often become the hard core discipline problems of the school and are a tribulation to all those who deal with them. Not only are they a blight on the school's record, not only are they blatant troublemakers for all concerned, but no one is certain how to cope with them in a school setting. Even when a teacher tries to work with them, these pupils usually proceed so slowly that the teacher's patience is sorely tried and she may feel like giving up, too. Although working with them one at a time is beset with heavy enough problems, teaching a group is even more taxing. In dealing with such pupils, the teacher must consider ways to overcome interfering reactions and find suitable methods and materials so that they can benefit from schoolwork.

This chapter will discuss ways to improve these pupils' attitudes toward reading and ways to reach them through adapted methods and special materials. Then detailed descriptions will illustrate how various teachers salvaged such pupils in three different high schools and how one pupil was handled who needed individual tutoring. The ways these teachers dealt with their pupils may serve as a guide to others who meet similar situations.

Improving Attitudes toward Reading

Teachers who try to help such pupils must first of all have confidence that all is not lost. They need not despair, even when they gaze upon distraught, belligerent, tormented youngsters. Despite their utter misery, their lack of surface appeal, they can be transformed. Not only can their façade be penetrated, but they desperately need a forceful, inspiring influence in their lives—much more perhaps than their more fortunate contemporaries. Such an influence can cause them to drop their armor and start afresh.

The teacher who is determined enough to try realizes that such pupils must feel that someone cares about them and believes in them enough to help them help themselves. When the pupils see in addition that there are all kinds of useful and meaningful things to learn about and that they can actually master them, feelings of competency as well as an improved relatedness to the world about them are engendered. Through the teacher's respect, through reaching their basic desire to know and to grow, through connecting schoolwork with their personal lives and feelings, these pupils may finally emerge as more earnest and resolute.

Ways to Handle Severely Retarded Readers

Besides overcoming entrenched resistance and finding qualified teachers, the major considerations in handling severely retarded readers center around setting realistic goals and finding ways to reach them in a learning situation. It is not that these pupils need anything so different from other young people. They have the same strivings for self-exploration and knowledge of the practical and esthetic world around them as the others do. It is just that their poor academic skills have alienated them from school life. To bring them back, we must have a realistic view of their problem and adapt the program to their present situation. They may then absorb the essentials that will carry over into their life after they leave school and at the same time enable them to experience the joy of a job well done in the classroom. Each school and each teacher must plan and improvise according to the pupils' stage of development, the subject matter to be taught, and the materials available. Therefore, no specific prescriptions can be offered. Instead, some over-all suggestions will be stated concerning goals, adaptation of the program, and the finding of suitable reading matter. These suggestions can then be modified to fit the particular pupils that a teacher may find before her. As already stated, examples of how teachers handled actual classes are included at the end of this chapter.

Setting Realistic Goals

As in all cases of reading disability, diagnosis determines individual expectations and circumscribes the goals that are realistic for such pupils. Diagnosis has been discussed in Chapters 2 and 3. However, for pupils with such severe difficulty, more reliance should be placed on informal rather than standardized measures in order to obtain a truer picture. Trial lessons, as described in Chapter 2, are particularly suitable in evaluating the needs of such pupils. Also, prognosis should be tentative because these pupils have failed for so many years that they are likely to have developed antipathy toward formal examinations of any kind, and test scores tend to underestimate their ability.

Therefore improvement—even though very slow—is the realistic goal. Even those pupils who are far behind can and should be able to improve. Perhaps their extreme disability will prevent their ever reaching their potential, but they can move ahead; their poor foundation and years of failure may cause severe handicaps, but they can be surmounted to some extent. Perhaps they will never reach the ideal; perhaps they will never even rise to average standards. But they can do better. Hopefully these pupils can all be brought up to at least sixth or seventh grade reading level before they leave school. This is the minimum for their getting along in our world. But even if this minimum is not reached, every effort must be made to prepare them to fit into society, to help them better their vocational chances, and to see that they get as much out of school as they can.

Adapting the School Program to Pupils with Severe Reading Disability

First the pupil's word recognition abilities are investigated. If he can learn by a visual approach he can be introduced immediately to meaningful material as discussed in the case of Matthew in this chapter and Lloyd in Chapter 10. However, cases are occasionally found where a pupil has special difficulty with this method. If such a pupil can learn by the phonic method he might use a series similar to the *Royal Road Readers*, which are based on a phonic system. If neither of these approaches proves feasible it may be necessary to employ the visual-motor or kinesthetic method. All of these are described in Chapter 5. Some materials particularly suitable for developing word recognition techniques for the older pupil are listed in this chapter on Page 148. Others are listed in Appendix C.

In helping these pupils understand their various subjects, the teacher first presents material orally, visually, and concretely. For example, some adults have neither the time nor patience to wade through complicated material, but will be able to go back to it after they have, let us say, seen a movie on the subject. Likewise, pupils can gain the needed information when the teacher presents the subject in ways that help them compensate for their lack of foundation skills. In other words, reading fits into the total framework, but the teacher cannot count on independent use of books the way she can with better prepared pupils.

Thus the teacher depends heavily on films, recordings, dramatic productions, oral discussion, and the like for elaboration of the subject before books are used and tries in every way to humanize the material. This usually gets the pupils thinking and responding actively and helps them surmount their listlessness and resistance. Although they need to develop a broader background and vocabulary and to extend their skills just as other pupils, this cannot be done in the usual ways. In fact, formal practice on techniques, such as finding the main idea and important details, rate, and so on, must be delayed until the pupils learn to apply their thoughts and efforts to the subject matter under discussion, regain sufficient confidence and discipline to undertake study-type reading, and develop enough competence to proceed more independently. When they reach this point they can benefit from instruction similar to that described in Chapter 7. In the meantime, the teacher assumes an active role and wherever possible evokes interest in the topic, relates factual material to their personal lives, and shows them that discovery of the information can have real value.

Those who work with such pupils are well aware that most of them have little desire to learn academic subjects. They are usually not even willing to undertake them for secondary goals, such as a means toward higher education or improvement of their status. So they need presentations that come alive and emphasize those aspects that make sense to them at their present stage. Later on they may be able to absorb more abstract approaches, but their attitude at the beginning is usually "What does this mean to me?"

The teacher can introduce the text by building concepts and new vocabulary and raising questions. Then she guides the class to find the answers. This procedure has been described in Chapter 7. However, with such poor readers, she places emphasis on discussion and oral reading in order to compensate for their minimal reading ability. She postpones expectation for more independent work until they are capable of doing it.

These pupils can also engage in a certain amount of simple supplementary reading. Books of historical and informational interest with low vocabulary are becoming more available. These books are less difficult than their regular texts. Publishers such as Garrard Press, Bobbs-Merrill, and Webster have developed many such books. Typical selections can be found on Page 148 of this chapter and in Appendix B. Naturally, the pupils cannot be expected to do extensive research, particularly in the beginning. But they can be encouraged to do more than they have ever done before. When assignments are clear-cut and properly circumscribed, they can experience the satisfaction of finding answers without fruitless effort and discover that they actually can obtain information they wish from reading material.

After the preparatory discussion, collaborative textbook work, and supplementary reading, the teacher helps the pupils organize information into a logical and useful order. That which the teacher and class consider sufficiently important can be compiled into notebooks for future reference. This helps them remember what they have learned and can also be used for review purposes and for tests.

The Place of Test Taking

The taking of tests by pupils with severe reading disability deserves special comment. Their general attitudes of extreme indifference or acute anxiety apply here also. Some of the children, for example, have failed for so many years that another failure rolls off their backs. Others have a great deal of apprehension about attaining the required reading level for promotion. Or, as graduation looms near, still others may have a great stake in passing tests, either because getting a certificate or diploma has intrinsic meaning or because it is crucial for their future job placement. Whatever the ramifications, passing tests creditably can play a specialized role with such pupils. The new experience may be, for instance, an added factor in renewed effort; it may be concrete evidence that they really are not as stupid as they have always felt; best of all, it can engender personal pride and satisfaction.

Therefore, it is important that the teacher explain the purpose and place of tests. If the pupils perceive a test as something punitive or devastating, she tries to relieve their fears. She explains that the test will be used only as a measure for assessing understanding of the subject matter and to help clarify ambiguous points. The teacher makes certain that the pupils know that tests will be based directly on their work in class. They should be familiar with the content because of their previous class discussions and notes.

Short quizzes, oral or written, with two or three simple questions can serve as a start. Tests may be objective or essay, closed or open book, depending on the teacher's preference. The important point is that they be related directly to the material covered in class and formulated in such a way that the pupils have every fair chance of doing well on them. As short a time as possible should intervene between taking tests and learning the results. Tests can be corrected in class by the pupils themselves and marks deemphasized. Questions which are answered incorrectly may be discussed in class, or pupils can be directed to sources where they can find the necessary information. Ultimate knowledge of the material, not right and wrong answers, is stressed so that the pupils come slowly to care about what they are learning and how they are improving.

When the pupils realize a measure of success through competency on tests and increased understanding of the subject matter, they may feel an entirely new sensation—a sharp sense of accomplishment. It may not be outstanding according to some standards, but for them it is remarkable enough.

As pupils have concrete evidence that they are learning and becoming informed about different issues and individuals, they have a chance to develop some dignity. This may diminish their outbursts and their antipathy toward school. When they consider, in addition, that they are no longer second-class citizens and that they are improving beyond their wildest expectations, they react with untold pride. Too often in the past, they have been relegated to the jobs of errand boy, blackboard washer, or bulletin board monitor. In a situation designed to compensate for their difficulties and promote competence, this need no longer be. Instead of standing on the periphery or failing abysmally, these pupils become an integral part of their group. As they acquire further knowledge, skill, and insight, they begin to gain a feeling of triumph. This enhances their concept of themselves and their status in relation to school. From angry, unruly pupils they can slowly pull themselves upward and can develop a sincere desire to learn more on their own.

Choosing Suitable Material

Interesting material for older pupils with very low reading ability is necessarily extremely limited. The lower the level of readability, the narrower the choice and the less appealing the story is likely to be. For authors to write interesting, let alone mature, reading matter with very few words which must be repeated constantly, is next to impossible. Therefore, it is impractical to rely on content to tempt the pupil. Instead, it is best to choose reading matter that is as acceptable as possible and to depend on skillful presentation. For example, when a teacher starts working with a fifteen-year-old who is practically a nonreader, there tends to be a minimum of embarrassment and resentment if she offers pamphlets and books that are designed especially for adults. *Men in the Armed Forces,*[1] with a correlated workbook, *First Steps in Reading English,* and stories about the Brown family in *Home and Family Life Series,* at approximately first and second grade level, are ostensibly for foreign-born adults learning English. Older pupils generally react favorably to such material due partly perhaps to the illustrations and characters which represent adults and partly to their relief on discovering that people even older than they have serious reading problems.

Such material should be presented as an introduction only to give the pupils the boost they need and to crumble some of the hard, ingrained distaste for reading. This clears the way for accepting any books that must be used. Changing the material frequently is advisable also. Indeed, prolonged use of any one book at this level usually proves undesirable because so many of them have limitations. Sometimes the teacher might wish to present books chosen from among a large number of simple series published by Benefic Press, such as the *Jim Forest* or *Dan Frontier* series. At other times she might use informational items from school newspapers, such as *My Weekly Reader* or *Scholastic Magazines,* at beginning reading levels. As soon as some basic word recognition skills are developed, a simple collection of sayings for autograph albums like *Yours Till Niagara Falls* can prove appealing. It offers ideas for signing yearbooks and the like and is popular with pupils who have no sign of reading difficulty. *Bennet Cerf's Book of Laughs* can add some spice and humor to the program. In other words, the structure must of necessity include a great deal of experimentation together with artful handling in order to compensate for the serious problems involved.

At second grade level, choices of books are similar to those described above. Books in all the series mentioned go up to at least third grade level. One series, *The Deep-Sea Adventure Series,* start at high second grade level. It is particularly attractive to those who enjoy finding out about

---

[1] All materials listed here, graded according to reading level, can be found in Appendix B.

the mysteries of ocean life. In addition, there are some occupational booklets, among which are the second grade editions of *Gas Stations*—a particular favorite—and the Experimental Curriculum Research Publications, such as *Getting a Job in the Garment Trades* and *Shopping in the Supermarket*. There are also certain suitable workbooks that start at second grade level and continue through fourth grade and higher. Among others are *New Practice Readers* and *Reader's Digest Reading Skill Builders*. The SRA *Laboratory*, elementary edition, is also appropriate. Then, too, there are appropriate school newspapers with reading levels from elementary grades through high school. At all levels, selections can be chosen that relate to curriculum topics.

Coordinated with this type of material should be workbooks containing practice material for teaching word recognition. Among those best suited for older pupils are *Diagnostic Tests and Remedial Exercises in Reading, My Own Reading Exercises*, Book 2, and *Remedial Reading Drills*.

Books written at third grade level provide a somewhat wider choice. Also it is possible at this stage and onward to select reading matter more directly related to basic information and the more significant aspects of our cultural heritage. This emphasis is important because we want to round out, as stated in previous chapters, the foundation and background knowledge that these pupils have missed. For example, there are many biographies which may be tied in with various periods in history. Among those offered at third grade level by Garrard Press are: *Abraham Lincoln, Samuel F. B. Morse*, and *Leif the Lucky*. For pleasure reading, there are sports, mystery, and adventure stories. Each of the following books at third grade level, for example, is one of a series with at least one other book on the same level and several on higher levels: *Mystery of Broken Wheel Ranch, Ten Great Moments in Sports*, and *Pilot Jack Knight*.

Pupils who can handle fourth grade reading matter and above can be treated in ways similar to those described in Chapter 7. Of course, where methods or materials are too immature they should be avoided. More grown-up stories concerned with teen-agers' personal problems, such as dating, cars, and so on, are particularly apt. Some at fourth grade level are *Teen-Age Tales*, Books A and B, which are especially popular, and *Stories for Today*. Sources which build up background include comprehension workbooks, classics which have been rewritten, and numerous biographies of inventors, scientists, nurses, pioneers, and other historical figures. These may be chosen from those at fourth grade level, or above, listed in Appendix B.

Thus in choosing suitable books for older pupils with severe disability, the main goal is to whet their appetites, pick subject matter that is of general significance as well as related to topics being studied in school, and to find material that is not too overwhelming. Some of it may be frowned upon because it is rewritten and does not follow the richness of style and ideas portrayed by the original authors; some of it may be considered inconsequential. However, anything that can help pupils who have a serious reading difficulty get started serves an important function. Just as a convalescent may need to be coaxed to eat by means of attractive trays and special tidbits, so children with reading disability must be lured to read by providing them with exciting but uncomplicated reading matter. Books that are inherently too complex and involved quickly discourage pupils whose reading power is weak, and they end up reading nothing.

The ways in which several teachers handled various situations with severely retarded readers in junior and senior high school follow. The programs can be adapted to similar school situations. Their accounts show graphically how, even under the most trying circumstances, difficult pupils can be salvaged.

An Individualized Program for a Group with a Wide Range of Reading Retardation

A teacher[2] in a New York City junior high school was confronted with a group of 23 pupils in eighth grade. Not only were most of them extremely retarded in reading, but they were resistant to learning and had disciplinary problems besides. His own account follows:

"My most immediate need was to establish a classroom atmosphere in which discipline could be maintained without resorting to dire threats and punishments to which the boys had long become inured. I attempted to establish rapport by getting across the feeling that I was keenly interested in each member of the class. Various devices that had a noticeable effect in a relatively short time included visits to homes when pupils were ill, monthly birthday parties, and my participation in punchball games in which the boys could demonstrate their proficiency. Fortunately, I acquitted myself creditably on the ball field and gained status in their eyes. My position was made secure when, drawing on my musical ability, I performed rock and roll music for them at our parties! Day by day there was an improvement in class morale and deportment.

"A study of the pupils' record cards revealed a reading range of second to fourth grades. An informal textbook test, however, indicated that one

---

[2] Louis Simon, Junior High School 17, Manhattan.

boy was on a preprimer level, four were on first grade, and eighteen ranged from second to fourth grade reading levels. Results of the *Roswell-Chall Diagnostic Reading Test* revealed severe lacks· in almost all word recognition skills. The I.Q. range was from 66 to 104, and ages from thirteen to sixteen.

"I set up three reading groups, using the *Reader's Digest Reading Skill Builders,* but I soon realized that this plan would not work. I had no suitable material for the slowest group, nor had I the knowledge of how to devise my own. The two other groups had both been exposed to the *Skill Builders* in years past, and resented the grading on the covers. Furthermore, discipline problems arose because the groups could not work independently. Out of this confusion and frustration came the idea of an individualized reading program.

"I broached the plan to my principal and found a willing and sympathetic ear. Unfortunately, the purchase of books for this class was not possible since funds for the current year had already been spent. Asking the boys to bring books from home was out of the question. Most of them had never owned a book, and if they had, these probably would not have been suitable for this class.

"I finally reached a compromise solution by arranging a trip to the public library. Peace was made with the authorities by the payment of accumulated fines for past transgressions, and that afternoon my class returned to school with 23 library cards and a collection· of books."

Classroom Procedure

"The next four months were spent in reading library books during the English periods. Pupils were encouraged to recommend books that they found interesting, and these were freely exchanged. Volunteers for the privilege of reading a third grade level book, *Curious George,* or a book on magic to the five slowest readers were plentiful. The boys in this group would then read to each other, with assistance from me or another pupil.

"My time was spent in individual conferences during which I assisted with vocabulary, comprehension, and word recognition skills. The chief benefit lay in the opportunity for giving encouragement and individual attention. Almost magically, reading had become a 'good' period.

"Pupils were called for conferences in alphabetical order. We sat together at a desk in the rear of the room. A conference usually included some oral reading, a brief discusion of what the story was about, and some direct teaching or review on a needed skill.

"If little Helga was laboriously reading word by word, our conference time might be devoted in part to taking turns in reading so that her interest in the story might be maintained. At the same time, I provided a model for more fluent reading. I also made a note to assign a page in a workbook to help her in phrase reading.

"If Dominick was deeply absorbed in a book that was on his independent reading level, our conference might be merely a brief discussion of what had happened so far, a conjecture as to how it would end, and an admonition to be sure to let me know how the story turned out. But I made a note to steer Dominick to something more challenging for the next book, or the one after that.

"Each conference was an opportunity for diagnosis, skill teaching, vocabulary enrichment, and oral communication in a relaxed one-to-one relationship.

"I found that a touch of humor each day was of inestimable value in getting activities started or keeping them moving. One of the most effective devices was the 'daily chuckle.' Written with brush pen, a two- or three-line joke taken from a magazine or jokebook was displayed in the front of the room before the class arrived. The class looked forward to this little treat and vied for the privilege of reading or acting out the joke. Of course this could not take place until everyone was seated and ready for work.

"With a little practice, I developed a feeling for the type of humor which the children enjoyed most. The following are typical:

NED: What are you doing with a pencil and paper?
ED:　I'm writing a letter to my brother.
NED: Who're you kidding; you don't know how to write.
ED:　Sure, but my brother doesn't know how to read.

VISITOR: Why is your dog watching me while I eat?
HOST:　　Maybe it's because you're eating out of his plate.

"After a while pupils brought in jokes, and I appointed a rotating committee to select those to be posted.

"I learned that asking what was funny about a joke was not the unpardonable sin that it would be with a more sophisticated audience. The discussions that followed provided an ideal opportunity for oral communication, comprehension development, vocabulary enrichment, and exchanges of experiences in an atmosphere that was light and comfortable."

Records

"Since there were many stages of learning going on at the same time, I found that a record for each pupil's progress was advisable. An anecdotal account of each conference, results of diagnosis, assignments, and subjective evaluation of progress in skills and attitudes were kept in a notebook. A page or two was devoted to each pupil and was invaluable in helping my planning.

"Two records were maintained by the pupils. One was a mimeographed form on which the student indicated the title and author of the book being read, the number of pages read each day, the kind of reporting activity planned, new vocabulary, and a brief sentence or two on their reactions to the book. This form was helpful in eliminating squabbles about who was reading a particular book and also enabled me to maintain a check on the amount of reading being done.

"The other record was a large wall chart which listed the names of all the pupils and the titles of books they had read. Separate colored slips were available to paste next to each pupil's name. On the slip, pupils wrote the title of the book that they had completed and its author. Each color signified their opinion of the book. For example, a blue slip meant the book was 'excellent,' green indicated 'good,' yellow, 'fair,' and so forth. This device served as a record of accomplishment for each student and also guided other members of the class in their choice of a book."

Evaluation

"In January, after four months of individualized reading, standardized tests revealed some satisfying results. The average gain for the class was one year. Individual gains ranged from 2 months to 2.6 years. Fourteen pupils had scores over the 5.0 mark necessary for promotion to the next grade, as opposed to 23 pupils who began the term reading between pre-primer and fourth grade level.

"Other evidences of progress were equally heartening. The number of books each student had read ranged from four to fourteen. There was a decided improvement in fluency in written and oral communication. Most encouraging were the evidences of positive attitudes toward reading. It is a heart-warming sight to see a child linger in the room after the bell has rung, regretfully return his book to the cart,[3] and say as he leaves, 'Gee, that's a good story!' "

---

[3] With the assistance of the shop teacher, pupils built two bookmobile carts, so that books could easily be shared by many classes.

Mr. Simon's report shows what a devoted teacher can accomplish. It shows how a serious condition, which is prevalent in many urban areas, can be successfully handled. Certainly the needs of his pupils did not call for the level or type of teaching generally expected in the junior high school. But this is neither the pupil's, the teacher's, nor the school's fault. When confronted with such an unfortunate situation, the teacher must rise to the occasion or collapse in despair. Granted that many of us could not make home visits, play punchball in the yard, or play rock and roll music as did this teacher, but each one can find a way to reach his pupils after his own fashion, if he so desires.

Teaching Reading to a Homogeneous Group

The pupils in the next instance were sixteen to eighteen years of age in an ungraded class at a special school. They had been given up by almost everyone in the area. Their parents insisted that they get a high school diploma, so they were forced to remain in school beyond the usual age limit. The pupils all read at about fifth grade level. Their intelligence fell within normal range, 90–110. They were disinterested in school, surly, and unmanageable. The first day was spent amidst frequent explosions from firecrackers, "hot foots," and "cherry bombs." That night the teacher[4] contemplated, not lesson plans, but a scheme that might capture the hearts and feelings of these youths.

The next morning they were told that they would all be given a "diagnosis" to help them and the teacher to find out what they could do well and where they needed help.

The pupils were told that the test would not "count" for their school marks or as an official record of any kind. In fact the test booklet could be thrown out as soon as it had served its usefulness if they so wished. They were told that the test consisted of items which increased in difficulty; therefore they might find it harder to answer questions as they went along. In any case they would not be expected to get all the answers correct. The important thing was to assess the kinds of errors they made so that they could be taught to avoid such mistakes in the future. The process was compared to a physician's examination in which the patient might be told that his weight and height were proportionate, his general health good, but he was somewhat anemic. Just as a doctor would prescribe a regimen for bodily improvement, they, too, would be apprised of a way to increase their achievement.

---

[4] The teacher in this case was one of the authors, who taught in a special school in an urban area.

The *California Reading Test—Elementary*, for grades 4, 5, and 6, was chosen. After the students completed the test, they took turns coming to the desk for their "diagnostic interpretation." In contrast to orthodox procedure, the test was scored immediately with the pupil, so that he could be shown exactly where his strengths and weaknesses lay. This took the mystery out of the test taking and engendered a feeling of collaboration and self-respect in the student. Of course this had to be handled most skillfully to avoid undue anxiety regarding failure. Each one came away with as much concrete, constructive information as possible. For example, one child did very well on answers requiring factual information that was imparted in the paragraphs, but could not "read between the lines" for implied data. Another was excellent at understanding the main idea, but poor on recall of details; another showed misunderstanding of directions but strong vocabulary; whereas two boys received a high degree of accuracy in responses but were penalized by time, and so on. Each child was given some immediate suggestions for overcoming his difficulty and shown some of the materials he might be working with for practice. They were told that time would be set aside to practice each day in class.

The effect of this procedure was electric. There seemed to be two important reactions. One, the students felt that someone might really be trying to help them, and secondly, the selections offered indicated that there might be something of true interest for them. It was not "the same old hard, boring stuff," as one student commented later.

From that day forward, discipline problems diminished although they never disappeared completely. But it was clear that a spirit had been captured; from dispirited, disruptive young people, they were willing to try again. In order to keep up their morale, the teacher continued to foster feelings of competence. Periods in social studies, English, science, and math were conducted in a group, while the particular skills were practiced individually for a half hour, three times a week. At that time the teacher helped with and checked their work. Besides using some fourth and fifth grade comprehension workbooks, they worked with materials such as crossword puzzles specially prepared for those with reading disability, directions for card tricks, fortune-telling cards, magic books, simple science experiments, and *Weekly Reader* and *Scholastic Magazines* at appropriate levels. Simple books with high appeal, such as *Alec Majors, The Trojan War,* and *The Spanish Cave* helped develop more fluency and speed in their reading. Such material proved dramatic, compelling, and sufficiently different to stimulate their curiosity. In addition, they were encouraged to bring in anything with which they wished help, such as driver's manuals, menus, and the like.

In each subject area, lively discussions and explanations preceded every reading lesson. The pupils learned a wealth of facts and ideas pertinent to the subject matter before reading the text. In this way, demands never became overwhelming. The pupils used textbooks to fill in their knowledge rather than as a source for independent gathering of information. Many times subject matter was related to personal experience in order to evoke attentiveness. For example, when learning about the Food and Drug Administration, the students were asked, "Have you ever seen the purple stamp on meat? Have you ever, to your knowledge, eaten meat without this stamp?" Sometimes discussions combined general student attitudes and subject matter. For example, in discussing the Constitution of the United States, the students thought that perhaps a class constitution would help them maintain better order. Thus, they decided to draw up their own class constitution. It is reproduced here in its original form, including errors:

CONSTITUTION OF CLASS _____

ARTICLE 1 There shall be no throing of books, erasers, chalks, pensils, can
Sec. 1 openors, paper airplanes and spit balls and other thing that go in that catogory.

Sec. 2 There shall be no giving hot foots handeling of other persons while class is being conducted and you can do as you wish as long as it doesn't affect any one else. There shal be respect for the person in charge and Prophanity shall be kept to respected minimum. This constatution shall be respected by the person huo sines this, and if not respect shall leave the class.

Through communicating to the students her desire to help them and by making available actual means for improvement, the teacher helped these boys to make slow but steady progress during the term. Although they never turned into "model" pupils, they became a cohesive unit willing to listen, reasonably well behaved, and with a less antagonistic attitude toward learning.

Handling a Large Number of Retarded Readers Using Material Parallel to the Regular Junior High School Curriculum

The students consisted of 120 children with reading disability divided into four classes of thirty children each. Their I.Q.'s ranged from 76 to 115, and they were between eleven and thirteen years of age at the beginning of the seventh grade. Their reading test scores ranged from nonreaders to sixth grade with most children reading at fourth grade level.

The four classes remained intact for some of their lessons with their regular class teachers and consolidated for others under supervision of two reading teachers.[5] A total of nine periods a week was devoted to various skills related to the language arts. For two of these periods, the four classes met together in the auditorium for instruction with the reading teachers. The reading teachers collaborated with the regular classroom teachers in planning the language arts periods. Their account follows:

"Since independent reading was so poor, we planned first to train the pupils to listen critically to tape-recorded dramatizations of literary master-pieces. The selections were the same as those being read by the other seventh graders who had no reading difficulty.

"The first lesson was always presented through a radio broadcast. They listened to the WNYE broadcast of a famous work of literature over the public address system in their individual classrooms. Before the broadcast, we introduced new vocabulary, elaborated difficult concepts, and discussed the main characters. The classroom teachers wrote pertinent information on the board in each classroom. For example, in introducing the tape of O. Henry's 'Ransom of Red Chief' (part of our unit on the nineteenth-century short story), we told the children about such aspects of the author's life as are reflected in his work: O. Henry was in jail for a while, so he knew criminals very well and wrote about them with a sense of humor. Because of this, the children saw the need for a pen name; an author in jail might have a hard time selling stories to a Victorian public. We also explained the idea and use of a plot.

"We set aside the second literature lesson of the week for the follow-up of our presentation, which was also broadcast. At this time, the four classes gathered together in the auditorium so that the work could be more closely coordinated. We used an overhead projector instead of a chalkboard to present the major points and the unfamiliar words in the story. After hearing the story, we encouraged the children to answer questions about it. We responded to acceptable answers with praise and extra credit. Before long, the hands of at least three quarters of the youngsters waved before us.

"In our third lesson still dealing with O. Henry, we chose to emphasize the differences between the 'Ransom of Red Chief' and a newscast that we presented about kidnaping. First we asked the pupils to state the plot

---

[5] Mrs. Paula Fuld and Miss Helane Goldstein under the direction of Miss Grace Canary, Assistant Principal, Macomb's Junior High School, New York City.

as if it were a newscast. This 'reporting' served many purposes: (1) It provided the students with an interesting way to summarize and review the plot; (2) it helped us to elicit only the important events of the story; and (3) it heightened the differences between a news story and a story with literary merit. Then we helped the pupils see the differences between a newscast and the dramatic aspect of the story. 'What made the story more fun than the plot summary you have just given?' Now the children noted O. Henry's use of the surprise ending, the types of characters about which he chose to write, and the language used by the kidnapers in the story. We could also draw out how O. Henry's techniques and background were similar to those of other authors that the children had studied. Finally, the children began to appreciate literature as opposed to other forms of writing.

"In subsequent lessons we presented additional stories by the same author. The WNYE tapes did not fill our needs completely, however, and we had to dramatize our own adaptation of the 'Gift of the Magi.' After this, many of the children wanted more stories by O. Henry, so we encouraged them to read an adapted version of this author's works edited by Lou Bunce. This and similar books could be found in the lending libraries which we had established in our classrooms. The demand for the O. Henry stories continued long after the lessons had been completed.

"We continued our short story unit with 'The Necklace' by Guy de Maupassant. We wanted the children to see the similarity between two authors living at the same time, but in different countries. We elaborated facts about the authors' lives and their historical setting. As no broadcast dramatization or easy adaptation was available, we had to make our own tape. The end product was even more elaborate than we had anticipated. It included such sound effects as doors closing, a horse and buggy passing, wind blowing, and a Strauss waltz for the ball the Loisels attended. The children were very impressed by the story, but even more impressed by the fact that the tape had been made especially for them. They even expressed interest in helping to make the tapes in the future.

"An important outcome of our program was helping the children develop a rexographed notebook which included paragraphs written by groups of about twelve children under the guidance of the classroom teacher. Children with less verbal ability drew illustrations of their favorite scenes. The content of the notebook included articles on critical evaluations of the stories under discussion, information on the authors' lives, or comments concerning the historical background of the times in which the authors lived. Curiosity about the contributions of the other children, as well as the unusually attractive appearance of the rexographed pages, encouraged the children to read the composite notebook. Because the ideas had been contributed by the students in their own words, the prose tended to be simple enough for the children to read easily. The sheets could also be used later for review.

"Another important aspect of our program concerned testing the children on the stories and information which we discussed. In line with conquering defeatist attitudes, both testing and reviewing procedures were designed to ensure success for most of the children. First, thorough review in class eliminated the necessity for independent study at home. This was unsuited to most of the children due both to chaotic home conditions and lack of sufficient independent study skills. We also prepared them for the format of the test through rexographed review sheets and gave them practice in following directions similar to those that would be on the test. Fears of the testing situation were handled through open discussion of the pupils' feelings and reactions toward taking tests. We then staged a mock testing situation for practice. Finally we administered the test over the broadcasting system, with the English teachers actively assisting in each classroom to be certain that everyone understood the directions. (The children also had their own copies of the test to read if they could.) This minimized failure due to inability to accurately read the questions on the test. The few who did not succeed on the first test took a second one after additional review.

"The results of the tests demonstrated that our approach had been successful. The pupils showed that they learned a great deal, enjoyed the stories, and received pleasure from learning 'regular' seventh grade content that they could discuss with any of their more able contemporaries. Not only the children, but also we who were teaching, had overcome discouragement."

Treatment of a Tenth Grader at First Grade Level

Finally, let us consider how an individual pupil might be handled. At sixteen years of age, Matthew, I.Q. 97, was in the tenth grade, reading at first grade level. He wanted to leave school but was afraid to do so. He said, "Maybe I won't be able to get a job. Nobody'll hire me. I can't even read a want ad or fill out a job application."

One of the authors was a reading specialist in the school at the time. She devoted twenty minutes, twice a week, to working individually with Matthew.

Sometimes using an entirely new method engenders hope, particularly in older children such as Matthew who are discouraged and feel that they will never learn. Therefore, she started by helping the boy read the want ads in the newspaper. Matthew developed a large sight vocabulary through such ads as: "Wanted—Bus Boy," "Truck Driver Wanted," "Help Wanted—Men," "Boys or Young Men Needed." Longer advertisements were used also. For example:

A Good Job
is worth
waiting for. . . .

N O W

HERE IT IS

We have an opening for an
Experienced

SHORT ORDER COOK

And we'll be happy to teach you
anything you need to know.

Write Box WCP 224, this newspaper, giving home address and
telephone number where you can
be reached.

Matthew worked on filling out application blanks, too. He quickly learned the words *name, address, telephone number.* Frequently, he brought in material from the newspaper at home and picked out ads or headlines that he wanted to learn. In addition, the visual-motor method (see Chapter 5) was used to reinforce sight words and to strengthen spelling words such as *experience* or *necessary.*

Since sight words offer only a limited means for recognizing words, and since Matthew was sufficiently motivated to profit from a concentrated phonic approach (which is too laborious for many pupils), making words from known sounds was emphasized. The workbook *Remedial Reading Drills* was used a great deal to teach the sounds of many letters. Associative picture cards (see Chapter 5) were available at the outset if Matthew had particular trouble remembering a sound. Matthew then practiced figuring out phonetic words. He was so interested that he would go through two or three phonic exercises from Hegge, Kirk, and Kirk in one lesson, first looking at the words and sounding them out, then writing them from dictation.

Later he learned the vowel sounds and the rules governing their long and short sounds. He could then apply this knowledge to words he found on signs, such as *Bus Stop, Drugs, Live Bait,* and *Cleaner.* Some special material was composed with short sentences, such as "This is Bill. He has a job. He works every day. He is a bus boy." However, he used published material at first grade level as soon as possible. Workbooks and narrative material with mature format such as those mentioned earlier in this chapter were presented. In addition, Matthew brought in miscellaneous reading matter that interested him—restaurant menus, safety signs from shop, road signs from the driver's manual. His application and effort became greater and greater as his confidence increased. He finally reached low fourth grade level when he left the school. Although this was far from ideal, even this low reading achievement would enable him to continue improving on his own.

The foregoing accounts show that extremely poor readers who have already given up are able to gain a fair degree of skill and confidence. Even though achievement may not always have been spectacular in terms of potential, the startling fact is that these pupils became sufficiently interested to improve and to keep on trying. Their teachers were able to succeed despite the obstacles and unfavorable conditions prevalent in so many of our crowded urban schools. With ingenuity, dedication, and hard work, they were able to change attitudes of doom and degradation to those of anticipation and animation.

When such pupils are ready to leave school, they can be told that education need never stop. Once they are out in the world they can always return to night school, to adult education courses, or whatever. Some may eventually reach their intellectual capabilities even though it takes them many years to do so. Some may yet enter college when they themselves wish to work hard enough for it; some may even enter careers which require exacting academic preparation. If they have learned the rudiments of academic skills, they no longer need to scoff at educational pursuits. But if they lack the barest essentials they may indeed be absorbed into the morass of delinquent, antisocial, and wretched people with whom urban societies are becoming more and more familiar.

Suggestions for Further Reading

FEATHERSTONE, W., *Teaching the Slow Learner*. New York: Bureau of Publications, Teachers College, Columbia University, 1951, Ch. VII.

FISHER, B., "Group Therapy with Retarded Readers." *Journal of Educational Psychology*, 44 (1953), pp. 354–60.

INGRAM, CHRISTINE, *The Education of the Slow-learning Child.* New York: Ronald Press, 1960.

JERSILD, A., and HELFANT, K., *Education for Self-understanding.* New York: Bureau of Publications, Teachers College, Columbia University, 1953.

JEWETT, A., *Improving Reading Instruction in the Junior High School.* U.S. Dept. of Health, Education and Welfare. Office of Education, Bulletin No. 10. Washington, D.C.: Government Printing Office, 1957.

JOHNSON, O., *Education for the Slow Learners.* Englewood Cliffs, N.J.: Prentice-Hall, 1963, Part II.

KIRK, S., and JOHNSON, G., *Educating the Retarded Child.* Boston: Houghton Mifflin, 1951.

RUSSELL, D., *Children Learn to Read.* Boston: Ginn, 1961, pp. 394 ff.

৯ 9

The Bright High School Student
Who Is Not Achieving
up to Capacity

৯ The bright high school student who reads up to grade level but still is not functioning up to his potential presents a reading difficulty of such a subtle nature that it has probably gone undetected until he has reached high school. He was able to continue up to this point and obtain fairly satisfactory marks despite his lack of interest, his dearth of outside reading, and his minimal application to his studies. The more rigorous requirements of high school, however, often bring his difficulty to light for the first time.

In educational parlance, such a student is called an underachiever. His teachers consider him disinterested and difficult to reach. The pupil himself is at a loss to know where the trouble lies. He is weary of being told by parents and teachers alike "You could do much better if you only applied yourself. You have the potential; why don't you use it?" These empty phrases only arouse more anxiety and guilt in the student because he knows that he is not stupid, yet he realizes that something seems radically wrong.

Diagnosis

The first step in helping such a student is to diagnose the problem. Techniques used in this connection are discussed in earlier chapters. For the convenience of the examiner, however, in evaluating the reading of students at upper levels, some appropriate tests and comments on their use follow: *Cooperative English Tests, Revised—Reading Comprehension* (grades 9–12; 12–college); *Cooperative Sequential Tests of Educational Progress—Reading* (grades 10–12); *Iowa Silent Reading Tests—Advanced* (grades 9–college); *Nelson-Denny Reading Test* (grades 9–college).[1] It is not necessary to administer an entire test. Selected subtests dealing with vocabulary, speed of reading, and paragraph comprehension are the most pertinent. They can be administered in three quarters of an hour or less. In analyzing errors on these subtests, the teacher can obtain clues as to the student's difficulties and may discover why his scores are low.

Wherever possible, test results are interpreted to the student in a constructive manner. The teacher might find that the student displays a high degree of accuracy in his answers but is penalized by time or that he has misread words that look alike, and so on. As the pupil becomes aware of his ineffective approach and finds out what he can do about it, he becomes more interested in receiving help. In this way, diagnosis lays the groundwork for future cooperation and sustained effort.

Dealing with Bright Underachievers

The approaches necessary for effective assistance include finding ways to help the student overcome his basic distrust of himself, locating reading matter and workbook exercises to surmount specific weaknesses in reading, and assisting with any other aspect of his schoolwork which interferes with his functioning. These include handling assignments, improving rate of reading, and the like.

It is not always possible for underachievers, even with help in reading, to suddenly obtain the grades or test scores predicted for them. In fact, if overemphasis is placed in this direction, it may produce even lower scores due to increased tension or resistance. Instead of repeatedly admonishing them to improve and reminding them of their untapped possibilities, the authors discuss with the students the ways in which they might handle their problems. We also indicate the various alternatives available even if their achievement scores do not rise appreciably. We point out that their lives will not be ruined if they fall short of the high standards set for them. We may mention that famous scientists, presidents of colleges, and other outstanding men did not always receive high grades in high school or attend well-known universities.

Furthermore, we have observed that although many with whom we have worked eventually ranked high in their classes, achieved outstanding scores on their college boards, and entered the colleges of their choice, these incentives rarely were effective at the outset. Thus, the student is

---

[1] Tests mentioned in this chapter are listed in Appendix A.

helped to gain insight into his strengths and his deficiencies. He is shown how he can improve his skills and cope with the problem at hand.

Choosing Narrative Material

The teacher chooses stories, classics, novels, and the like that touch upon universal human experiences. The most important objective is to find something that will impress the student sufficiently to read further on his own. A story that directly relates to a personal need or problem can have a powerful influence. Not only can it heighten his interest in reading, but sometimes it can be forceful enough to help him relate better to other individuals and to his most important responsibility—schoolwork.

Sometimes the teacher must search long and diligently through anthologies, comprehension exercises, and workbooks before she can find material which will move the students.[2] But when she does, the impact will be unmistakable. Then their inherent interest will carry them along. But many times this does not happen. The student reads grudgingly or merely to improve his school grades. This is an acceptable start. Reading to obtain higher marks can improve the student's functioning in school and can open the door to future academic plans that are more in line with his ability. Rather than deplore such an attitude, the teacher accepts it for the time being and realizes that as the student matures, he may develop sounder goals. In the meantime, every effort is made to find appealing short stories and articles that will serve as a springboard to other books.

Sometimes one brief, dramatic story will have a lasting effect and inspire the student to read more. For example, a young boy who rarely read for pleasure or enjoyment completed a short story by Steinbeck in an anthology. He became fascinated with Steinbeck's style of revealing a character's secret thought. Before this he considered that he alone had "bad thoughts." He felt that he was the only one who said one thing and thought another. The story made such an impression on him that he began reading everything by Steinbeck that he could find. He finally became an avid reader of a variety of authors.

Selection and Use of Workbooks

Besides compelling narrative material, it is important to use a variety of comprehension exercises dealing with separate fields. This offers the stu-

---

[2] To help the teacher find suitable material, a specially selected list of books and workbooks is included in this chapter, pp. 166–9.

dent a wealth of background information and new vocabulary in a short span of time. Besides broadening background and vocabulary, which the student decidedly needs, these selections develop flexibility in reading. Also, choosing articles from social studies, science, current affairs, and the like approximates the reading that the student needs for his textbooks; hence it develops study skills as well. (Of course the student who does not transfer these skills to actual texts needs further supervised practice.)

Articles are selected with care so that time is not wasted on irrelevant or poorly constructed ones. The main criteria for selection include intrinsic interest of the subject matter, a wide choice of content and style, clear exposition of paragraphs, and properly constructed questions. If the teacher makes it a practice to preview the articles and answer the questions herself, she can soon discover which are most suitable. She may also discover which to discard as too difficult, ambiguous, or inappropriate.

The instructor shows the students how different articles will be used. Some selections are very short; others are two thousand words or longer. They include newspaper articles, technical reports, informational material, and so forth. The types of questions vary also. Some are followed by one or two questions that seek the main idea; others have about ten questions that search out details. Some questions are reflective, others inferential, and so on. In handling these materials, the student practices shifting his pace from one to the other. He learns when to read carefully and when to skim. He aims for efficiency in reading rather than increased rate per se. (A more extensive discussion of rate is offered on pages 169 ff. of this chapter.)

As an additional aid, the instructor selects two or three pertinent articles on reading theory from workbooks such as *Study Type of Reading Exercises* or *Reading Skills* (see Appendix C). They contain suggestions on organization of ideas, remembering what is read, reading to get the author's thought, and so on.

After the student has completed a selection and corrected his work, he may find that keeping a record of his accuracy or his rate of reading score is a beneficial incentive for improvement. But another student might find it too threatening, since there is apt to be wide fluctuation in performance. Some derive benefit from working under the pressure of a stop watch; others find that this detracts from their concentration. The student experiments under the instructor's guidance until the latter finds the method that best suits the student. Also, it is enlightening for the student to discuss the nature of his errors after he has completed the comprehension exercises. For example, did he misunderstand a question due to its ambiguity or insufficient familiarity with the subject? If so, he might be told to leave such questions out in the future and answer the rest. (Perhaps he will have time at some point to use an encyclopedia or other source to obtain the information.) If he makes wild guesses, he must learn to read more accurately. If he confuses his personal reactions or past knowledge with the information specifically stated in the paragraph, he must learn to make the distinction between them. If he tends to read every word, he can be encouraged to read for ideas; if he skims too rapidly and loses the details, he should be shown the value of becoming more precise.

The student continues working in this way for as long as necessary. For most students, ten to twenty sessions are sufficient to show them what they need and how to proceed independently. After completing instruction, a student can always return for occasional practice whenever he feels the need. But the more responsibility he assumes for incorporating the skills he has acquired into his general reading and school assignments, the more he should be able to improve his reading efficiency.

The materials listed below offer a variety of subject matter in a condensed form for practice in comprehension on a high school level. For more advanced students, material at college level is listed on Page 171 and in Appendix C.

Materials For Practicing Comprehension Skills

BOOKS

U. Leavell and Matilda Bailey, *The Mastery of Reading Series.* New York: American Book Co., 1956. Six books for grades 7 through 12. Revised editions. Each book includes exercises in comprehension, rate, vocabulary development, interpretation, critical evaluation, use of source material, organization, fact finding, cause and effect relations, and so on. Accompanying workbooks are available for grades 7, 8, and 9.

	Reading Level
Worlds of Adventure	7
Worlds of People	8
Worlds to Explore	9
The World of Endless Horizons	10
The World of America	11
The World and Our English Heritage	12

R. Pooley *et al., America Reads Series.* New York: Scott, Foresman, 1953. Four books for grades 9, 10, 11, 12. Each book has an accompanying "Think It Through" workbook, with exercises in comprehension and vocabulary development.

	Reading Level
Good Times through Literature	9
Exploring Life through Literature	10
The United States in Literature	11
England in Literature	12

W. D. Sheldon *et al.*, *The Track Two Adventures in Literature Series.* New York: Harcourt, Brace & Co., 1956. Each book is an anthology of biography, poetry, articles on the West, industry, history, and so forth. The series has two "tracks." Track One is used for regular classes, while Track Two is simpler in style and readability level.

	Reading Level
Adventures for Today	7–9
Adventures in Living	8–10
Adventures for Americans	9–11
Adventures in Modern Literature: 4th edition	10–12

P. Spencer and T. Robinson, *Reading and Study Series.* Chicago: Lyons & Carnahan, 1954. The books include exercises in rate of reading, how to read a newspaper, vocabulary development, readings in history and science, organizing information, using source material, and so on.

	Reading Level
Driving the Reading Road	7
Progress on Reading Roads	8

WORKBOOK-TYPE MATERIAL

	Reading Level
H. Covell *et al.*, *Reading Laboratory,* IVa, College Prep Edition, Science Research Associates. Selections offer a wide variety of material on different subjects. Besides exercises in rate and comprehension, it includes "Listening—Notetaking Builders" to practice fundamental skills of lecture note taking. Answer keys available.	8–14

	Reading Level
W. Guiler and J. Coleman, *Reading for Meaning.* Lippincott. Each workbook contains selections followed by exercises in central thought, organization, summarizing, details, total meaning, and so on.	9–12

	Reading Level
Eleanor Johnson, *Modern Reading.* Merrill. Each article is followed by exercises in comprehension and vocabulary practice.	Bk. 2: 8–10 Bk. 3: 9–12

Reading Level
9–12

T. McCall and Lelah Crabbs, *Standard Test Lessons in Reading*, Book E. Bureau of Publications, Teachers College, Columbia University. Each brief paragraph is followed by multiple-choice questions. Answer keys available.

Reading Level
9–12

Ruth Strang, *Study Type of Reading Exercises*, for secondary schools. Bureau of Publications, Teachers College, Columbia University, revised edition. Each of the 1,000-word reading exercises is based on description and explanation of good reading habits. The student practices rate while reading about the theory and practice of efficient study.

Vocabulary Development

Although bright pupils who are poor students may have developed an adequate vocabulary for their general needs, they find it increasingly difficult to compete with students of comparable ability who have acquired a much larger vocabulary through reading a variety of material during the years. Furthermore, high schools are placing more and more stress on extending knowledge of words because of the weight given to vocabulary subtests on the comprehensive and scholastic aptitude examinations.

In helping to enlarge vocabulary, the student might keep an alphabetized notebook in which he writes unfamiliar words together with a definition and a simple sentence in which each is used. Other means for increasing vocabulary include practice with verbal analogies, classification of words, and replacing an incorrect word in a sentence. Examples of materials that offer practice in vocabulary development are annotated below.

MATERIALS FOR PRACTICING VOCABULARY SKILLS

The Cebco Company, 104 Fifth Ave., New York 11, N.Y., puts out stencil sheets which can be duplicated, so that each student receives a copy of all exercises. The sets consist of a series of vocabulary-building exercises that help to develop precision in the use of words and in the comprehension of reading matter. For high school seniors.

H. C. Hardwick, *Words Are Important*. Hammond. Eight booklets are available. The selection of words for the various books has been based on Thorndike and Lorge, *Teachers' Word Book of 30,000 Words*. Answer keys available.

	Grade Level
Junior Book	7
Introductory Book	8
Simplified Edition	
Regular Edition	
First Book	9
Second Book	10
Third Book	11
Fourth Book	12
Fifth Book	13

J. R. Orgel, *College Entrance Reviews in English Aptitude*. Educators Publishing Service, 301 Nassau Street, Cambridge 39, Mass. The booklets are designed primarily to practice for college entrance tests. Answer keys available.

S. Taylor *et al., Word Clues.* Educational Developmental Laboratories, Huntington, N.Y. A programmed instruction workbook for self-teaching of vocabulary. For use with junior and senior high school students.

	Grade Level			Grade Level
Book G	7		Book J	10
Book H	8		Book K	11
Book I	9		Book L	12
			Book M	13

Vis-Ed English Vocabulary Cards, 207 S. Perry St., Dayton, Ohio. 1,000 separate cards with which to study English vocabulary. On each card a word is printed with its pronunciation and an example of its proper use in sentence form. On the reverse side of the card is its definition. For high school students.

A. Works, *Vocabulary Builders*. Manter Hall School, Cambridge, Mass. Gives practice in vocabulary, using new words in context; also offers exercises in prefixes, suffixes, and roots, analogies, synonyms and antonyms, and words commonly confused. Answer keys available.

	Grade Level
Book 1	12
Book 2	11
Book 3	10
Book 4	9
Book 5	8

Rate of Reading

Today more than ever, a great deal is heard about rate. Some reading centers claim that they can increase an individual's rate of reading to the upper hundreds and even thousands of words per minute. To achieve or maintain such astronomical speed is in our experience most unusual. Besides, rate should always be governed by purpose and be assessed in conjunction with comprehension.[3] There is no "normal" or average rate of reading. For general reading, some authorities have considered 300 words per minute fairly adequate. According to Nila Banton Smith, "The average (adult) reader covers about 250 words per minute. Very good readers read 500 or 600 words per minute. Occasionally there is a person who reads at the phenomenal rate of 1,000 words per minute, or in rare instances even faster."[4]

How do we determine rate, and how do we decide who should have training in it? Rate is measured by subtests on the regular reading examinations listed previously in this chapter. It is but one portion of a diagnosis which includes evaluation of advanced word recognition techniques, vocabulary, comprehension, and so on. Rate scores must always be evaluated in connection with comprehension. For instance, students who score in the ninetieth percentile in rate and the twentieth percentile in comprehension are bound to run into trouble in high school and college, obviously not because of rate, but because they get so little from their reading. In addition to looking at the scores of rate and comprehension, it is important to investigate the student's own thoughts on the matter. Is he overwhelmed by the questions on examinations? Is he spending an inordinate amount of time on his homework? Does he consider that his rate in general is excessively slow?

If the test results confirm the impression that rate improvement is indicated, then the instructor works out an appropriate program with the student.

Students who need to speed up their reading and are able to work on their own may profit from a workbook which explains the theory of efficient reading at the same time that it measures the student's rate and comprehension. Some students find that this is all the work that they need. However, these students are in the minority. Most individuals wish for some direction and guidance. This is where the teacher can provide the necessary stimulus and the systematic checking that keep the student going. If he is motivated adequately, he can make good progress.

The program consists of practice with appropriate material. All the reading matter suitable for practice in comprehension is also appropriate for rate and vice versa. However, for correcting answers and measuring words per minute, it is convenient to have material that contains the number of

---

[3] L. Carillo and W. Sheldon, "The Flexibility of Reading Rate," *Journal of Educational Psychology*, 43 (1952), pp. 299–305.

[4] Nila Smith, *Read Faster and Get More from Your Reading* (Englewood Cliffs, N.J.: Prentice-Hall, 1958), p. 3.

words in the selection, conversion tables for finding rate, individual answer keys, and the like. For bright high school juniors and seniors and college students, the following materials are particularly appropriate. Content is at college reading level.

MATERIAL SUITABLE FOR PRACTICING RATE AND COMPREHENSION IN READING

WORKBOOKS

W. Baker, *Reading Skills*. Prentice-Hall.
J. Brown, *Efficient Reading*, alternate edition. D. C. Heath.
R. Cosper and G. Griffen, *Toward Better Reading Skill*. Appleton-Century-Crofts.
L. Miller, *Increasing Reading Efficiency*. Henry Holt.
P. Shaw and A. Townsend, *College Reading Manual*. Thomas Y. Crowell.
Ruth Strang, *Study Type of Reading Exercises, College*. Columbia University Press.

BOOKS

H. Carter and Dorothy McGinnis, *Effective Reading for College Students*. Dryden Press.
Nila Smith, *Read Faster and Get More from Your Reading*. Prentice-Hall.

In addition to such practice, the student must agree to undertake some independent reading at home which he does regularly for approximately a half hour. It is recommended that the student choose reading matter that does not make excessive demands on concentration. Magazine articles, short stories, novels, fiction, and so on are suggested. He forces himself to read these as fast as he possibly can, making certain that he understands reasonably well what he reads. Several weeks or months of such practice usually result in much more facile reading ability. For a detailed discussion of procedures for an individual with a slow rate of reading, see the case of Jerry in Chapter 10.

Most students are able to read more rapidly after they undertake the program just described. However, there are always some who do not increase their rate to a satisfactory degree. Such students may develop so much concern about the number of words they read per minute that their progress is often impeded. Where this occurs, the instructor may help the student by discussing some of the ways in which he might compensate for his slow reading. For example, he might set aside a little more time for daily studying than he ordinarily does. Or he might take four courses rather than five a year, or he might take additional credits in summer school. Adopting these alternatives would provide him with enough time to study so as to complete assignments without working under undue pressure. Apprising the student of such choices serves to decrease his anxiety about his inadequate rate of reading. As he gains a more realistic attitude toward his problem, he is usually able to function more effectively.

The Place of Machines in Improving Rate

The subject of rate would not be complete without some mention of the use of machines. Various types of pacing machines, tachistoscopes, and other devices for quick exposure of words, phrases, and connected reading have long been in use. They have some desirable aspects as well as limitations. On the positive side, students are frequently intrigued by them. Thus they heighten motivation.[5] They may give students the initial boost that they need in developing a faster rate, or they may help to overcome a long-standing habit of slow reading. Also, machines may lend a more mature atmosphere for study. Students may feel less embarrassed doing exercises in rate and comprehension with the aid of films or a reading accelerator than with workbooks.

However, there may be little carry-over from the machine to the normal reading situation. A machine represents an artificial learning situation that is rarely available outside of school. It also leads to some distortion in the reading process.[6] Furthermore, any program still depends on the person who leads it. Without skillful personal guidance, the use of machines is likely to develop into a meaningless procedure. Therefore, a period of guided reading without mechanical devices should follow any program that depends on machines.

The most widely used instruments include pacing machines, projectors for specially constructed reading films, and tachistoscopes. Some of those that deserve consideration are described below.[7]

Pacing Machines

Pacing machines for individual practice use a simple principle of a shutter which gradually slides down over a printed page line by line. It

---

[5] W. Perry and C. Whitlock, "Clinical Rationale for a Reading Film," *Harvard Educational Review* (1954), pp. 6–27.

[6] A. Gates, "News and Comment," *Elementary School Journal, 62*, No. 1 (1961), pp. 1–13.

[7] For further discussion on the advantages and disadvantages of machines in reading programs, see O. Causey and W. Eller, *Starting and Improving College Reading Programs* (Fort Worth, Texas: Texas Christian University Press, 1959), Part I, and R. Karlin, "Machines and Reading: A Review of the Research," *Clearing House, 32* (1958), pp. 349–52.

usually covers the material over which it passes in order to prevent looking back. The reader can use his own material and set the control at the desired speed.

> *AVR Rateometer.* Audio Visual Research, 531 South Plymouth Court, Chicago, Ill.
> *SRA Reading Accelerator,* Model III. Science Research Associates, 57 W. Grand Street, Chicago, Ill.

Reading Films

Reading films consist of a printed page projected onto a screen. A bar of light illuminates consecutive phrases of prepared material; the remainder of the page on the screen remains dimmed. The viewer is forced to read at the prescribed rate as he follows the pace of the light strip. The speed of projection can be increased by the instructor from less than 200 words to approximately 500 words per minute.

> *Harvard University Reading Films, Second Series.* Adapted for 16 mm silent projector, The Harvard University Films, produced by William Perry and Charles Whitlock, Cambridge, Mass., Harvard University Press, 1948. (For college students and adults.)
> *Iowa Reading Films, College Series.* Bureau of Audio-Visual Instruction, State University of Iowa, Iowa City, 1958. (For college students.)
> *Iowa High School Films,* Bureau of Audio-Visual Instruction, State University of Iowa, Iowa City, 1950. (For high school students.)
> *The Controlled Reader.* Educational Developmental Laboratories, Huntington, N.Y. (For beginning reading through adult levels.)

Tachistoscopes

Tachistoscopes allow exposure of single words, numbers, phrases, and so on for very short periods. The purpose is to speed up recognition of small units with the hope that this ability will be transferred to reading connected material. However, research studies show conflicting evidence about their value.[8] Exposure usually ranges from one second or more to fractions of a second. Power-driven tachistoscopes include:

> *The Keystone Overhead Projector and Flashmeter.* Keystone View Co., Meadville, Pa.
> *Perceptoscope.* Perceptual Developmental Laboratories, 6767 Southwest

[8] *Ibid.*, pp. 55–9.

Ave., St. Louis 17, Mo. (This instrument is both a tachistoscope and a projector.)

Hand-operated tachistoscopes include:

Flash X. Educational Developmental Laboratories, Huntington, N.Y.
Pocket-Tac. The Reading Institute, 116 Newberry St., Boston, Mass.

Meeting Academic Requirements and Assignments

As is well known, high school requirements become more stringent as students advance. Students who are reading less well than they are able may find their assignments becoming more and more arduous. All the reasons that have been enumerated contribute to this predicament. The students' foundations may remain inadequate, their vocabulary insufficient, their rate slow, and their confidence low. Beside the suggestions described, it is sometimes profitable to give the student a little extra direction in assignments. For example, helping him to look for suitable references or guiding him in organizing the salient features for an outline can be beneficial. Concrete explanations as to the format and scope required in a term paper can bring about satisfactory results.

In organizing their studies, some students find the *SQ3R Method* helpful.[9] This formula stands for "Survey, Question, Read, Recite, Review." In essence, this technique suggests (1) glancing over chapter headings for major points; (2) turning paragraph headings into questions; (3) reading to answer the questions; (4) looking away from the book, briefly reciting to oneself, then writing down the information, and finally (5) reviewing the lesson for major points.

Whatever the method used, the student needs continued encouragement. One cannot always live up to a theoretical potential nor work at the peak of one's efficiency. But a student can be helped to improve his techniques, accelerate his effectiveness, and increase his power of functioning.

Coping with Examinations

Another problem of major importance concerns pupils who often become overconcerned and panicky over intensive examinations. Particularly in the latter years of high school, tests such as the *College Boards* cause heightened fear and anxiety. Students who have minimum achievement become particularly unnerved by them. They may react similarly to class

---

[9] F. Robinson, *Effective Study* (New York: Harper & Brothers, 1961).

tests, too. Although there is no cure, there are certain things that have proved alleviating.[10] The teacher and pupil can discuss the latter's approach toward taking tests. Does he "freeze"? Does he make "careless" errors in mistaking directions? They can discuss how many people "go blank" when faced with an important test; in fact, it is almost universal for everyone to have anxiety before, during, and even after taking tests. The student can then take actual examinations for practice. This makes the ordeal more commonplace and lessens some of its overpowering tension. In addition, he is advised to exert reasonable effort on each test item, but not puzzle too long over any one of them. If there is time, he can always return to a question he left out. If an answer is omitted, the student learns caution in placing the next mark properly. (Too often a "skipped" question throws off subsequent markings.) On an essay-type examination, he is encouraged to read all the questions first; this sometimes yields valuable hints for answering several of them. Learning to gauge time correctly is also of paramount importance. After practice tests are taken, the teacher and student can score them jointly. Incorrect responses can be accounted for on the spot. Reviewing his errors can help the student gain insight into the nature of his mistakes. Finally, assuring him that there are still colleges that accept students without examinations takes away the unrealistic fear that his whole life depends on a test.

Fallacy of Prediction from Test Scores Alone

Evaluating ability and suggesting choices for the future entails the use of predictive measures. That is, it includes mapping out courses of study and future academic plans on the basis of test scores and teachers' evaluations of the student. But foretelling human outcomes is at best a risky undertaking. The largest factor, motivation, still remains a mystery. Demosthenes, the severe stutterer, became an accomplished orator. Winston Churchill supposedly failed English composition three times, yet his prose is impeccable. Those considered "most likely to succeed" in high school yearbooks often turn out to be miserable failures. Furthermore, the growth spurt from late adolescence to maturity makes prophecy hazardous.

Therefore, let us not in this overtesting age be influenced by quantitative scores and other mechanical measures alone. Let us not be misled even by the most careful and extensive assessment of a student who, in his present stage, shows less academic aptitude than is considered desirable. Those

---

[10] H. Kalish, N. Garmezy, E. Rodnich, and R. Bleke, "The Effects of Anxiety and Experimentally Induced Stress on Verbal Learning," *Journal of General Psychology*, 59 (1958), pp. 87–95.

who deal with all forms of reading problems are still puzzled over outcomes. Some mediocre students in high school have become brilliant achievers in college. Some students whose test scores suggested that they were not college material have entered the army and a few years later have become sufficiently interested to seek college admission. There they have made creditable and even brilliant records. Other students whose "verbal" scores were significantly higher than their "math" scores on scholastic aptitude tests were strongly advised against pursuing the science, mathematics, and physics studies which attracted them. Yet many who ignored this counsel have turned out to be successful in these fields. There are some students who have suffered from reading difficulty throughout their first twelve years of schooling and are still miserable spellers. Through sheer determination and adherence to their goals, they have become doctors, lawyers, engineers, or whatever else they wished. We have known pupils who were told to give up the idea of college completely. Against this advice not only did they go to college, but, in many cases, they went on to graduate study.

The opposite situations have also obtained. Students who were scholarship material in high school have failed in college; those who were told that they would make excellent Ph.D. material never were able to withstand the academic strain. Thus an experienced teacher or counselor imparts as many of the skills as possible. When a certain amount of failure seems unconquerable, the "door must be left open." The situation is assessed as fairly as possible, but decisions remain tentative. Tremendous change can occur outside the confines of formal education. Life circumstances, inspiration, and growth processes between eighteen and thirty years of age and even older have as yet to be investigated. No one knows when maturation reaches its zenith. People continue to learn throughout their lives, and striving need never stop. Our most important contribution to those who have academic difficulty is to lessen their sense of failure so that they have an opportunity to make use of whatever abilities they may have.

Suggestions for Further Reading

BRACKEN, DOROTHY, "Appraising Competence in Reading in the Content Areas," in *Evaluation of Reading*, ed. Helen Robinson. *Supplementary Educational Monographs,* No. 88. Chicago: University of Chicago Press, 1958.

GRAY, W., "New Approaches to the Study of Interpretation in Reading." *Journal of Educational Research,* 52 (1958), pp. 65–7.

HEILMAN, A., *Principles and Practices of Teaching Reading.* Columbus, Ohio: Merrill, 1961, pp. 266–7.

ROBINSON, HELEN, "Promoting Maximal Growth among Able Learners." *Supplementary Educational Monographs,* No. 81. Chicago: University of Chicago Press, 1954.

The Reading Teacher, December, 1954, entire issue devoted to "Improving Reading in the Content Areas"; February, 1958, entire issue devoted to "Efficient Reading in Each Curriculum Area"; and December, 1961, entire issue devoted to "Reading as Thinking."

STRANG, RUTH, McCULLOUGH, CONSTANCE M., and TRAXLER, A., *The Improvement of Reading,* 3d ed. New York: McGraw-Hill, 1961, pp. 369–76.

೭ 10

Illustrative Case Histories

ೆ Over the years, the authors have often been asked by psychiatrists, psychologists, and other workers, "What actually takes place during remedial treatment?" The cases presented in this chapter have been selected from our files to illustrate the nature of the remedial process with children ranging from a brain-damaged boy to an underachiever of high intelligence.

There are some instances in which the reading problem is cleared up in as few as six or seven sessions. We have not selected such cases for description, gratifying though they may be, since they are easily treated and pose no special difficulty. More often it takes a much longer period before any achievement is apparent, and occasionally remedial instruction has to be continued for a number of years. Sometimes this is due to the slow development of certain children who, although gifted intellectually, cannot apply themselves easily to the demands of schoolwork due to uneven physiological growth. This is illustrated in the case of Guy, who was treated for a year and a half and whose progress was followed from third grade through his junior year in college. Sometimes prolonged remedial treatment is necessary because the youngster has been neglected for so long that it requires painstaking care to get him back on the road toward learning. This is discussed in the case of Lloyd, a potential delinquent who was becoming antagonistic, contrary, and belligerent.

In treating such children, there is no magic that can be invoked; neither is there dramatic success most of the time. Many pupils manifest a sporadic pace of learning; many need extensive retraining. Often the process is so complex and takes so long that even the best-intentioned parents and school personnel become impatient. However, when they are able to understand the difficulties that the child is undergoing, when they realize that something

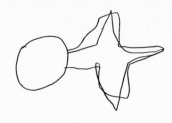

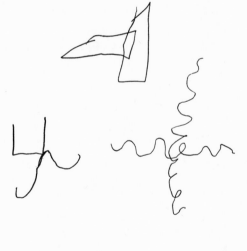

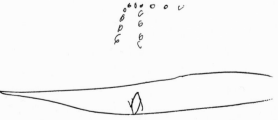

FIGURE 1. Frank: age eight years (59% of the size of following figures).
(Cf. pp. 199-205.)

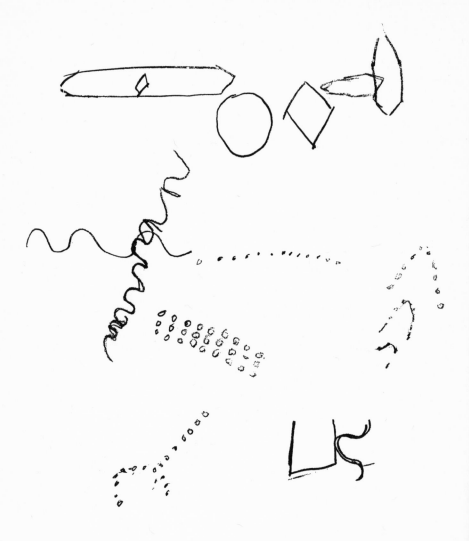

FIGURE 2. Frank: age ten years, three months. (Cf. pp. 199-205.)

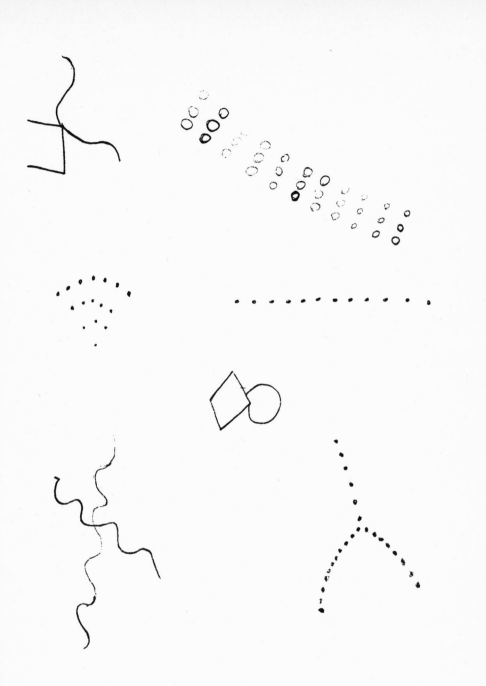

FIGURE 3. Frank: age fourteen years. (Cf. pp. 199-205.)

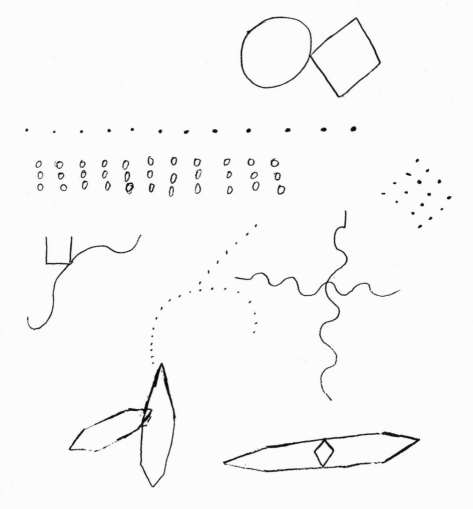

FIGURE 4. Frank: age seventeen years, one month. (Cf. pp. 199-205.)

can be and is being done, when they are agreeable to altering standards in the light of the child's immediate development and achievement, this understanding alone has a striking impact on the pupil. Indeed, without it, he is seriously handicapped.

Attitudes play a major role in remedial sessions, too, as does knowledge of appropriate teaching procedures. In fact, both the spirit and the content of the sessions are the crux of remedial instruction. The tutor who knows which methods to try and how to experiment with different books and materials and, in addition, continues to have trust and confidence in the pupil's inherent strengths can mobilize the resources of the child toward a fresh start. The tutor realizes that wide fluctuations in performance or infinitesimal gains are integral parts of the picture. He uses all his ingenuity to reassure the child by pointing out what he has already accomplished and what he can do; he also finds ways to inspire him to put forth renewed efforts despite his handicaps. How the authors attempted to do just this is described in the following six cases, which we consider representative of the many variations in causation and treatment.

Lloyd

At the age of 15, Lloyd, I.Q. 78, was still a nonreader. He was unruly and rebellious, on the road to becoming a hardened delinquent. The psychiatrist at the mental health clinic which Lloyd attended had many interviews with him but considered psychotherapy contraindicated. He concluded that what Lloyd needed most was to learn enough to be able to get a job and take care of himself in a satisfactory fashion. Since no school would accept him, he was referred to one of the authors for individual instruction. During remedial sessions, he acquired sufficient reading and arithmetic skills to find a job. More than that, he slowly dared to hope that he could improve. Through his relationship during remedial sessions he came to feel that all was not lost for him—that maybe he could make a new start.

History

Lloyd was suspended from school at 12 years 8 months of age because the school considered him lazy, disturbing, defiant, and disinterested. The school reported that they could not keep him because he "has no respect for authority. He cannot be trusted at any time. He is bold, insolent and does not accept corrections. He sulks, pouts, lies and never admits he is wrong. He is failing in all classwork, does not appear interested, is untidy and disorganized." It was the school's recommendation that behavior and achievement were so deviant that arrangements should be made for institutional care for the boy.

The psychiatrist at the mental health clinic did not agree that Lloyd should be institutionalized. He tried to work out educational plans for the boy. He found Lloyd very eager to cooperate. However, the one school that was willing to accept him would do so only if they might place Lloyd, then fourteen, in a third grade class. The psychiatrist felt that despite the boy's drive to gain some education sitting in a third grade class would have been too humiliating for him, especially since he was an important member of a group of boys in his neighborhood who planned many activities together.

Lloyd was living with his maternal grandmother and two older brothers. He and his brothers were born out of wedlock. None of his family was particularly concerned with him. Thus he wandered about for almost three years while workers at the agency were trying to find suitable placement for him. One of the authors worked with him three times a week. Traveling to these sessions involved taking three buses and took approximately two hours, but Lloyd never missed a lesson.

Test Results

Revised Stanford-Binet Intelligence Scale, Form L

C.A.	15 yrs. 11 mos.
M.A.	11 yrs. 8 mos.
I.Q.	78

Wechsler-Bellevue Intelligence Scales

C.A.		15 yrs. 11 mos.
Verbal Scale	I.Q.	76
Performance Scale	I.Q.	79
Full Scale	I.Q.	75

It was immediately clear why Lloyd could not do his homework and experienced so much difficulty in school. Not only was his intelligence low, but there was definite evidence of neurological impairment on these and other psychological tests. This finding explained Lloyd's inability to develop effective word-analysis techniques throughout the years. Reading tests revealed that he was a total nonreader, unable to read even the simplest material at preprimer level. Because of his poor visual memory and inability to synthesize sounds, both the visual-motor and phonic methods were found entirely unworkable. The only method by which Lloyd could learn was a whole-word approach.

Remedial Treatment

After reading the school's reports, the author who treated Lloyd was prepared to deal with a hostile, aggressive, resistive boy. Instead she found a very cooperative one, serious in attitude and eager to learn. Even though this boy had far to travel, he always arrived early. Indeed, these sessions seemed to be the only source of order and meaning in his life at this time.

Lloyd had three sessions a week for one and a half years, excluding summer vacations. He was so eager to learn that it was possible to start with the regular published materials at preprimer level. The correlated workbooks were used to give additional practice in the new words learned. Because of his poor auditory discrimination, some time was spent at each session on developing phonic readiness. Pictures of common objects were cut out of newspapers and magazines and pasted on cards. The name of each object was printed underneath its picture; on the reverse side the word appeared alone. Lloyd enjoyed learning in this way and was most responsive as he gradually saw evidence of progress. He was also able to learn consonant sounds by associating them with representative pictures. As soon as his knowledge of consonant sounds developed, he could learn by a word-family procedure. Thus, if he knew the word *light,* he was able to figure out *sight, right, fight,* and so forth.

The level of difficulty in the graded series of readers and workbooks was increased gradually. Because it was so difficult for Lloyd to remember, learning to read was a slow process for him. He never was able to blend sounds together, despite his persistence in trying to do so. Thus his ability to develop independence in word recognition was limited. Every bit of achievement entailed real effort on his part. Yet he did not become overly discouraged.

By the time Lloyd read at second grade level, he started taking home simple books which he was able to read by himself. He was now past sixteen years of age, and a new approach was introduced. He was taught words which he would be likely to encounter on signs, labels on foods and medicines, menus, and help-wanted advertisements. He responded enthusiastically to this approach and seemed to derive great satisfaction from his attainments. Each word had to be taught not only in capital letters but in lower case as well, since there was no carry-over in his learning. It was as if he were learning two different languages. Some of the words taught this way were:

Help Wanted	Men	Employees
Boy Wanted	Women	No Smoking
Danger	Boys	Fire Escape
Poison	Girls	Doctor
Keep Off	Fire Extinguisher	First Aid
Keep Out	Live Wires	Employment Agency
Stop	Fare 15 Cents	Dynamite
Go	Bus Stop	Wet Paint
Walk	Beware of Dogs	Hands Off
Don't Walk	Out of Order	Electric Rail
Wait	Glass	Elevator
Entrance	In	Telephone
Exit	Out	Box Office
Up	Hospital	Thin Ice
Down		

Since the summer was approaching and instruction would be interrupted, Lloyd had become interested in finding a job. He started reading the want ads, such as:

> Boy Wanted—Dishwasher
> No experience necessary
> Call at 765 North Street
> Between 3 and 5 P.M.

He had reached the point where the little reading knowledge that he had was being applied in a practical and constructive way. This proved highly significant in his future adjustment because he could connect it directly with his daily experiences. Since Lloyd was never accepted at any school, it was imperative that he have some meaningful way of applying his reading outside the remedial sessions. This was accomplished by using word lists that served as a source of protection and assistance to him. Thus, even the meager ability he acquired in reading simple materials afforded him some personal satisfaction and a sense of achievement.

Part of each session was spent on strengthening his ability in simple addition and subtraction of numbers. He learned to count change and became proud that he could keep track of his money.

Toward the end of the remedial treatment, Lloyd expressed the hope that he would be able to get a job working with his brothers on the railroad. The mental health clinic which was following his progress confirmed this as a job possibility. Therefore, "Live Wires," "Electric Rail," "Dynamite," and other related signs were added to his growing functional reading vocabulary. An illustration of material which the writer made up for Lloyd to read follows:

> Today is Thursday, June 5, 1957. This is the last month that I will be coming here. I have learned to read and to add and subtract. When I leave here, I will go to an EMPLOYMENT AGENCY that says HELP WANTED, because I want a summer job. I will walk in and say, "Good Morning. My name is Lloyd Brown. I am looking for a job." "What can you do?" "I can wash dishes, help in the kitchen, and be very handy."
>
> After I leave the employment agency, I will take an ELEVATOR to the first floor. If I am very hungry, I will go to a DINER and eat some lunch. This is what I will have: Tomato soup, Ham sandwich, Milk, and Cake.
>
> My brother has a friend who will help me get a job next winter working on a railroad. These are the signs I will have to look out for: ELECTRIC RAIL, LIVE WIRES, LOOK OUT, KEEP OUT, KEEP AWAY, STOP, LOOK, LISTEN, DANGER, TUNNEL, TRAIN COMING, WATCH OUT.
>
> If I hurt my hand, I will go to a box marked FIRST AID. I will look for IODINE, ALCOHOL, COTTON, BAND AID, or GAUZE. I may also want ASPIRIN.

At the end of a year and a half, remedial work was terminated. Lloyd had shown growth in every way. The remedial treatment appeared to have alleviated the strong feelings of inferiority that resulted from his school failure. It seemed likely that Lloyd would be able to find work. At this point, there was no question of institutionalization. Had he experienced continued rejection on all sides, however, and remained totally illiterate, he might have committed antisocial acts, become a burden to himself and society, and become less amenable than ever to change.

Guy

The case of Guy, age 8 years 11 months, is in direct contrast to the previous one. Guy was referred at the end of his third year in school because he was reading, with difficulty, at beginning third grade level despite the fact that he was very bright, with an I.Q. of 131.

Delayed maturation seemed to be the primary cause of Guy's difficulty, but his problem was complicated by all the secondary emotional reactions that set in when he became so acutely aware of always tagging along at the end of the class. What can be done for such a child? His physiological growth cannot be accelerated. According to the psychological examination, therapy was not indicated. Instead, the report stated that Guy needed to become more proficient in his schoolwork so as to counteract his loss of self-esteem. Could remedial instruction be effective under such circumstances? How this boy was handled and how he responded are discussed in the following pages, which describe treatment and follow-up over a period of more than twelve years.

History

There was nothing unusual in Guy's developmental history except that his walking and talking were somewhat delayed. His teachers considered him to be fairly well adjusted. The kindergarten and first grade teachers described him as independent and a leader in his class. He had a good sense of responsibility and was sought after by his friends.

Test Results

Revised Stanford-Binet Intelligence Scale[1]
C.A.   8 yrs. 11 mos.
M.A. 11 yrs. 8 mos.
I.Q.   131

Cornell-Coxe Performance Scale
C.A.   8 yrs. 11 mos.
M.A. 11 yrs. 1 mo.
I.Q.   123

Bender Visual-Motor Gestalt Test and *Human Figure Drawings* test showed evidence of maturational lag in visual-motor development and coordination.

Gates Advanced Primary Test	Grade Level
Word Recognition	3.1
Paragraph Reading	3.2
Gates Reading Diagnostic Test	
Word Pronunciation	2.7
Gray Oral Paragraphs Test	2.9

On the *Gates Diagnostic Test,* Guy showed only rudimentary phonic knowledge. He knew most of the consonant sounds, but did not know any of the short vowel sounds. However, he did fairly well on the test of

---

[1] All tests and materials listed here can be found in Appendixes B and C, except those which have direct references in this chapter.

auditory blending. Trial lessons of word study indicated that the phonic approach could be used and that he could also learn by the visual-motor method.

On the surface, by merely looking at the grade scores, one might not consider this a very severe disability. However, Guy attended a school where most of the children possessed very high intelligence, so that practically all of his classmates were reading well above grade level. Guy, on the other hand, whose intelligence ranked among the highest, was barely able to handle a simple third grade book at the completion of the third grade in June. His reading was highly inaccurate. When confronted with unknown words, his guesses were based either on the sound of the first consonant or on the configuration of the word. Thus he would say "soon" for "same" and "guard" for "green," as he had no knowledge of how to analyze words otherwise. His reading ability, as far as the school was concerned, was totally unsatisfactory. He himself, when interviewed, seemed very discouraged about himself. He stated, "I read terribly, just terribly. Everyone reads better than me!"

Remedial instruction was started at once during summer vacation. Guy was apathetic about getting help. He had reached the point, after only three years of schooling, where he had already experienced sufficient humiliation and failure to have little faith in anybody's ability to help him. Nevertheless, he came for remedial instruction because his mother insisted. He did not show enough fight to oppose her, and his attitude at the beginning was very passive. The sentiments which he implied amounted to, "Well go ahead and teach me. Nobody else could. See what you can do, but don't expect anything from me."

How to raise even a glimmer of response in this child was a challenge. Finding materials that would accomplish this was very difficult. Furthermore, at the time Guy was referred, there was a dearth of books specially devised for children with reading disability. Therefore, the writer searched through the available series of graded readers for stories which this child might find satisfying. Finally, he liked one tale, "The Good Flea and the Wicked King," adapted from Victor Hugo. This was found in *Fun and Frolic*, a third grade reader. We read this story almost as one might read a play. Guy took the part of the flea, and the writer read the part of the wicked king and also those sections which involved narration. (See Appendix B for a complete bibliography listed according to reading level.)

This story lent itself to dramatization. As Guy identified with the little flea who outwitted the king, he appeared to be carried away by the story. He seemed to lose his self-consciousness about the mechanics of reading and even read with feeling the parts where he was able to express anger toward the king who was causing so much trouble. Thus some participation on his part was effected. Among the other stories in this book which he found appealing were "Pekka and the Rogues" and "The Monkey and the Crocodile."

From this book we went on to another third grade reader, *Tall Tales*.[2] Guy found some of these stories sufficiently satisfying to maintain his interest and effort during the initial stages of instruction. In general, then, the work during the summer was fruitful.

After the 14th session, when Guy was about to enter fourth grade, a book at that level, *Let's Look Around*, was introduced. Stories were still selected with care. Among those chosen were well-known ones such as *Dr. Doolittle and the Pirates, The Three Golden Apples*, and *The Golden Goose*. When he was able to handle more difficult fourth grade material, he was given the *Cases of Sherlock Holmes*. He found this book so engrossing that he took it home between sessions to read on his own. From this point on, finding recreational reading matter presented little difficulty.

During initial sessions, he often appeared troubled about the discrepancy between his performance and that of his classmates. The writer could only accept his discouragement as perfectly understandable and explain that sometimes these things take a long time, but that eventually he would "get there." She explained that, like him, some people grow slowly, just as plants do. Had he ever planted seeds and seen some sprout quickly while others trailed along? Guy showed that he understood this only too well as he sighed acceptingly and said, "I sure hate this 'slow' business."

Word recognition procedures also had to be taught in a manner which would elicit Guy's participation.

Therefore, the writer outlined a program, together with Guy, covering the skills he needed to master to enable him to deal independently with words. She told him that she would use many means of helping him. She demonstrated briefly how workbooks, games, and other devices could be helpful in this connection.

With the structure of skills to be taught clearly set up, the writer proceeded to present them in varied ways. Some of the techniques to which Guy responded in a positive manner were the use of phonic strips, which he brightly referred to as the machine for teaching letter sounds; true and false sentences from *Eye and Ear Fun*, Book I, which always aroused his interest; and dictation of phonetic words, which gave him the satisfaction of knowing he could really apply the phonic knowledge he had acquired.

---

[2] S. Artley and W. Gray, *Tall Tales* (Chicago: Scott, Foresman, 1948).

He also reacted favorably to games such as the Group Sounding Game which provided additional practice in word analysis.

As Guy's reading became more fluent, emphasis shifted to expanding his vocabulary and developing comprehension and study skills as described in Chapter 7. Special vocabulary pertaining to social studies and science material was taught through the lists found in the *Handbook of Technical Vocabulary*. It was explained that each subject has its own specific vocabulary. For instance, the words *decimal, quotient,* and *denominator* are associated with mathematics; *monoxide, molecules,* and *litmus paper* are scientific terms.

Throughout fourth grade Guy had one session a week. Shortly after he entered fifth grade, the following scores were obtained:

Metropolitan Achievement Test—Intermediate	Grade Level
Reading	6.6
Vocabulary	6.8
Gray Oral Paragraphs Test	6.2

Thus he had reached the point where it seemed safe to discontinue instruction. He was then given suggestions for continuing his reading independently and was told he might return from time to time to discuss his work, if he so desired.

In evaluating the case at this point, we can say that Guy progressed as well as one might have expected. He made sufficient gains to do creditable work in school; his word-analysis skills improved markedly, but were not perfect; reversal errors persisted, and occasionally configurational errors were apparent such as *demolish* for *diminish.*

In this respect, Guy is typical of many children with reading disability. They rarely ever master skills completely. This is due to the nature of the learning process, which does not always take place in as orderly a fashion as a tutor might wish. Rather, children with reading disability learn and remember partially and are able to utilize only to some degree what they have absorbed. Even with the most systematic and precise instruction, these children often remain unsteady and wobbly in their reading. This uncertainty constantly plagues them, lowers their self-esteem, and accounts in part for their rarely becoming the avid readers and solid students that their natural endowments suggest they should be. The authors question whether most children with reading disability ever develop the great love for reading which all reading teachers express as their goal. If so, it usually comes much later in the student's life when he becomes truly stimulated in some special fields; at such time he may find reading interesting and rewarding. This is just what happened to Guy. He did not ask for help again until he was in twelfth grade. At that time he was planning to go to a leading liberal arts college and thought that he might need help in increasing his rate of reading. He was tested and achieved the following scores:

The Nelson-Denny Reading Test	Percentile as Compared with 12th Grade Students
Vocabulary	90
Paragraph Reading	93
Total	92
Rate	68

Iowa Silent Reading Test—Advanced	Percentile as Compared with 12th Grade Students
Rate	48
Comprehension	91
Directed Reading	77
Word Meaning	93
Sentence Meaning	82
Paragraph Comprehension	74

The results on the *Nelson-Denny Test* indicated that Guy's reading comprehension was very satisfactory and close to what might be expected for his mental level, but his rate of reading was slow. The *Iowa Test* scores were somewhat lower. Thus he might profit from training in more rapid reading.

Guy was eager to obtain such aid. He showed a mature attitude and expressed a desire to read widely before entering college. Therefore, he did a considerable amount of work on his own with a minimum of guidance. He read books faster than his customary rate and used workbooks designed for improving reading at the college level. At the last follow-up, Guy was in his junior year at college. His reading was most satisfactory at this time and no longer stood in the way of his achieving academic success.

Polly

Polly was first seen at about nine and one half years of age, when she had completed two months of the fourth grade. Her teacher reported that she was able to read aloud fairly well, but was failing social studies and science.

According to the school report, Polly was a conscientious and willing young-ster, but she just couldn't seem to apply herself. She did very poorly on tests as well as in class discussion and did not seem to understand the basic con-cepts of the subject matter. Polly seemed oversensitive about her work, cried when she got poor marks, and worried unduly about tests.

History

Polly's parents reported that she had always been shy and retiring. This became even more apparent when she entered school, where she did not relate well to children. Otherwise, the developmental history was within the normal range.

At school she did not do well in first grade, but showed some improve-ment in second. She did somewhat average work in third grade. Polly's parents had been concerned about her shyness and poor relationships. They therefore consulted a psychiatrist when she was five and one half years old. He treated Polly for a little over a year at that time and considered that sufficient improvement had been accomplished to terminate treatment. When Polly's fourth grade teacher complained of her work, the psychiatrist saw Polly for an interview. He felt that Polly's low achievement was beginning to interfere with her emotional adjustment. He advised that an evaluation of her abilities be undertaken.

Test Results

Wechsler Intelligence Scale for Children
Verbal	I.Q.	101
Performance	I.Q.	93
Full Scale	I.Q.	97

	Grade Score
Gilmore Oral Reading Test	4.4
Metropolitan Achievement Test—Elementary	
Reading	3.5
Vocabulary	4.6

Roswell-Chall Diagnostic Reading Test
Showed fairly good background in word-analysis skills. However, she seemed uncertain of some of the short vowel sounds.

In addition to the above tests, Polly was given *Human Figure Drawings* and the *Bender Visual-Motor Gestalt Test* as well as trial lessons (see Chapter 2). The latter consisted of comprehension exercises to determine where her difficulty in this area lay. The examiner also had an interview with both parents and a consultation with the psychiatrist.

After assessing all the factors, it was concluded that Polly, according to her reading and intelligence scores, was achieving close to what might be expected. However, qualitatively there did seem to be certain definite limitations with respect to comprehension. Also oral reading was somewhat hesitant and labored. To complicate the picture further, Polly, a girl of average intelligence, attended a class in which most of the children were considerably brighter than she. This situation was becoming overwhelming for her since she felt so inferior to the others. Certainly the emotional reactions of inadequacy, insecurity, and timidity seemed to be encroaching on Polly's self-concept, and it was feared that she might revert to her former shyness.

It was therefore decided to obtain another evaluation of personality factors. (Projective tests had been administered previously when psychotherapeutic treatment was originally instituted.) The findings of the second examination ruled out the presence of neurosis of a serious nature. However, it seemed likely that the emotional difficulties which Polly was exhibiting were a reaction to her unfavorable situation. Unfortunately, in this school there was no other class available which would be more suitable for a child with Polly's abilities.

Recommendations

Since no change could be made in the school situation, it was decided to try to help Polly use more effectively the ability she did have. She would return to psychotherapy once a week for supportive treatment. Remedial instruction would be undertaken on a trial basis once a week to see whether comprehension skills could be strengthened sufficiently for Polly to achieve more satisfactorily in school and also to attempt to develop more fluency in oral reading. Reading instruction was initiated despite the fact that Polly could not be considered a disability case according to strict interpretation. This was done because the authors consider that remediation can always be attempted when a child shows possibility for improvement and where poor functioning in school is serving as an upsetting factor in the child's life. Thus the reading expectancy ratio of one year's retardation below the mental age[3] is used only as a guide while the additional factors involved are considered also. In this particular case, it seemed likely from the qualitative measures that some positive gains might result if the subject matter

---

[3] This is described fully in Chapter 2.

could be made more understandable to her and reading and study skills could become more facile and efficient.

Remedial Treatment

Since Polly's word recognition skills were for the most part adequate, the sessions were devoted mainly to oral and silent reading. *Far East Stories,* a book at third grade level, was introduced first. It was read alternately by Polly and the author who treated her. The oral reading allowed a natural basis for assessing her lacks in understanding. Discussion of the content was encouraged wherever indicated. In addition, social studies and science subject matter were read either silently or orally, whichever was deemed more suitable. Sometimes Polly's school texts were used, sometimes workbooks.

Beside the texts, selections from the *Reader's Digest Reading Skill Builders,* Books II and III, and Stone and Grover workbooks, *Practice Readers,* were used wherever appropriate and coordinated as much as possible with current schoolwork. For instance, the class was studying plants in science. *Practice Readers,* Book I, offers many short articles on this subject in Unit E, "Plants and Seeds." Polly learned many necessary facts from these selections plus some additional ones that she was proud to share with her classmates.

As Polly became more accustomed to reading for a purpose, her tendency to read word by word lessened. She was encouraged to read "thoughts" and not words, and in this way phrasing was developed. As a relationship began to evolve between her and the author, she became more self-confident and less fearful of making errors. This seemed to make her performance smoother also, and after about four months, hesitations disappeared altogether.

But Polly did not make comparable progress in comprehension and study skills. As already pointed out, most of the class members were considerably more able than Polly. They were so alert and articulate that no matter how well Polly was helped to prepare her work, class discussion was often far over her head. Polly herself told the author, "Everyone there is better than me. I get most of the assignment when I'm with you, but when I get to school, everyone's talking way up there somewhere! My sister says that with everyone doing so much for me on the outside, I should be the star pupil. But I guess I'm hopeless!"

After a conference with the class teacher, it was decided that other procedures should be tried. For instance, she could be responsible for bringing in pictures and other visual aids on the different topics being considered in class. She also could be in charge of the bulletin board which was to display related pictures that other pupils brought in. Finally, she could be given special assignments related to the class topic but not as demanding—assignments that she could be sure to manage.

In addition to providing better means for class participation and specialized work for Polly in this fashion, the teacher and principal both agreed with the author that wherever possible, standards could be revised for Polly. In classwork and on report cards, she could be marked according to effort and accomplishment and in terms of what she could do, not according to what the rest of the class was accomplishing.

This plan worked to much better advantage. Polly learned a great deal from her special assignments and took pride in contributing something worth while. Polly's parents helped, too. For example, when Hawaii was under discussion, Polly's mother gathered Hawaiian newspapers, pictures, a genuine grass skirt, and other native articles from friends and neighbors.

These changes increased Polly's self-respect and confidence. She progressed much more satisfactorily for the rest of the year, obtained no failures whatsoever, and began to feel more acceptable as a pupil. Therapy and remedial instruction were discontinued toward the end of the fourth grade.

The next year an "average" class was available to Polly, and here she managed well. She is now in eighth grade in junior high school. She remained through the years in a group whose standards of achievement stayed within her reach. Her parents report that she no longer battles with her homework every night; the frustration of trying to keep up with pupils much more capable than she has diminished considerably.

Louise

Many children whose reading has been satisfactory in the elementary school suddenly become overwhelmed when faced with the type of reading required at the junior high school level. This is the problem which Louise, age 12 years 6 months, I.Q. 111, experienced. She read at about sixth grade level, but needed special direction in the skills necessary at the upper elementary and junior high school levels.

History

Louise was referred for remedial instruction when she was in grade seven. Her parents reported that her schoolwork was adequate throughout the elementary grades. Even though there were no complaints about her reading, her parents observed that she never went to the library or engaged in any recreational reading. However, when she reached seventh grade and had to write book reports and read difficult social studies texts, she seemed completely lost.

Louise, a very attractive girl with a vivacious manner, was friendly, warm, and charming. She showed a good deal of anxiety about school. She reported that she never got beyond the first chapter of any book because she became too discouraged with the task of reading an entire book. Furthermore, she became nervous and upset after English and social studies classes because her teacher rigidly upheld extremely high standards. The teacher said, "I am not concerned when I see adolescents fall apart as this girl is doing. She will have to pick herself up again. . . . It is my duty to prepare them. . . ." Thus coordination of private remedial tutoring with the school was difficult. It became necessary to help Louise accept the attitude of the teacher and to continue working with her on her basic reading problem.

Test Results

Revised Stanford-Binet Intelligence Scale
    C.A.   12 yrs. 7 mos.
    M.A.   14 yrs. 0 mos.
    I.Q.   111

	Grade Score
Gray Oral Paragraphs Test	5.5
Metropolitan Achievement Test—Advanced	
Reading	6.5
Vocabulary	6.9
Iowa Silent Reading Test—Elementary	
Rate	3.8
Comprehension	5.3

Louise's oral reading was highly inaccurate. There were mispronunciations, insertions, and omissions of parts or entire words. Her word recognition skills were well below average for seventh grade pupils. The fifth grade score, however, probably underestimated her ability to some extent because of her marked anxiety connected with reading. On the silent reading test her achievement was considerably better. However, when confronted with paragraphs which appeared difficult, Louise merely skipped over them rather than try to read them and experience failure.

On the Iowa test not only was her rate of reading excessively slow, but her responses on Part I were so inaccurate that the rest of the test was not administered.

Remedial Treatment

Louise had two 45-minute sessions a week for 30 weeks. The remedial program stressed accuracy in oral reading and development of comprehension and study skills. Later on she was also given help in increasing rate of reading.

For oral reading, Louise was started on the story of *Homer Price and the Donuts*, fifth grade readability level. We have found that using humorous material at the outset has many values. It causes anxious children to relax, while those who are resistive become more amenable to treatment. After a few sessions, it was possible to use materials which paralleled the school curriculum in English literature. Thus she was reading an adapted version of *The Prince and the Pauper*. (The original book was a school assignment.)

Part of each session was spent working directly in her social studies text. Louise learned how to vary her reading according to her purpose—in some instances to prepare oral reports for class, in others to pass brief weekly quizzes, and, of most importance, to understand what the material in the text was designed to impart. Along with development of study skills, she needed help with the specialized vocabulary she encountered in the various content areas.

Silent reading skills were developed further through use of comprehension workbooks listed in Chapter 7. As Louise's power of comprehension and word-analysis skills increased, emphasis on ways of increasing her rate was gradually introduced. Materials which were found helpful in this connection were chosen from *Driving the Reading Road, Modern Reading Skilltexts*, Books I and II, and *Worlds of Adventures*. The number of words in each selection was counted, and records of words per minute and degree of comprehension were carefully kept. As her competence in all reading skills improved, the level of difficulty was gradually raised in both oral and silent reading materials. Louise's assigned readings from school remained difficult for her, so that for quite sometime it was necessary to supply her with adapted versions of the classics such as *Ivanhoe* and *Lorna Doone*. Lack of flexibility in the school's standards of expectation kept Louise's morale and functioning at uneven levels. Her performance depended to a great degree on her teachers' and parents' attitudes. When they were critical, rejecting, and demanding, improvement was impeded. They seemed to feel that if Louise would only try harder her problems would be solved. Such attitudes placed a greater burden on the writer, who had the responsibility of counteracting them and keeping Louise on an even keel.

For example, Louise came in particularly discouraged one day when she received a grade of D in social studies on her report card. She blurted out, "I am a failure." This led to a discussion of the meaning of grades and the many factors involved in determining them. It was pointed out how teachers' judgments may be based not only on objective data such as test scores, but may also be influenced by impressions gleaned from pupils' behavior in class. As an illustration, they talked about two students who received the same grade of C on a mid-term exam. One student chose to sit way off in a corner in the last row of the room, appeared very bored, and never volunteered answers to any questions the teacher raised. The other student sat toward the front of the room, evinced interest in what was going on, and occasionally asked to have a point clarified which she did not understand. When the time came for evaluating these students' work for report cards, if the teacher were in doubt about whether to give a grade of C or D, classroom behavior would certainly enter into such appraisal. The student whose attitude appeared to be negative and disinterested might receive a grade of D, whereas the teacher might be more kindly disposed toward the one who exerted some effort in class and give her a grade of C.

Louise appeared surprised at the idea that a report card mark was not an absolute rating of one's ability. As our relationship became more secure, it was possible to guide her toward more effective methods of studying and to point out ways in which she might participate more actively in class sessions. Furthermore, it was suggested that, as soon as she realized that she was unable to understand the subject matter being presented, she talk it over with her teacher after class.

At the following session, Louise reported that it took a great deal of courage to speak to her teacher about suggestions as to how she might improve her work in social studies. However, she considered the conference somewhat helpful in that at least her teacher probably modified the image she had of her as a totally disinterested pupil. On Louise's part, she recognized that she had to assume responsibility for her own achievement.

Thus, instead of seeing everything in terms of success or failure, Louise gained insight into her role in influencing her achievement and also the relationship between her approach to the school situation and her teacher's reaction to her.

There were many occasions when Louise felt disappointed in her performance. At such times some of the facets of her problem were talked about and possible ways of helping herself were explored. Frequently just sympathetic recognition of the difficulties she encountered in school helped to tide her over the humps.

The type of supportive handling described in this case can have a therapeutic effect. It can make the difference between prolonged failure, where the student appears to become frozen in a pattern of defeat, and the beginning of improvement. When some success is achieved, the process is gradually reversed and the student begins to adjust more satisfactorily in school. This is what happened in Louise's case. Further evidence of her progress is reflected in the results of comparable achievement test scores which follow:

	Seventh Grade	
	Oct.	June
Gray Oral Paragraphs Test	5.5	8.0
Metropolitan Achievement Test—Advanced		
Reading	6.5	9.0
Vocabulary	6.9	9.6
Iowa Silent Reading Test—Elementary		
Rate	3.8	6.3
Comprehension	5.3	8.4

When remedial treatment was discontinued, Louise was able to handle material above grade level and in line with expectancy for her mental age. Her rate was still slow, but certainly improved. She could handle her textbooks and read stories for recreation. However, of most significance, she had a more optimistic outlook and had developed some confidence in her abilities.

At the last follow-up, Louise was in tenth grade. Though reading is not among her favorite pastimes, she does pick up a book voluntarily now and then. Since her reading skills are good enough to enable her to function well in school, any deeper interests in articles, newspapers, and books may have to await a later stage, when she is more eager for them.

Jerry

Jerry was 16 years 8 months of age in eleventh grade. His reading problems were typical of those found frequently in bright high school and college students who do poorly on examinations and do only average work in school. Jerry was a very intelligent boy, I.Q. 137, who was unable to function up to his potential in school because of inadequate reading skills. He studied longer and harder than his classmates. When confronted with examinations, he developed considerable anxiety because he was never able to complete enough items to obtain scores in line with his ability.

History

This referral was made by a psychiatrist because Jerry was so worried about his school problems. His intelligence quotient on the *Wechsler-Bellevue* was 137 for the Full Scale with a Verbal I.Q. of 137 and a Performance I.Q. of 129.

Test Results

Results of the *Iowa Silent Reading Test—Advanced,* as compared with eleventh grade students, were:

	Percentile
Rate	29
Comprehension	70
Directed Reading	56
Word Meaning	92
Sentence Meaning	79
Paragraph Comprehension	75

Further analysis of Jerry's responses indicated a high degree of accuracy on comprehension questions, but because of the brief time limits of the test, he could not answer enough questions to achieve higher scores.

Thus he required help in improving his rate of reading. He needed to develop flexibility in his reading so as to learn to vary his rate according to the demands of the material and the purpose for which he was reading. Apparently he was using one rate for all reading matter and one which was excessively slow and inefficient. Above all, he needed assurance that he could be helped and that his problem could be alleviated. He seemed quite discouraged and disheartened. His reading problem loomed up as something threatening and, as he described it, "like a cloud constantly hanging over me with all doors to my future closed." He was fearful of making mistakes and overreacted whenever he answered comprehension questions incorrectly.

Remedial Treatment

Before remedial work was started, Jerry was given an interpretation of the test findings. He was reassured about his intelligence. (Jerry, like many others in his position, seriously questioned the adequacy of his intellectual capacities.) He was told that his comprehension on the intelligence test was superior. On his reading test record, it was pointed out to him that he showed a high degree of comprehension on the items answered, but his scores were lowered throughout the test because of his slow rate. The way to overcome his problem was outlined to him.

He seemed deeply interested, and as the problem became concretized at each session his anxiety lessened considerably. For example, to increase his rate he was told he must read at home daily for 15 to 30 minutes, forcing himself to read faster than he generally did. It was suggested that the material he should choose for practice in rapid reading might be short stories, digest-type articles, mystery stories, in fact anything that did not demand too much concentration, in order to maintain his rate at a high level without affecting his comprehension. In the meantime he was seen once a week for a 45-minute session. During that period, he was given a wide selection of material, and a record was kept of his rate and level of comprehension.

Articles were chosen on a variety of subjects from *Modern Reading Skilltexts*, Book 3; *Study Type of Reading Exercises*, College Level; *SRA Better Reading*, Book 3; *SRA Reading Laboratory*, selections at eleventh, then twelfth, grade levels; *The World of America;*[4] *The World of Our English Heritage.*[5] After ten sessions, the reading material was chosen from textbooks designed to improve reading at college levels, such as *Efficient Reading*, alternate edition; *Toward Reading Comprehension;* and *Improving Reading Ability*.

Jerry was started with fairly easy materials for a boy with his abilities. But gradually, as he gained confidence, it was possible to introduce much more challenging ones with difficult comprehension questions. Many different subjects were selected, with different formats and varied questions, in order to present typical reading matter which he was likely to encounter in his college subjects. Comprehension questions involved high levels of

---

[4] Matilda Bailey and U. Leavell, *The World of America* (New York: American Book, 1951).

[5] Matilda Bailey and U. Leavell, *The World of Our English Heritage* (New York: American Book, 1951).

thinking such as making inferences, critical evaluation, and recognizing the author's intent.

Selected articles from *Study Type of Reading Exercises* were used to reinforce the theoretical aspects of reading improvement at advanced levels. Some time was spent on the use of skimming as a technique. However, not too much emphasis was placed on this skill because of the risk that he might learn how *not* to read if he did too much skimming, scanning, and skipping. (Skimming is a handy technique when judiciously used. Our experiences, though, with some students who failed in high school and college have shown that they placed too much emphasis on speed and skimming and not enough on comprehension. Thus we expect bright students to achieve between 90 percent and 100 percent in response to comprehension questions. Otherwise their rate or other reading skills are considered inadequate.)

Jerry had a total of twenty sessions. His anxiety regarding his ability to pass examinations had decreased markedly. This was probably due to his increasing ability to handle fairly difficult material. The next time he took his *College Board Examinations* he did well enough to be admitted to a college with high standards. In a follow-up on Jerry's case, it was discovered that he did very well in college and is currently engaged in graduate study.

Frank

Frank, I.Q. 88, a boy with neurologic impairment, was first seen when he was 7 years 6 months of age. He repeated first grade and still was a total nonreader. He could not understand basic concepts in arithmetic either. Because of his extreme difficulty in learning, Frank's prognosis for improvement was unfavorable. However, Frank did learn, albeit slowly. This case describes the techniques and materials used for remedial treatment and includes follow-up information until Frank reached eighteen years of age.

History

Frank was an only child. His father was in the advertising business. His mother was a conscientious woman who worked as a secretary.

Frank's mother reported that her pregnancy was normal but labor was prolonged and difficult. During Frank's first years, there was evidence of delay in all areas of development, including teething, sitting, standing, walking, and talking. Frank's parents considered him a nervous and restless child. He did not play well with others.

Although Frank had been in first grade twice, he still could not grasp even the simplest instruction in schoolwork. His experiences in school had been most unfortunate. An extremely unsympathetic teacher demanded work which was far beyond his capacity. She was impatient with him because "he refused to learn."

Test Results

Frank was referred by a psychologist who reported an I.Q. of 88 on the *Stanford-Binet Intelligence Scale.* The Rorschach record at that time revealed an unstable personality. There were indications that Frank's approach to reality was confused and distorted. Some of his responses suggested the possibility of organic brain damage. His reactions were those of an extremely immature boy with a marked learning disability. A severe memory defect, together with reactions resembling nominal aphasia, confirmed the Rorschach impressions of organic neurological impairment, as did the *Bender Visual Gestalt Test.* Therefore, Frank was referred for a neurological examination. The findings revealed brain damage.

The neuropsychiatrist considered psychotherapy inadvisable. Instead he recommended remedial teaching, along with an educational program adapted to Frank's level of functioning and his adjustive needs. Consultations with several neuropsychiatrists over a period of time continued to confirm these recommendations.

Remedial Treatment

Frank was seen for remedial reading twice a week. (His mental age was 6 years 8 months at the time.) Each session lasted about 45 minutes and was divided into very brief activities so as to maintain Frank's interest and attention. He reacted very favorably from the outset. A good relationship was established easily and has been maintained throughout the years. The author who worked with him has remained as educational consultant to Frank and his family. Re-evaluation was undertaken annually long after remedial instruction was discontinued.

When remedial work was started, Frank was given very simple materials at preprimer level. It was evident almost immediately that Frank could not cope with them. Thus reading readiness materials were substituted. These he accepted readily. Because of Frank's extreme immaturity, he responded enthusiastically to such materials. He would clap his hands like a young child to show his pleasure and delight as he performed the simple tasks required in these readiness books. He experienced success at each session and was most responsive to encouragement.

Because of Frank's poor muscular coordination, readiness activities were an integral part of the program. Exercises in visual discrimination were introduced at the simplest level. Gradually he was given increasingly difficult items, until he reached the point where he was able to recognize words through associating them with pictures. To develop auditory discrimination, exercises were chosen from *Building Word Power*,[6] which provided opportunity to integrate the work in both visual and auditory discrimination.

A typical session would include (1) cutting, pasting, drawing, and matching exercises in readiness books; (2) work in auditory and visual discrimination, presented through game-type procedures; and (3) reading to Frank, which he enjoyed immensely. The latter served many purposes. It provided experiences of sheer delight in listening to stories, thereby engendering awareness that books contain something pleasurable and worth while. This served to counteract the very traumatic experiences related to reading which he had in school. Some of the stories offered therapeutic possibilities as discussed in Chapter 4. The tutor noticed that Frank was particularly delighted with stories selected from *It Happened One Day*, such as "The Lion and the Mouse," where the little mouse comes off victorious; "Jack and the Beanstalk," where Jack conquers the giant; and "Drakesbill," where a little duck eventually triumphs over a king. Apparently Frank identified in each instance with the helpless creatures who became heroes in the end and seemed to sigh with relief as each one overcame his lowly status.

Thus each session provided feelings of success and well-being for Frank. He came for his lessons regularly and willingly. He always put forth excellent effort and felt he was gaining in achievement. Along with the reading, help was also given in arithmetic.

Gradually, Frank developed a sight vocabulary. He also learned to read the names of colors connected with concrete illustrations. But abstract words such as *here, the, get, this, will*, and so fourth, were impossible for him to learn as yet.

Difficulty in recalling names and in associating words with pictures persisted for the first two years of tutoring. Frank frequently groped for names of animals or objects with which he was completely familiar. For

---

[6] D. Durrell and Helen Sullivan, *Building Word Power* (Tarrytown-on-Hudson, N.Y.: World Book, 1945).

example, he looked at a picture of a cow and after being unable to name it said, "Eats hay"; for "top" he said, "Spinning thing"; for "barn," "You find it on a farm." And vice versa when he saw the word *cow* in print, he said, "I can't think of its name, but I'll find its picture." He quickly glanced through the book and said, "It's this." Also, when he saw the word *elephant* in print and could not name it, he said, "I know what it is, let me draw it." He sketched it hurriedly and then suddenly called out, "Elephant!"

Words that had seemed thoroughly learned were forgotten. Sometimes Frank could read a word correctly in four successive sentences and then fail to recognize it in the fifth sentence. In fact, various kinds of memory defects had been manifested repeatedly. He could not remember names of the characters in the books which he read. (They were always quickly supplied.) When he could not recall a word he would say, "Don't tell me what the word is. You're supposed to think of the right word." He would try to remember by such means as closing his eyes and trying to visualize the object. He would try very hard and become upset when he was unable to recall words. Again encouragement was given. The word would be supplied to him while he was told, "Soon you'll be able to remember it."

During this period, many methods of word study were tried, including the kinesthetic, but the only successful one was the visual, and this to a limited degree. Since he had no other means of figuring out words, he would continue to confuse words of similar configuration, such as *doll* for *ball*, *pig* for *big*, *pig* for *dog*, *letter* for *kitten*, and so on.

After nine months, there was improvement in his visual and auditory discrimination. At this time, the preprimer *We Look and See*[7] was introduced along with its correlated workbook. He continued with the other preprimers in this series, and by the end of one year, he was ready for his first hard-covered book—a primer. He was also beginning to learn the names and sounds of letters. Correlated with this was work in writing, using material from the same publisher as his reader, *We Talk, Spell and Write*, Book 1 followed by Book 2. Even though Frank was in a special class, in which he had been placed following the outcome of the neurological examination, school still presented problems. Frank reported, "The other kids make fun of me. The teacher gets angry with me. Then I go home and pester my mother and father because I get so angry about what the kids did to me. My mother and father have a right to scold me because I pester them so much."

Frank continued to learn very slowly. There was much fluctuation and

---

[7] W. Gray *et al.*, *We Look and See* (Chicago: Scott, Foresman, 1946).

variability in his performance, but nevertheless learning gradually took place. When Frank was 9 years 6 months of age and after two years of work, he was able to handle a high first grade reader, *Our New Friends*.[8] He enjoyed this book and found it very " 'citing." His infantile speech patterns persisted as an integral part of his language disability. He was even more pleased when he could read *I Know a Story*, a first grade book which contained folk tales. When he was 10 years 3 months of age, he was given an easy second grade reader. At this point, he was actually capable of reading the folk tales in *It Happened One Day*, "The Lion and the Mouse," "The Three Little Pigs," and "Jack and the Beanstalk," which he had enjoyed so much when the tutor read them to him. He still remained enchanted with these stories. He took home supplementary reading material at first grade readability level.

Around this time it was possible to introduce the word-family approach. He had learned letter sounds somewhat, through practice in the remedial sessions and in workbooks, but mainly he learned them by playing *Go Fish*. As soon as he learned these sounds, he discovered how new words could be formed by changing the initial consonants.

Eye and Ear Fun, Book I, was used in connection with the teaching of word-analysis skills; and the Group Word Teaching Game, played like Bingo, helped reinforce his learning of the Dolch 220 basic sight words.

It would be too cumbersome to mention all the materials used with Frank. Only those will be commented on when changes in procedures or levels took place. By the age of 11 years 1 month, Frank could read *Aesop's Stories*, at third grade readability level. Word-analysis skills were improving. He was able to learn consonant combinations. Go Fish, Set II, was particularly helpful in this connection. But he still experienced difficulty in blending sounds together. Through the use of exercises in *Happy Times with Sounds*, Book II, he was able to learn some means of figuring out phonetic words, probably through word comparisons, even though he could not blend auditorily. Also, he was able to write phonetic words which were dictated to him. By the age of 11 years 6 months, he was able to read a high third grade book.

Between the ages of twelve and thirteen, there was considerable improvement in his word recognition skills. He was at last able to use a phonic approach. In all probability, some integration in the central nervous system had taken place which facilitated this ability. This is commented on further at the conclusion of this case. In addition, silent reading materials at third grade level were introduced. He showed decided interest in ma-

[8] W. Gray *et al.*, *Our New Friends* (Chicago: Scott, Foresman, 1946).

terials found in various workbooks and enjoyed reading them. The comprehension questions were simple enough for him and resulted in a high degree of success. His persistence and effort were maintained at a high level throughout the sessions. When Frank was thirteen years of age in seventh grade, reading at fourth grade level, the regular weekly remedial sessions were discontinued, but contact was kept up with the school. Thereafter, Frank was seen about twice a year, then once a year up until age 18. Progress continued to be apparent as evidenced in the test results which follow:

Age in Years		Grade Score
8 to 10	For the first two years, Frank's reading was too low to be measured by standardized tests.	Nonreader
10	Metropolitan Achievement Test Primary I	2.3
12	Metropolitan Achievement Test Primary II	3.3
15	Metropolitan Achievement Test Elementary	4.6
17	Metropolitan Achievement Test Intermediate	7.5
18	Stanford Achievement Test Advanced	10.1

Roswell-Chall Diagnostic Reading Test administered at fifteen years of age showed mastery of phonic skills.

When Frank was eighteen years old, he had completed his work at school, and satisfactory vocational plans were made for him. Reading was at tenth grade level, and arithmetic, which had presented an even more difficult problem for many years, was at seventh grade level.

This degree of proficiency meant that Frank could function adequately in the areas he needed. He could read popular fiction, biography, and current events, which would open new vistas, broaden his horizons, and continue his education. In this way he would begin to accumulate knowledge and become more and more sensitive to and understanding of the world around him.

In retrospect, this case shows the snail's pace at which severely impaired children learn. Had Frank been given up as hopeless during the period when evidence of progress was almost imperceptible, it is difficult to predict what might have happened. It might be surmised that his adjustment would have been totally inadequate and that most avenues in school and in work would have been closed to him.

Prefixed to this chapter are reproductions of four *Bender Visual-Motor Gestalt Tests* administered to Frank between the ages of 8 and 17 years. Marked changes in visual-motor coordination, perceptual development, and integrative capacity are apparent in his performance on successive records.

It is interesting to note that as Frank's development in these areas proceeded, it was not only reflected in his handling of the *Bender Visual-Motor Gestalt Tests,* but was also evidenced in his ability to synthesize sounds as well as perform better in other aspects of his reading.

What caused this acceleration especially around preadolescence and beyond can only be conjectured. Heightened neurophysiological development immediately suggests itself. However, one must also take into consideration the possible contribution of continued perceptual training. Added to these a very important unifying force—Frank's ability to utilize all of his capacities more effectively because of his growing sense of adequacy—might account for his marked improvement. Hence, any one factor or the interaction of many could explain the striking changes in the tests which precede this chapter.

Thus it can be seen that remedial treatment covers a wide range and variety of problems. The remedial specialist coordinates his work with other workers in the field whenever indicated, keeps in mind the reality factors surrounding each pupil, helps in any way possible to foster competency in schoolwork, and, above all, promotes the very best qualities that are present in every individual. Remediation is more than imparting techniques; it is more than therapeutically oriented treatment. It is a situation that is personal and unique in all cases. Such experience can make the difference between a life of failure and a life of acceptance and harmony.

ठ APPENDIX A

Representative Tests*

READING-READINESS GROUP TESTS
ठ

Can be administered individually or in a group.

Gates Reading-Readiness Tests (Bur. of Pub., T.C., Columbia U.)

Consists of five subtests measuring visual and auditory discrimination. The first four subtests—picture direction, word matching, word-card matching, and rhyming—can be administered to a group. The fifth subtest—reading letters and numbers—must be given individually.

Range	Time	Forms
None suggested (useful in K-1)	None suggested	One

Lee-Clark Reading-Readiness Test (Calif. Test Bur.)

Consists of four subtests measuring various aspects of visual discrimination and linguistic development. Subtests 1 and 2 are concerned with discrimination of letter symbols, subtest 3 with vocabulary and ability to follow instructions, subtest 4 with discrimination of word symbols.

Range	Time	Forms
K-1	20 min.	One

Metropolitan Readiness Tests (Harcourt, Brace & World)

Content is entirely pictorial. Yields three readiness scores—reading, number, and total.

Range	Time	Forms
K-1	App. 60 min.	R or S

Monroe Reading-Aptitude Tests (Houghton Mifflin)

A series of individual and group tests in vision, hearing, motor control, language, speed of oral reading, and articulation. Group tests can be administered to about a dozen children at a time.

---

*Compiled with the assistance of Joel Weinberg.

Range	Time	Forms
K-1	Group: 30–40 min.	One
	Ind.: 10–15 min.	

Murphy Durrell (Harcourt, Brace & World)

Consists of three subtests measuring auditory discrimination, visual discrimination, and learning rate.

Range	Time	Forms
K-1	Subtests 1 & 2: app. 60 min.	One
	Subtest 3: app. 20 min.	

New York Reading-Readiness Test (N.Y.C. Bd. of Educ.)

Consists of two subtests—concepts and word matching. A check list is included to help the teacher appraise aspects of the child's reading readiness.

Range	Time	Forms
K-1	None suggested	A or B

READING TESTS

California Reading Tests (Calif. Test Bur.)

A series of group achievement tests, each consisting of two parts, vocabulary and comprehension. The parts, in turn, are divided into three or four sections for diagnostic purposes. Each test is also available as a part of a battery in the corresponding California Achievement Test.

Test	Range	Time	Forms
Lower primary	1–2	35–50 min.	AA, BB, CC, or DD
Upper primary	3–L4	35–50 min.	AA, BB, CC, or DD
Elementary	4–6	35–50 min.	AA, BB, CC, or DD
Junior high	7–9	35–50 min.	AA, BB, CC, or DD
Advanced	9–14	35–50 min.	AA, BB, or CC

Cooperative English Tests, Test C—Reading Comprehension (Educ. Testing Svc.)

A group test which has two parts, vocabulary and reading. It yields three subscores—vocabulary, speed, and level—and a total reading comprehension score based on both parts.

Test	Range	Time	Forms
Lower level C1	7–12	40 min	R, T, Y, or Z
Higher level C2	Superior 11 and 12 graders plus college students		

Cooperative Sequential Tests of Educational Progress—Reading (Educ. Testing Svc.)

A group test designed to test reading comprehension.

Range	Time	Forms
4–6	70 min.	4A or 4B
7–9	70 min.	3A or 3B
10–12	70 min.	2A or 2B
13–14	70 min.	1A or 1B

Davis Reading Test (Psych. Corp.)

Yields two scores—level of comprehension and speed of comprehension. Can be scored by hand or machine; for group or individual use.

Range	Time	Forms
11–13	40 min.	1A, 1B, 1C, or 1D

Dolch Basic Sight Word Test (Garrard)

A group test to determine children's knowledge of the 220 Dolch Basic Sight Words.

Range	Time	Forms
None suggested, but words should be known by end of grade 2	None suggested	One

Durrell Analysis of Reading Difficulty, new ed. (Harcourt, Brace & World)

An individual test which provides information on silent and oral reading, listening comprehension, word analysis, phonetics, pronunciation, and difficulties in writing and spelling.

Range	Time	Forms
1–6	30–40 min.	One

Durrell-Sullivan Reading-Capacity and -Achievement Tests (Harcourt, Brace & World)

The reading-capacity test is a group test composed entirely of pictures; it consists of two subtests—word meaning and paragraph meaning—both measuring understanding of spoken material. It measures ability to understand spoken language as an indicator of potential reading ability. The reading-achievement test measures silent reading comprehension. It has subtests in word meaning and paragraph meaning and optional tests in spelling and written recall. The primary test is made up of the easier parts of the intermediate subtests in word and paragraph meaning.

Test	Range	Time	Forms
Primary	2–4	40–45 min.	A
		Optional tests: 15–20 min. total	
Intermediate	3–6	30–40 min.	A
		Capacity achievement: 30–35 min.	A or B
		Optional tests: 15–20 min. total	

Durrell Analysis of Reading Difficulty (Harcourt, Brace & World)

Consists of a series of diagnostic reading tests for testing an individual child. The oral reading subtest consists of eight paragraphs of increasing difficulty. Yields scores in accuracy, rate, and comprehension. A check list for word recognition difficulties is provided.

Range	Time	Forms
1–6	App. 7 min. for oral rdg.	One

Gates Advanced Primary Reading Tests (Bur. of Pub., T.C., Columbia U.)

A group test containing two subtests, one measuring word recognition and the other paragraph reading.

Test	Range	Time	Forms
AWR (word recognition)	2.5–3	15 min.	1, 2, or 3
APR (paragraph reading)	2.5–3	25 min.	1, 2, or 3

Gates Basic Reading Tests (Bur. of Pub., T.C., Columbia U.)

Five aspects of reading are measured by this group test: reading to appreciate general significance, reading to note details, reading to understand precise directions, level of comprehension, and reading vocabulary. The subtests also measure reading rate and comprehension.

Test	Range	Time	Forms
GS, ND, UD	3.5–8	8–10 min.	1, 2, or 3
LC, RV	3.5–8	20 min.	1, 2, or 3

Gates-McKillop Reading Diagnostic Tests (Bur. of Pub., T.C., Columbia U.)

A diagnostic battery to be administered individually to pupils with reading difficulty. Tests oral reading, vocabulary, reversal errors, phrase perception, spelling, visual perception, and auditory techniques. Each subtest can be used independently.

Range	Time	Forms
1–8	None suggested	I and II

Gates Reading Survey (Bur. of Pub., T.C., Columbia U.)

Provides group tests designed to measure vocabulary, comprehension, rate, and accuracy of interpretation. Can be used in coordination with above-listed Gates reading tests and is available with IBM answer sheets.

Range	Time	Forms
3–8	50–60 min.	1, 2, or 3

Gates Primary Reading Tests (Bur. of Pub., T.C., Columbia U.)

Contains three subtests measuring word recognition, sentence reading, and paragraph reading, respectively.

Test	Range	Time	Forms
PWR (word recognition)	1–2.4	15 min.	1, 2, or 3
PSR (sentence reading)	1–2.4	15 min.	1, 2, or 3
PPR (paragraph reading)	1–2.4	20 min.	

Gilmore Oral Reading Test (Harcourt, Brace & World)

An individual test consisting of ten paragraphs scaled in difficulty, with comprehension questions. Yields three scores—accuracy, comprehension, and rate. A check list of word-recognition difficulties and a record for errors on each paragraph are provided.

Range	Time	Forms
1–8	15–20 min.	A or B

Gray Standardized Oral Reading Paragraphs Test (Public Sch. Pub. Co.)

An individual test consisting of twelve paragraphs arranged in order of increasing difficulty. Yields one grade-level score based on a combination of rate and accuracy. Accuracy is determined by avoidance of errors in pronunciation, omissions, insertions, repetitions, and substitutions.

Range	Time	Forms
1–8	3–8 min.	One

Iowa Every Pupil Tests of Basic Skills (Houghton Mifflin)

A group test consisting of two batteries of four tests each measuring silent reading comprehension, including paragraph meaning and vocabulary; work-study skills; basic language skills; and basic arithmetic skills. Each of these tests may be purchased separately. For most of the tests in the advanced battery, special IBM answer sheets are available. An examiner's manual is included in each package.

Test Battery	Range	Time	Forms
Elementary	3–5	App. 70 min.	L, M, N, or O
Advanced	5–9		L, M, N, or O

Iowa Silent Reading Test (Harcourt, Brace & World)

A group test including measures of comprehension, vocabulary, skills in locating information, and rate of reading.

Test	Range	Time	Forms
Elementary	4–9	50 min.	Am, Bm, Cm, or Dm
Advanced	9–college	45 min.	Am, Bm, Cm, or Dm

Iowa Test of Basic Skills (Houghton Mifflin)

Five areas are included in this group test: vocabulary, reading comprehension, language skills (spelling, capitalization, punctuation, usage), work-study skills (map reading, reading graphs and tables, knowledge and use of reference materials), and arithmetic skills (concepts and problem-solving).

Answers are marked on separate answer sheets which may be hand- or machine-scored. Test booklet is reusable.

Range	Time	Forms
3–9	None suggested	One

Metropolitan Achievement Tests (Harcourt, Brace & World)

A series of five batteries of group tests covering areas indicated below. Partial batteries (excluding science and social studies information) are available for the fifth through eighth grades.

PRIMARY I

Consists of tests in word knowledge, word discrimination, reading, and arithmetic (concepts and skills).

Range	Time	Forms
1	Battery: 85 min.	A or B
	Reading: 60 min.	

PRIMARY II

Contains tests of word knowledge, word discrimination, reading, arithmetic (problem-solving and concepts), and spelling.

Range	Time	Forms
2	Battery: 100 min.	A or B
	Reading: 65 min.	

ELEMENTARY

Contains tests in same areas as Primary II plus arithmetic computation and language.

Range	Time	Forms
3–4	Battery: 147 min.	A or B
	Reading: 40 min.	

INTERMEDIATE (partial)

Contains all tests as elementary except for word discrimination and also has language subtests (two in all) and a language study-skills subtest.

Range	Time	Forms
5–6	Battery: 171 min.	A or B
	Reading: 40 min.	

ADVANCED (partial)

Contains same tests as intermediate battery plus language subtest (three in all).

Range	Time	Forms
7–9	Battery: 171 min.	A or B
	Reading: 40 min.	

Monroe Diagnostic Reading Test (Stoelting)

An individual diagnostic test of word recognition, spelling, and arithmetic. Errors indicate direction of remedial work especially in problems of word recognition.

Range	Time	Forms
Any age	None suggested	One

Nelson Silent Reading Test (Houghton Mifflin)

A group test composed of two parts—vocabulary and paragraph comprehension. Self-marking.

Range	Time	Forms
3–9	Vocabulary: 10 min.	A or B
	Paragraphs: 20 min.	

Nelson-Denny Reading Test, rev. ed. (Houghton Mifflin)

A group test measuring three aspects of reading—vocabulary, comprehension, and rate. Provides a score in each of these areas and a total score. A modification of normal administration procedure has also been developed for adults. In addition to norms for grades 9 through 16, special adult norms are provided.

Range	Time	Forms
9–16 plus	30 min.	A or B

Roswell-Chall Diagnostic Reading Test (Essay Press, Box 5, Planetarium Station, New York 10025)

An individual test which provides an estimate of strengths and weaknesses in word recognition and points up instructional needs of pupil.

Range	Time	Forms
Elementary	10 min.	I or II

Roswell-Chall Auditory Blending Test (Essay)

An individual test which evaluates the pupil's ability to blend sounds into words when the sounds are presented orally.

Range	Time	Forms
Elementary	5 min.	One

Stanford Achievement Tests (Harcourt, Brace & World)

A series of group tests with four batteries covering the areas and the grade levels listed below. A special edition with separate answer sheets for machine-scoring is available.

PRIMARY

Includes tests of paragraph meaning, vocabulary, spelling, arithmetic reasoning, and arithmetic computation.

Range	Time	Forms
1.9–3.5	Battery: 80 min.	J, K, L, M, or N
	Reading: 30 min.	J, K, L, M, or N

ELEMENTARY

Includes tests in same areas as primary battery, plus a language test. The reading part, covering only comprehension and vocabulary, is available as a separate test, for hand-scoring.

Range	Time	Forms
3–4.9	Battery: 215 min.	J, K, L, M, or N
	Reading: 35 min.	J, K, or L

INTERMEDIATE

Includes tests in same areas as elementary battery. Reading part is available separately.

Range	Time	Forms
5–6	Battery: 140 min.	J, K, L, M, or N
	Reading: 40 min.	J, K, L, or M

ADVANCED

Includes tests in same areas as intermediate. Reading test is available separately.

Range	Time	Forms
7–9	Battery: 140 min.	J, K, L, M, or N
	Reading: 40 min.	J, K, L, or M

Traxler High School Reading Test (Public Sch. Pub. Co.)

A group test which measures rate of reading, comprehension, and ability to locate main ideas. Rate is based on reading of social science material; location of main idea, on reading of social science and natural science textbook material.

Range	Time	Forms
10–12	30 min.	1 or 2

Traxler Silent Reading Test (Public Sch. Pub. Co.)

A group test measuring vocabulary, rate, comprehension, word meaning, and paragraph meaning.

Range	Time	Forms
7–10	50 min.	1, 2, 3, or 4

Wide-Range Achievement Test (Psych. Corp.)

An individual test measuring oral reading, spelling, and arithmetic computation.

Range	Time	Forms
Age 5 to adult	None suggested	One

DIAGNOSTIC TESTS

Gates-Russell Spelling Diagnostic Tests (Bur. of Pub., T. C., Columbia U.)

Individual tests comprised of spelling words orally; pronouncing words; naming letters for letter sounds; spelling one syllable; spelling two syllables; word reversals; spelling attack; auditory discrimination; visual, auditory, kinesthetic, and combined spelling methods.

Range	Time	Forms
None suggested	None suggested	One

Morrison-McCall Spelling Scale (Harcourt, Brace & World)

Consists of eight spelling lists, each ranging from easy to difficult, of fifty words. The same lists can be used in all grades.

Range	Time	Forms
2–8	None suggested	One

See also subtests of the California, Metropolitan, Stanford, and any other standardized achievement test batteries that contain separate spelling tests.

GROUP INTELLIGENCE TESTS

California Test of Mental Maturity (Calif. Test Bur.)

Offers a variety of items with separate language and non-language sections.

Range	Time	Forms
K-adult	Full test: app. 90 min.	One
	Language: app. 40 min.	

Davis-Eells Games (World)

Items are designed to be relatively culture free. Problems are presented pictorially instead of verbally.

Range	Time	Forms
6–12 years	Primary—gr. 1: 2 30-min. periods	A
	gr. 2: 2 30-min. periods	
	Elementary—gr. 3–6: 2 50–60 min. periods	A

Kuhlmann-Anderson Intelligence Tests (Personnel)

Includes thirty-nine tests consisting of many booklets so that a choice to fit an individual class's ability is possible. Below fifth grade content is largely non-reading.

Range	Time	Form
6 years–adult	45 min.	One

Kuhlmann-Finch Intelligence Tests (Amer. Guid. Svc.)

Content for first and second grades requires no reading. Content in higher grades is largely non-verbal.

Range	Time	Forms
6–18 years	25 min.	One

Lorge-Thorndike Intelligence Tests (Houghton Mifflin)

This test is a non-verbal test for the lower grades. The tests for the fourth grade and over have verbal and non-verbal portions.

Range	Time	Forms
K-12	34 min.	A or B

Otis Quick-Scoring Mental Ability Tests (Harcourt, Brace & World)

The Alpha Short Form is a group intelligence test requiring no reading; the Beta Test is a group intelligence test which requires reading.

Range	Time	Forms
1–4	25 min.	Alpha Short Form
4–9	30 min.	Beta Test

Pintner-Cunningham Primary Test (World)

The test is composed entirely of pictures which are marked by the pupils according to the examiner's oral directions.

Range	Time	Forms
K-2	25 min.	A, B, or C

Pintner-Durost Elementary Test (World)

This test is in two scales, either of which may be used alone or in combination. Scale 1, picture content, is administered wholly by oral directions and requires no reading on the part of the child; scale 2, reading content, requires reading.

Range	Time	Forms
2–4	45 min. for each scale	A or B

INDIVIDUAL INTELLIGENCE TESTS

To be used by psychologists.

Arthur Point Scale of Performance Tests (Harcourt, Brace & World)

Range	Time	Forms
5 years–adult	App. 60 min.	One

Cornell-Coxe Performance Ability Scale (Harcourt, Brace & World)

Range	Time	Forms
6–15 years	App. 60 min.	One

Stanford-Binet Intelligence Scales (Houghton Mifflin)

Range	Time	Forms
2 years–adult	App. 60 min.	L, M, or L-M

Wechsler Adult Intelligence Scale (Psych. Corp.)

Includes verbal, performance, and total I.Q. scores. It is a revision of the Wechsler-Bellevue Intelligence Scale.

Range	Time	Forms
16 years–adult	App. 60 min.	One

Wechsler-Bellevue Intelligence Scale (Psych. Corp.)

Includes verbal, performance, and total I.Q. scores.

Range	Time	Forms
15 years–adult	App. 60 min.	I or II

Wechsler Intelligence Scale for Children (Psych. Corp.)

Scores yield verbal, performance, and total I.Q.'s.

Range	Time	Forms
5–15 years	App. 60 min.	One

PROJECTIVE TESTS OF PERSONALITY

To be used by psychologists; there are no alternate forms or time limits for these tests.

Children's Thematic Apperception Test (Psych. Corp.)

Range
3–10 years

Human Figure Drawings (Thomas)

Range
Nursery school-adult

Rorschach (Psych. Corp.)

Range
Nursery school-adult

Thematic Apperception Test (Psych. Corp.)

Range
Elementary school-adult

MISCELLANEOUS TESTS

To be used by psychologists; there are no alternate forms or time limits for these tests.

Bender Visual-Motor Gestalt Test (Psych. Corp.)

A clinical test involving copying visual designs.

Range
6 years–adult

Benton Revised Visual Retention Test (Psych. Corp.)

A test involving copying visual designs.

Range
8 years–adult

Harris Tests of Lateral Dominance, rev. ed. (Psych. Corp.)

Tests of hand, eye, and foot dominance.

Range
6 years and up

Wepman Auditory Discrimination Test (Lang. Rsch. Ass.)

Tests to determine a child's ability to recognize the fine differences that exist between elements in English speech.

Range
Elementary school pupils

---

*May be used by teachers also.

Selected Books by Grade Level

ε∾ In using any compilation of graded books, the teacher's judgment plays an important role; no estimate of the reading level of a book can be entirely accurate. Many factors—the author's style and sentence structure and the child's interest in the subject matter, his experience, and his understanding of the concepts—affect the ease or difficulty of a book for a particular child. Nor is the score a child achieves on a standardized reading test always a reliable indication of the level of book he can handle. Therefore readability levels, including those indicated on this list, should be used only as guides. To be sure that a book is appropriate, the teacher must try it out with her pupils. Sometimes, however, teachers have difficulty deciding on the reading level of a book. They know they cannot always rely on publishers' estimates either. Thus it is helpful to use certain readability formulas which rate a book according to grade level.[1]

---

[1] Those which are most widely used at the primary level are G. Spache, "A New Readability Formula for Primary-Grade Reading Materials," *Elementary School Journal,* 53 (1953), pp. 410–13, and L. Wheeler and E. Smith, "A Practical Readability Formula for the Classroom Teacher in the Primary Grades," *Elementary English,* 31 (1954), pp. 397–9. At elementary and advanced grades, those worthy of consideration are E. Dale and Jeanne Chall, "A Formula for Predicting Readability," *Educational Research Bulletin,* 27 (1948), pp. 11–20, and D. Russell and H. Fea, "Validity of Six Formulas as Measures of Juvenile Fiction," *Elementary School Journal,* 52 (1951), pp. 136–44. Some compilations based on readability formulas that may be helpful to the teacher in selecting children's books are Phyllis Fenner, *The Proof of the Pudding* (New York: John Day, 1957), Geneva Hanna and Mariana McAllister, *Books, Young People and Reading Guidance* (New York: Harper, 1960), Nancy Larrick, *A Teacher's Guide to Children's Books* (Columbus, Ohio: Charles E. Merrill, 1960), Florence Roswell and Jeanne Chall, *Selected Materials,* rev. ed. (New York: City College, 1963), G. Spache, *Good Reading for Poor Readers,* rev. ed. (Champaign, Ill.: Garrard Press, 1960), Ruth Strang *et al., Gateways to Readable Books,* 3rd ed. (New York: Wilson, 1958), and Ruth Tooze, *Your Children Want to Read* (Englewood Cliffs, N.J.: Prentice-Hall, 1957).

Beginning at the fourth grade, teachers who deal with children who have reading disability have specific requirements for book lists. They often wish to know which books contain short stories and brief articles suitable to class and individual work, which books can be recommended for independent reading, and at which level certain classics have been adapted. Thus for fourth grade and above, the following list has been divided into these three categories. In compiling the books in these categories, the authors have borne in mind the resistance that many children with reading disability show toward full-length books. Such pupils frequently read brief articles and stories, then become engrossed in longer works. To entice the pupil to read full-length books independently without becoming overwhelmed by them, the authors have chosen those which many such pupils have found absorbing.

Many simplified classics are available at a variety of reading levels. Sometimes the same classic has been adapted by several publishers at levels ranging from fourth grade to senior high school. Only a small sampling of these classics is presented here. For complete listing and information regarding levels, such publishers as Globe; Sanborn; Scott, Foresman; Webster; Random House; Garrard; and Laidlaw, who are well known for adapting the classics, should be consulted.

For further differentiation as to characteristics and suitability of books, the following symbols have been used:

* Reading level as indicated; especially useful for junior high school students.

** Reading level as indicated. Mature format and contents, especially useful for senior high school students.

· Part of a series; other books on various reading levels.

LOW FIRST GRADE

Author	Title
· Battle	*Jerry* (Benefic)
· Hurley	*Dan Frontier* (Benefic)
· ————	*Dan Frontier and the New House* (Benefic)
· McCall	*Bucky Button* (Benefic)
· ————	*Button at the Zoo* (Benefic)
· Wasserman	*Sailor Jack* (Benefic)
· ————	*Sailor Jack and Eddy* (Benefic)
· ————	*Sailor Jack and Homer Potts* (Benefic)
Wenkart	*At a Zoo* (Wenkart)

FIRST GRADE

Author	Title
· Battle	*Jerry Goes Fishing* (Benefic)
· ——	*Jerry Goes Riding* (Benefic)
° · Bright and Mitchell	"The Home and Life Family Series": *A Day with the Brown Family* (Croft)
· Chandler	*Cowboy Sam* (Benefic)
· ——	*Cowboy Sam and Porky* (Benefic)
· ——	*Cowboy Sam and Shorty* (Benefic)
· Cordts	*Tommy O'Toole and Larry* (Benefic)
· Dolch	*Dog Pals* (Garrard)
· ——	*Tommy's Pets* (Garrard)
· ——	*Zoo Is Home* (Garrard)
° Gibson and Richards	*First Steps in Teaching English* (Pocket Books)
Guilfoile	*Nobody Listens to Andrew* (Follett)
· Huber	*I Know a Story* (Row, Peterson)
· Hurley	*Dan Frontier Goes Hunting* (Benefic)
· ——	*Dan Frontier with the Indians* (Benefic)
King	*Mabel the Whale* (Follett)
· McCall	*The Buttons at the Farm* (Benefic)
· ——	*The Buttons and the Pet Parade* (Benefic)
· Rambeau	*Jim Forest and Ranger Don* (Harr Wagner)
· ——	*Jim Forest and the Bandits* (Harr Wagner)
° Robertson	*Veteran's Reader* (Steck)
° Wasserman	*Sailor Jack and Bluebell* (Benefic)
· ——	*Sailor Jack's New Friend* (Benefic)

SECOND GRADE

Author	Title
Angelo	*Just Be Patient* (Winston)
· Battle	*Jerry Goes on a Picnic* (Benefic)
° · Bright and Mitchell	"The Home and Family Life Series": *Making a Good Living* (Croft)
· Cerf	*Book of Laughs* (Random House)
· Chandler	*Cowboy Sam and Freddy* (Benefic)
· ——	*Cowboy Sam and the Rodeo* (Benefic)
° · Coleman, *et al.*	*The Sea Hunt* (Harr Wagner)

* · ———	*Treasure under the Sea* (Harr Wagner)
· Cordts	*Tommy O'Toole at the Fair* (Benefic)
· Corson	*Peter and the Unlucky Rocket* (Benefic)
· ———	*Peter and the Big Balloon* (Benefic)
· Dolch	*Animal Stories* (Garrard)
· ———	*Dog Stories* (Garrard)
· ———	*Circus Stories* (Garrard)
· ———	*Folk Stories* (Garrard)
· ———	*Horse Stories* (Garrard)
· ———	*Irish Stories* (Garrard)
· ———	*Pueblo Stories* (Garrard)
———	*Why Stories* (Garrard)
· Eastman	*Sam and the Firefly* (Random House)
· Elkin	*The Big Jump* (Random House)
* · Experimental Curriculum Research Publ.	*Shopping in a Supermarket* (N.Y.C. Bd. of Educ.)
———	*Getting a Job in a Restaurant* (N.Y.C. Bd. of Educ.)
———	*Getting a Job in the Garment Trades* (N.Y.C. Bd. of Educ.)
* · Goldberg and Brumber	"Rochester Occupational Reading Series": *Gas Stations* (Syracuse Univ.)
* · Harding and Burr	*Men in the Armed Forces* (U.S. Armed Forces Inst.)
	Servicemen Learn to Read (U.S. Armed Forces Inst.)
· Hoff	*Danny and the Dinosaur* (Harper)
· ———	*Sammy the Seal* (Harper)
· Holland	*A Big Ball of String* (Random House)
· Huber, *et al.*	*It Happened One Day* (Row, Peterson)
· Hurley	*Dan Frontier and the Wagon Train* (Benefic)
· McClintock	*A Fly Went By* (Random House)
· McKee	*Come Along* (Houghton Mifflin)
· ———	*On We Go* (Houghton Mifflin)
Morrison	*Yours Till Niagara Falls* (Thos. Y. Crowell)
· Norman	*A Man Named Columbus* (Coward McCann)
· ———	*Johnny Appleseed* (Coward McCann)
* · Rambeau	*Jim Forest and the Mystery Hunter* (Harr Wagner)
* · ———	*Jim Forest and Dead Man's Peak* (Harr Wagner)
· Seuss	*The Cat in the Hat* (Random House)
· ———	*The Cat in the Hat Comes Back* (Random House)
· Shane and Hester	*Doorways to Adventure* (Laidlaw)
· Stolz	*Emmett's Pig* (Harper)
· Wasserman	*Sailor Jack and the Target Ship* (Benefic)

THIRD GRADE

Author	Title
* · Agle and Wilson	*Three Boys and a Mine* (Scribner)
* · Allen	*Great Moments in American History* (Follett)
* · ————	*Ten Great Moments in Sports* (Follett)
* · Anderson	*Friday, the Arapaho Indian* (Row, Peterson)
* · ————	*Squanto and the Pilgrims* (Row, Peterson)
* · Anderson and Johnson	*Pilot Jack Knight* (Row, Peterson)
* · Ardizzone	*Little Tim and the Brave Sea Captain* (McGraw-Hill)
· Austin, ed.	*John Paul Jones* (Garrard)
· ————	*Samuel F. B. Morse* and many other biographies (Garrard)
· Battle	*Jerry Goes to the Circus* (Benefic)
· Beals	*Chief Black Hawk* (Row, Peterson)
· Bendick	*First Book of Airplanes* (Watts)
· Berry	*Leif the Lucky* (Garrard)
· Bishop	*The Five Chinese Brothers* (Coward McCann)
* · ————	*Lafayette* (Garrard)
* · Bright and Mitchell	"The Home and Family Life Series": *The Browns at School* (Croft)
* · Carmer	*Henry Hudson* (Garrard)
· Chandler	*Cowboy Sam and the Indians* (Benefic)
· ————	*Cowboy Sam and the Rustlers* (Benefic)
* · Coleman, *et al.*	*Submarine Rescue* (Harr Wagner)
· Colver	*Abraham Lincoln* (Garrard)
· Cordts	*Tommy O'Toole and the Forest Fire* (Benefic)
· Corson	*Peter and the Moon Trip* (Benefic)
· ————	*Peter and the Two-Hour Moon* (Benefic)
· ————	*Peter and the Rocket Ship* (Benefic)
* · Crowley	*Tor and Azor* (Oxford)
* · Dagliesh	*The Smiths and Rusty* (Scribner)
· Dolch, ed.	*Aesop's Stories*, adapted (Garrard)
————	*Andersen Stories* (Garrard)
————	*Bible Stories* (Garrard)
————	*Fairy Stories* (Garrard)
————	*Far East Stories* (Garrard)
* ————	*Greek Stories* (Garrard)
————	*Ivanhoe* (Garrard)
* ————	*Robin Hood Stories* (Garrard)
* ————	*Stories from Japan* (Garrard)
· ————	*Stories from Mexico* (Garrard)

° · Eisner	*Buried Gold* (Follett)
° · ———	*Mystery of Broken Wheel Ranch* (Follett)
° · Epstein	*George Washington Carver* (Garrard)
° · Friedman	*Dot for Short* (Morrow)
° · ———	*Sunday with Judy* (Morrow)
° · Goldberg and Brumber	"Rochester Occupational Reading Series": *Bakeries, Restaurants and Cafeterias* (Syracuse Univ.)
° · Haywood	*Betsy's Little Star* (Morrow)
° · ———	*Eddie and Luella* (Morrow)
· Huber, *et al.*	*After the Sun Sets* (Row, Peterson)
· Hurley	*Dan Frontier, Sheriff* (Benefic)
· Johnson and Jacobs	*Treat Shop* (Charles E. Merrill)
· Kissen	*Straw Ox* (short plays) (Houghton Mifflin)
° · Lane	*All about the Insect World* (Random House)
° · Latham	*Samuel F. B. Morse* (Garrard)
Leeming and Miller	*Riddles, Riddles, Riddles* (Watts)
Mellon	*A Treasure Chest of Humor* (Hart)
° · Rambeau	*Jim Forest and Lone Wolf Gulch* (Harr Wagner)
° · ———	*Jim Forest and the Flood* (Harr Wagner)
° · ———	*The Mystery of Morgan Castle* (Harr Wagner)
Rey	*Curious George* (Houghton Mifflin)
° · Seylar	*Mary Elizabeth and Mr. Lincoln* (Follett)
· Shane and Hester	*Doorways to Adventure* (Laidlaw)
· Wasserman	*Sailor Jack Goes North* (Benefic)
° · Wilkie	*Daniel Boone* (Garrard)
· Witty, *et al.*	*Fun and Frolic* (Heath)

FOURTH GRADE

SHORT STORIES AND SELECTIONS

Author	*Title*
° · Beauchamp, *et al.*	*Discovering Our World,* Bk. I (science) (Scott, Foresman)
Bennet, *et al.*	*Wonder and Laughter* (Silver Burdett)
· Bond and Cuddy	*Days of Adventure* (Lyons & Carnahan)
· ———	*Stories to Remember,* classmate ed. (Lyons & Carnahan)
° Bunce, ed.	*O. Henry's Best Stories* (Globe)
° ° Cass	"Adult Educ. Series": *How We Live* (Noble & Noble)
° · Coleman, *et al.*	*Frogmen in Action* (Harr Wagner)
° · ———	*The Pearl Divers* (Harr Wagner)

* •	Commager	*First Book of the American Revolution* (Watts)
**	Dale	*Stories for Today* (Gov't. Printing Office)
*	Experimental Curriculum Research Pub.	*Shopping in the Supermarket* (advanced level); (N.Y.C. Bd. of Educ.)
•	———	*Getting a Job in a Restaurant* (advanced level); (N.Y.C. Bd. of Educ.)
•	———	*Getting a Job in the Garment Trades* (advanced level); (N.Y.C. Bd. of Educ.)
** •	Goldberg and Brumber	"Rochester Occupational Reading Series": *Bakeries* (Syracuse Univ.)
** •	———	"Rochester Occupational Reading Series"; *Restaurants and Cafeterias* (Syracuse Univ.)
•	Gray, *et al.*	*Days and Deeds* (Scott, Foresman)
* •	Haywood	*Betsy and Billy* (Harcourt, Brace & World)
** •	Heavey and Stuart	*Teen-Age Tales,* Bks. A & B (Heath)
•	Huber, *et al.*	*It Must Be Magic* (Row, Peterson)
•	Johnson and Jacobs	*Magic Carpet* (Charles E. Merrill)
•	Kissen	*Bag of Fire* (short plays) (Houghton Mifflin)
•	Kottmeyer, ed.	*Cases of Sherlock Holmes* (Webster)
* •	———	*Greek and Roman Myths* (Webster)
* •	———	*Old Testament Stories* (Webster)
•	Larrick, ed.	"Jr. Science Series": *Book of Beavers* (Garrard)
•	———	"Jr. Science Series": *Book of Electricity* (Garrard)
•	———	"Jr. Science Series": *Book of Flying* (Garrard)
•	———	"Jr. Science Series": *Book of Stars* (Garrard)
•	———	"Jr. Science Series": *Book of Trees* (Garrard)
•	McKee	*High Roads* (Houghton Mifflin)
•	Russell, *et al.*	*Roads to Everywhere* (Ginn)

SUPPLEMENTARY READING

•	Anderson	*Blaze Finds the Trail* (Macmillan)
* •	Anderson and Regli	*Alec Majors* (Wheeler)
	Atwater	*Mr. Popper's Penguins* (Little, Brown)
	Bennett	*The Hidden Garden* (Day)
	Bice	*A Dog for Davie's Hill* (Macmillan)
•	Biemiller	*Star Boy* (Holt)
	Bjorklund	*Rodeo Roundup* (Doubleday)
•	Child Study Assn. of America	*Read to Yourself Storybook* (Crowell)

* ·	Clark	*First Men in Space* (Follett)
·	Cleary	*Henry Huggins* (Morrow)
	Clymer	*Treasure at First Base* (Dodd, Mead & Co.)
	Collodi	*Pinocchio* (Random House)
	Corbett	*Susie Sneakers* (Crowell)
** ·	Dagliesh	*The Davenports Are at Dinner* (Scribner)
** ·	Dressell and Hirsch-Zeno	*The Strange Paper Clue* (Row, Peterson)
** ·	————	*Find Formula X-48* and other mystery stories (Row, Peterson)
·	Gates	*State Trooper* (Macmillan)
·	————	*Cross-Country Trucker* (Macmillan)
·	————	*Keepers of the Lights* (Macmillan)
*	Gelman	*Football Fury* (Doubleday)
* ·	Guthridge	*Tom Edison* (Bobbs-Merrill)
·	Haywood	*"B" is for Betsy* and others (Harcourt)
·	————	*Eddie's Pay Dirt* (Wm. Morrow)
·	————	*Little Eddie* and others (Morrow)
·	Heffernan, *et al.*	*Desert Treasure* (Harr Wagner)
·	Higgins	*Stephen Foster* (Bobbs-Merrill)
·	Holland	*No Children, No Pets* (Knopf)
* ·	Ketcham	*Dennis the Menace* (Holt)
	————	*Baby Sitter's Guide by Dennis the Menace* (Holt)
* ·	Kottmeyer, ed.	*King Arthur and His Knights* (Webster)
* ·	————	*Robin Hood Stories* (Webster)
* ·	————	*Trojan War* (Webster)
	Krasilovsky	*The Man Who Didn't Wash His Dishes* (Doubleday)
·	Lindgren	*Pippi Longstocking* (Viking)
* ·	MacGregor	*Miss Pickerell and the Geiger Counter* (Whittlesey House)
* ·	————	*Miss Pickerell Goes to Mars* (Whittlesey House)
·	McCloskey	*Centerburg Tales* (Viking)
* ·	Monsell	*Susan Anthony* (Bobbs-Merrill)
·	Moore	*The Snake That Went to School* (Random House)
* ·	Orbaan	*Civil War Sailor* (Doubleday)
* ·	Parker	*Carol Heiss—Olympic Queen* (Doubleday)
	Preston, ed.	*Barrel of Laughs* (Scholastic Magazines)
* ·	Rambeau	*The Mystery of the Missing Marlin* (Harr Wagner)
·	Russell, *et al.*	*Roads to Everywhere* (Ginn)
*	Schleyer	*Stories for Today's Youth* (Globe)
	Seltzer	*Sweetie Pie* (Berkley)
	Seuss	*If I Ran the Zoo* (Seuss)
	————	*Yertle the Turtle* (Seuss)

* · Snow	*Samuel Morse* (Bobbs-Merrill)
* · Spencer, *et al.*	*Finding New Trails* (Lyons & Carnahan)
* · Stevenson	*Booker T. Washington* (Bobbs-Merrill)
* · ———	*Clara Barton* (Bobbs-Merrill)
* · ———	*George Carver* (Bobbs-Merrill)
** · Stevenson	*Treasure Island,* adapted (Scott, Foresman)
* · Van Riper	*Lou Gehrig* (Bobbs-Merrill)
* · ———	*Will Rogers* (Bobbs-Merrill)
* · Wagoner	*Louisa Alcott* (Bobbs-Merrill)
* · Weil	*Franklin Roosevelt* (Bobbs-Merrill)
White	*The Uninvited Donkey* (Viking)
* · Wilson	*Annie Oakley* (Bobbs-Merrill)
* · ———	*Ernie Pyle* (Bobbs-Merrill)
Winterfeld	*Castaways of Lilliput* (Harcourt)
Withers, ed.	*A Rocket in My Pocket* (poems) (Harcourt)
———	*Arrow Book of Jokes and Riddles* (Scholastic Magazines)
———	*Betty Crocker Junior Baking Book* (General Mills)
Wyndham	*Candy Stripers* (Julian Messner)

SIMPLIFIED CLASSICS

* Defoe	*Robinson Crusoe* (Random House)
* · ———	*Robinson Crusoe* (Garrard)
** · Hugo	*Les Misérables* (Globe)
* · Kottmeyer, ed.	*Robin Hood* (Webster)
· Moderow	*Six Great Stories* (Scott, Foresman)
* · Swift	*Gulliver's Stories* (Garrard)

FIFTH GRADE

SHORT STORIES AND SELECTIONS

* · Barker, *et al.*	*The Story of Our Country* (social studies text) (Row, Peterson)
· Beauchamp, *et al.*	*Discovering Our World,* Bk. II (science text) (Scott, Foresman)
· Cook	*Golden Book of the American Revolution* (Simon & Schuster)
· Gates, *et al.*	*Let's Travel On* (Macmillan)
· Gray, *et al.*	*Days and Deeds* (Scott, Foresman)
* Hamer, *et al.*	*Exploring the New World* (social studies text) (Follett)
· Huber, *et al.*	*They Were Brave and Bold* (Row, Peterson)

· Johnson and Jacobs	*Enchanted Isles* (Merrill)
· Larrick, ed.	"Rivers of the World": *The Mississippi* (Garrard)
———	"Rivers of the World": *The St. Lawrence* (Garrard)
· McKee	*Sky Lines* (Houghton Mifflin)
* · Moderow	*Six Great Stories,* adapted (Scott, Foresman)
· Parker	*Golden Treasury of Natural History* (Simon & Schuster)
* · Spencer, *et al.*	*Exploring New Trails* (Lyons & Carnahan)
** · Strang, *et al.*	*Teen-Age Tales,* Bks. 1–6 (Heath)
* · No Listed Author	*Stories Worth Knowing* (Gov't. Printing Office)

SUPPLEMENTARY READING

** · Baker	*Juarez of Mexico,* adapted (Webster)
** · ———	*Simon Bolivar,* adapted (Webster)
Barker	*The Story of Our Country* (Row, Peterson)
* · Beals	*Buffalo Bill* (Wheeler)
* · ———	*Chief Black Hawk* (Wheeler)
* · ———	*Davy Crockett* (Wheeler)
* · ———	*Kit Carson* (Wheeler)
** Becker	*Chimp in the Family* (Julian Messner)
* Bowman	*Pecos Bill* (Whitman)
· Brooks	*Freddy the Detective* (Knopf)
* Butterworth	*The Enormous Egg* (Little)
* Darling	*Baldy of Nome* (Knopf)
** · Doyle	*Cases of Sherlock Holmes,* adapted (Webster)
* · Du Jardin	*Wait for Marcy* (Lippincott)
** Edmonds	*The Matchlock Gun* (Dodd)
Freeman	*Fun with Cooking* (Random House)
———	*Fun with Chemistry* (Random House)
Gallant	*Exploring Mars* (Garden City)
Green	*Simple Tricks for the Young Magician* (Hart)
** · Harkins	*Punt Formation* (Morrow)
** Hickock	*Story of Helen Keller* (Grosset & Dunlap)
* Household	*Mystery of the Spanish Cave* (Little, Brown)
** · Jackson	*Squeeze Play* (Crowell)
** Lawson	*Ben and Me* (Little)
* Lewellen	*Tee Vee Humphrey* (Knopf)
* · Lindgren	*Mio My Son* (Viking)
* · Longstreth	*Elephant Toast* (Macmillan)
* · McCloskey	*Homer Price and the Donuts* (Viking)
* Montgomery	*Husky* (Holt, Rinehart & Winston)
* · Moody	*Little Britches* (Norton)
** · Piersall and Hirshberg	*Fear Strikes Out* (Little)
Pinkerton	*The First Overland Mail* (Random House)

	Stewart	*To California by Covered Wagon* (Random House)
❋ ·	Tucker	*Dan Morgan* (Wheeler)
·	Travers	*Mary Poppins* (Harcourt Brace)
❋ ❋	Villiers	*Windjammer's Story* (Louis de Rochemont, Cinemiracle Productions)
❋ ❋	Webster	*Daddy Long Legs* (Appleton-Century-Crofts)
·	Williams and Abrashkin	*Danny Dunn and the Anti-Gravity Paint* (Whittlesey House)
❋ ·	Wilson	*Herbert* (Knopf)
❋ ·	————	*Snowbound in Hidden Valley* (Julian Messner)
❋ ❋ ·	Winwar	*Napoleon and the Battle of Waterloo* (Random House)
·	Wooley	*Ginny and the New Girl* (William Morrow)

SIMPLIFIED CLASSICS

❋ ❋ ·	Dickens	*A Tale of Two Cities* (Webster)
❋ ❋	Dumas	*The Count of Monte Cristo* (Webster)
	————	*The Story of the Three Musketeers,* adapted (Sanborn)
❋ ❋ ·	Hugo	*Les Misérables* (Globe)
❋ ❋ ·	Melville	*Moby Dick* (Sanborn)
❋ ❋ ·	Poe	*The Gold Bug and Other Stories* (Webster)
	Sandrus	*Eight Treasured Stories* (Scott, Foresman)
❋ ❋ ·	Scott	*Ivanhoe* (Webster)
❋ ·	Twain	*Tom Sawyer* (Scott, Foresman)
	Verne	*Around the World in Eighty Days* (Scott, Foresman)
❋ ❋ ·	Wallace	*Ben Hur* (Webster)

SIXTH GRADE

SHORT STORIES AND SELECTIONS

❋ ·	Beauchamp, *et al.*	*Discovering Our World,* Bk. III (science text) (Scott, Foresman)
·	Bennett, *et al.*	*High Road to Glory* (Silver Burdett)
❋ ❋ ·	Burton and Mersand	*Stories for Teen-Agers,* Bks. 1–2 (Globe)
❋ ·	Gray, *et al.*	*Parades,* (Scott, Foresman)
·	Huber, *et al.*	*The Tales They Tell* (Row, Peterson)
·	Johnson and Jacobs	*Adventure Lands* (Merrill)
·	Kissen	*Crowded House* (Houghton Mifflin)
❋ ·	Meader	*Will to Win and Other Stories* (Harcourt Brace)
❋ ·	Spencer, *et al.*	*Traveling New Trails* (Lyons & Carnahan)

SUPPLEMENTARY READING

❋ ❋ ·	Alcott	*Little Women* (Little)
❋ ·	Anderson	*Fur Trappers of the Old West* (Wheeler)

* · Bliven — *The Story of D-Day* (Random House)
* · Boylston — *Clara Barton* (Random House)
** · ——— — *Sue Barton, Student Nurse* (Little)
* · Brink — *Caddie Woodlawn* (Macmillan)
* · Cleary — *Fifteen* (William Morrow)
* · Crouse and Crouse — *Alexander Hamilton and Aaron Burr* (Random House)
** de Kruif — *Microbe Hunters* (Harcourt)
** · de Leeuw — *The Story of Amelia Earhart* (Grosset & Dunlap)
** · Felsen — *Hot Rod* (E. P. Dutton)
* · Fisher — *Understood Betsy* (Holt)
** Forbes — *Mama's Bank Account* (Harcourt)
* · Frank — *Diary of a Young Girl* (Doubleday)
Freedman — *Mrs. Mike* (Coward-McCann)
* · Friedman — *The Janitor's Girl* (Morrow)
* Garfield — *Follow My Leader* (Viking)
* Holberg — *Restless Johnny: The Story of Johnny Appleseed* (Crowell)
* · Kjelgaard — *Irish Red* (Holiday House)
* · ——— — *Big Red* (Holiday House)
** · Leighton — *The Story of Florence Nightingale* (Grosset & Dunlap)
* · Lovelace — *Heaven to Betsey* (Crowell)
** · Malkus — *The Story of Winston Churchill* (Grosset & Dunlap)
** · Price — *The Story of Marco Polo* (Grosset & Dunlap)
* Smith — *The Hundred and One Dalmatians* (Viking)
* · Wilson — *Herbert* (Knopf)

SIMPLIFIED CLASSICS

* Coolidge — *Hercules and other Tales from Greek Myths* (Houghton Mifflin)
* · Cooper — *The Last of the Mohicans* (Scott, Foresman)
** · Dickens — *David Copperfield* (Scott, Foresman)
** · Eliot — *Silas Marner* (Scott, Foresman)
** · Hugo — *Les Misérables* (Laidlaw)
** · Kipling — *Captains Courageous* (Scott, Foresman)
** · Melville — *Moby Dick* (Scott, Foresman)
** Shakespeare — *Julius Caesar* (Globe)
* · Swift — *The Story of Lemuel Gulliver in Lilliput Land,* adapted (Sanborn)
Twain — *Huckleberry Finn* (Scott, Foresman)
* · ——— — *Tom Sawyer* (Scott, Foresman)
** · ——— — *The Prince and the Pauper* (Globe)
** Wyss — *Swiss Family Robinson* (Globe)

SEVENTH GRADE

SHORT STORIES AND SELECTIONS

** · Bailey and   *Worlds of Adventure* (American)
     Leavell

** · Brewton, *et al.*   *New Horizons through Reading and Literature*, Bk. 1
     (Laidlaw)

** · Gray, *et al.*   *Panoramas* (Scott, Foresman)

** · Russell, *et al.*   *Doorways to Discovery* (Ginn)

** · Spencer, *et al.*   *Driving the Reading Road* (Lyons & Carnahan)

SUPPLEMENTARY READING

**   Burnett   *The Secret Garden* (Lippincott)

** · Cavanna   *Angel on Skis* (Morrow)

**   Craig   *Trish* (Crowell)

**   Doss   *The Family Nobody Wanted* (Little)

** · Du Jardin   *Double Date* (Lippincott)

** · _____   *Practically Seventeen* (Lippincott)

**   DuMaurier   *Rebecca* (Doubleday)

** · Emery   *First Love, True Love* (Westminster)

** · _____   *Going Steady* (Westminster)

     Erdman   *The Edge of Time* (Dodd Mead)

** · Farley   *The Black Stallion* (Random House)

**   Garst   *Crazy about Horses* (Hastings)

     Giles   *Hannah Fowler* (Houghton Mifflin)

     Gipson   *Old Yeller* (Harper)

     Godden   *The Green Gage Summer* (Viking)

** · Guareschi   *The Little World of Don Camillo* (Farrar, Straus &
     Cudahy)

** · _____   *Don Camillo and His Flock* (Farrar, Straus & Cudahy)

** · Heinlein   *The Red Planet* (Scribner)

**   Hilton   *Goodbye, Mr. Chips* (Grosset & Dunlap)

**   Jewett   *Cobbler's Knob* (Viking)

**   Masters and   *Wilderness Teacher* (Rand McNally)
     Fowler

** · Meader   *Sparkplug of the Hornets* (Harcourt)

**   Richardson   *Second Satellite* (McGraw-Hill)

     Serraillier   *The Silver Sword* (Criterion)

**   Thompson   *Snow Slopes* (Longmans, Green)

** · Tunis   *All American* (Harcourt)

** · _____   *Go Team Go* (Morrow)

**   Ullman   *Banner in the Sky* (Lippincott)

**   Whitney   *Mystery on the Isle of Skye* (Westminster)

**   Wiggin   *Rebecca of Sunnybrook Farm* (Houghton Mifflin)

SIMPLIFIED CLASSICS

**	Blackmore	*Lorna Doone* (Globe)
** ·	Bronte	*Jane Eyre* (Globe)
**	Defoe	*Robinson Crusoe* (Sanborn)
** ·	Dickens	*Oliver Twist* (Laidlaw)
** ·	Homer	*The Odyssey* (Globe)
** ·	Scott	*Ivanhoe* (Globe)
** ·	Sewell	*Black Beauty* (Globe)
** ·	Stevenson	*Treasure Island* (Globe)

EIGHTH GRADE

SHORT STORIES AND SELECTIONS

** ·	Bailey and Leavell	*Worlds of People* (American)
** ·	Brewton, *et al.*	*New Horizons through Reading and Literature,* Bk. 2 (Laidlaw)
** ·	Lovrein, *et al.*	*Adventures for Today* (Harcourt)
** ·	Russell and Gunn	*Windows on the World* (Ginn)
** ·	Spencer, *et al.*	*Progress on Reading Roads* (Lyons & Carnahan)

SUPPLEMENTARY READING

** ·	Benary-Isbert	*Rowan Farm* (Harcourt)
** ·	———	*The Ark* (Winston)
**	Daly	*Seventeenth Summer* (Dodd)
**	Emery	*Senior Year* (Westminster)
** ·	Forbes	*Johnny Tremain* (Houghton Mifflin)
**	Forester	*The African Queen* (Modern Library)
**	Frank	*Diary of Anne Frank* (Doubleday)
	Godden	*Episode of Sparrows* (Viking)
** ·	Harkins	*Son of the Coach* (Holiday House)
**	———	*Young Skin Diver* (Morrow)
**	Hersey	*Hiroshima* (Knopf)
**	Heyerdahl	*Kon Tiki* (Rand McNally)
**	Hilton	*Lost Horizon* (Grosset & Dunlap)
**	———	*Random Harvest* (Little Brown)
**	Hunt	*Conquest of Everest* (Grosset & Dunlap)
**	Knight	*Lassie Come Home* (Winston)
**	Lederer and Burdick	*The Ugly American* (W. W. Norton)
** ·	London	*White Fang* (Grosset & Dunlap)

**	Lord	*A Night to Remember* (Holt)
**	MacLean	*Guns of Navarone* (Doubleday)
** ·	Meader	*T Model Tommy* (Harcourt)
**	Michener	*The Bridges at Toko-Ri* (Random House)
**	Montgomery	*Anne of Green Gables* (Grosset & Dunlap)
**	Moore	*The Baby Sitter's Guide* (Crowell)
**	Remarque	*All Quiet on the Western Front* (Little Brown)
**	Salinger	*Catcher in the Rye* (Grosset & Dunlap)
**	Smith	*A Tree Grows in Brooklyn* (Harper & Row)
**	Steinbeck	*Of Mice and Men* (Bantam)
**	———	*The Pearl* (Viking)
**	———	*The Short Reign of Pippin IV* (Viking)
**	Verne	*Twenty Thousand Leagues under the Sea* (Scribner)
**	Wells	*War of the Worlds* (Harper)

SIMPLIFIED CLASSICS

**	Austen	*Pride and Prejudice* (Globe)
**	Dickens	*A Tale of Two Cities* (Laidlaw)
**	Dumas	*The Count of Monte Cristo* (Globe)
**	Eliot	*Silas Marner* (Globe)
**	———	*The Mill on the Floss* (Globe)
**	Hawthorne	*The Scarlet Letter* (Globe)
**	Twain	*Connecticut Yankee* (Globe)

ॐ APPENDIX C

Games, Devices, and Workbooks

GAMES AND DEVICES FOR TEACHING SIGHT VOCABULARY

Title	Level
Basic Sight Vocabulary Cards (Garrard)	2–3
Grab: junior, senior, advanced (Dorothea Alcock, 107 N. Elspeth Way, Covina, Calif.)	1–5, according to set
Group Word Teaching Game (Garrard)	1–3
My Crossword Puzzle Book, Bks. I–II (Primary Educ. Svc.)	2 plus
Picture Word Cards (Garrard)	1
Read-O (Augsburg)	1–3
The Rolling Reader (Grolier)	1–3
Sight Phrase Cards (Garrard)	2 plus
Syllabascope Word Set (Wordcrafters)	4 plus
Take (Garrard)	3 plus

SUGGESTIONS FOR TEACHER-DEVISED GAMES

Dot Game[1]

The teacher can mimeograph a "dot picture" as in common "dot booklets," using consonants or blends for each dot. The sounds are pronounced, and the children draw a line for all the dots of the corresponding sound.

The Guessing Game[2]

After thirty-five words or so are learned, a guessing game that is a favorite with most children can be played. For example, the teacher wants to practice learning the sight words "found," "shall," "the," "you," and "put." The children already know Pat and Polly, who are characters in their reader, and they easily recognize the words "sees," "dog," "jump," "book," and "down." The teacher writes the following sentences on the blackboard:

---

[1] Devised by Stanley Hoffman.

[2] Nila B. Smith, *Learning to Recognize Words*. Out of print.

Polly *found* it.
Polly sees *the* dog.
Can *you* jump?
Put Pat's book down.
I *shall* go.

The words to be practiced are underlined. First the children read together all five sentences. The teacher then says, "I am thinking of one of the underlined words. Who can guess the word I am thinking?" The children take turns coming to the blackboard, pointing to the word they have chosen, and saying, "Is it the word 'the'?" If it is, he becomes the leader and is allowed to think of a word while the others guess. The children take turns for as long as desirable. (It is important that the child who guesses points to the chosen word, so that the teacher is certain that he had not thought one word and mistaken it for another of the underlined words.)

Learning Letters and Letter Sounds by Using Children's Initials[3]

When children are not too familiar with letters or letter sounds, the teacher can take small cards (about 3 x 5) and print a letter of the alphabet on each one in capital and lower-case form. The teacher then asks the child whose initials she holds up to stand. Also, whenever there is a reason to line up, the teacher can have the children take their places as she holds up their initials. Later, when the letters are better known, the teacher can ask the child who sits in front of or next to the child whose initials are held to stand. Still later, just the sounds of the pupil's initials might be used.

Ticktacktoe

A ticktacktoe frame is drawn on the blackboard or a piece of paper, and a list of words to be practiced is placed in full sight. Two individuals or two teams can play. The players choose who is to go first and who shall have the X's and O's. The pupil then says one of the words. If he is correct, he may place his mark next to the word and in any box he chooses in the ticktacktoe frame. (A mark is placed next to a word only to designate that it has already been chosen.) Another pupil then chooses a word and puts his mark in front of it and in the box he chooses. The game continues until one player gets three like marks in a row.

TEACHER'S REFERENCES FOR ADDITIONAL GAME SUGGESTIONS

DURRELL, D., AND SULLIVAN, HELEN, *Building Word Power*. Tarrytown-on-Hudson, N.Y.: Harcourt, Brace & World, 1941.

KINGSLY, B., *Reading Skills*. San Francisco, Calif.: Fearon Publishers, 1958.

Let's Play a Game. New York: Ginn, 1958.

Reading Activities for Middle Graders. New York: Ginn, 1958.

---

[3] Adapted by Helen O'Keefe of the Bellows School, Mamaroneck, N.Y., from D. Durrell, *Improving Reading Instruction* (Tarrytown-on-Hudson, N.Y.: World Book Co., 1956).

RUSSELL, D., AND KARP, ETTA, *Reading Aids through the Grades,* rev. ed. New York: Bur. of Publications, Teachers College, Columbia University, 1959.

RUSSELL, D., AND RUSSELL, ELIZABETH, *Listening Aids through the Grades.* New York: Bur. of Publications, Teachers College, Columbia University, 1959.

Tips and Games for the Classroom Teacher of Elementary Language Arts. New York: Metropolitan School Study Council, 1958.

WAGNER, G., AND HOSIER, M., *Reading Games.* Darien, Conn.: Grade Teacher Publication, 1961.

WORKBOOKS FOR PRACTICE IN WORD ANALYSIS

Author	Title	Level
Hargrave and Armstrong	*Building Reading Skills* (McCormick-Mathers)	1–6
Brueckner and Lewis	*Diagnostic Tests and Remedial Exercises in Reading* (Winston)	3 plus
Stone, *et al.*	*Eye and Ear Fun Books,* I–IV (Webster)	1–4
Thompson	*Happy Times with Sounds,* Bks. 2–3 (Allyn & Bacon)	2 plus
Stone	*Let's See* (Webster)	Primary
Bedwell and Hutchinson	*My Own Reading Exercises* (Prather)	2–6
Stone and Gatchel	*On the Way to Reading* (Webster)	Pre-primary
Meighan, *et al.*	*Phonics We Use,* Bks. A–F (Lyons & Carnahan)	1–6
	Phonics Stencils (Continental)	1–4
Wood and Barrows	*Reading Skills* (Holt, Rinehart, Winston)	6-12
	Reading Stencils (Continental)	1
Hay and Wingo	*Reading with Phonics* (Lippincott)	1–4
Hegge, Kirk, and Kirk	*Remedial Reading Drills* (Wahr)	All levels
Monroe, *et al.*	*We Talk, Spell and Write* (Scott, Foresman)	1–3

WORKBOOKS AND MATERIALS FOR COMPREHENSION, VOCABULARY, RATE, AND SPELLING

Author	Title	Level
Smith	*Be a Better Reader, I–III* (Prentice-Hall)	High 5–7
———	*Be a Better Reader, IV–VI* (Prentice-Hall)	10–12
Foster	*Developing Reading Skills,* A–C (Laidlaw)	4–7
Spencer and Robinson	*Driving the Reading Road* (Lyons & Carnahan)	7–9
Robinson, *et al.*	*EDL Study Skills Library*[1] (Educ. Dev. Labs)	4–9
Johnson	*Modern Reading Skilltexts,* Bks. 1–2 (Merrill)	7–10

Stone, Grover, et al.	*New Practice Readers*, Bks. A–G (Webster)	2–7
Gates and Peardon	*Practice Exercises in Reading*, Bks. III–VI (Bur. of Pub., T.C., Columbia U.)	3–6
Stone and Grover	*Practice Readers*, Bks. I–III (Webster)	3–6
Grover and Bayle	*Practice Readers*, Bk. 4 (Webster)	7–10
Spencer and Robinson	**Progress on Reading Roads* (Lyons & Carnahan)	9–10
Wagner, et al.	*Reader's Digest Reading Skill Builders*, Bks. II–VI; 2 at each level (Reader's Digest)	High 2–high 6
Anderson and Kinchelue	**Reader's Digest Advanced Reading Skill Builders* (Reader's Digest)	7, 8
Guiler and Coleman	*Reading for Meaning*, Bks. 4–12 (Lippincott)	4–12
Johnson	*Reading Skilltext*, Bks. 4–6 (Merrill)	4–6
Simpson	**SRA Better Reading*, Bk. 1 (Sci. Rsch. Ass.)	7–9
Parker	**SRA Reading Laboratories*, (Sci. Rsch. Ass.) Boxes of reading booklets. Approximately fifteen selections at each level. The following sets are available:	
	SRA Reading Laboratory, elem. ed.	2–9
	SRA Reading Laboratory, IIa	2–7
	SRA Reading Laboratory, IIb	3–8
	SRA Reading Laboratory, IIc	4–9
	SRA Reading Laboratory, IIIa; secondary ed.	3–12
	SRA Reading Laboratory, IVa; college prep. ed.	8–14
McCall and Crabbs	*Standard Test Lessons in Reading*, Bks. A–E (Bur. of Pub., T.C., Columbia U.)	3–7
Strang	**Study Type of Reading Exercises*, high school level (Bur. of Pub., T.C., Columbia U.)	9–12
Durrell	*Word Analysis Practice* (Harcourt, Brace & World)	4–6
Taylor, et al.	*Word Clues* (Educ. Dev. Labs.)	7–12

* Symbols are the same as those in Appendix B.

1 Designed to teach study skills through science and social studies. Three boxes at each grade level for each content area.

FOR IMPROVING READING ABILITY AT SENIOR HIGH SCHOOL AND COLLEGE LEVELS

Author	*Title*	*Level*
Shaw and Townsend	*College Reading Manual* (Crowell)	College
Wedeen	*College Remedial Reader* (Putnam)	College
Shaw	*Effective Reading and Learning* (Crowell)	College

Robinson	*Effective Study* (Harper)	College
Brown	*Efficient Reading*, alt. ed. (Heath)	College
Brown	*Explorations in College Reading* (Heath)	College
Morgan and Deese	*How to Study* (Harper)	College
Johnson	*Improve Your Own Spelling* (McGraw-Hill)	9–12
Stroud and Ammons	*Improving Reading Ability* (Appleton-Century-Crofts)	College
Miller	*Increasing Reading Efficiency* (Holt)	College
Johnson	*Modern Reading Skilltexts*, Bk. 3 (Merrill)	9–12
Gilbert	*Power and Speed in Reading* (Prentice-Hall)	College
Baker	*Reading Skills* (Prentice-Hall)	College
Perry and Whitlock	*Selections for Improving Speed of Comprehension* (Harvard)	College
Mersand	*Spelling Your Way to Success* (Barron's)	9–12 and college
Simpson	*SRA Better Reading*, Bks. 2–3 (Sci. Rsch. Ass.)	9–12
Strang	*Study Type of Reading Exercises*, coll. level (Bur. of Pub., T.C., Columbia U.)	9–12 and college
Spache and Berg	*The Art of Efficient Reading* (Macmillan)	College
Cosper and Griffen	*Toward Better Reading Skill* (Appleton-Century-Crofts)	College
Sherbourne	*Toward Reading Comprehension* (Heath)	College

DICTIONARIES

Basic Dictionary of American English (Holt, Rinehart & Winston)
Courtis-Watters Illustrated Dictionary (Simon & Schuster)
Golden Dictionary (Simon & Schuster)
Thorndike-Barnhart Beginning Dictionary (Doubleday)
Thorndike-Barnhart Junior Dictionary (Doubleday)
Webster's Elementary Dictionary for Boys and Girls (Merriam)
Webster's Picturesque Word Origins from Webster's International Dictionary (Merriam)

HAND TACHISTOSCOPES

Flash-X (Edl. Laboratories, 75 Prospect St., Huntington, N. Y.)
Pocket-Tac (116 Newberry St., Boston, Mass.)

❧ APPENDIX D

Word Lists

THE BASIC SIGHT VOCABULARY OF 220 WORDS[1]

a	buy	fly	how
about	by	for	hurt
after		found	
again	call	four	I
all	came	from	if
always	can	full	in
am	carry	funny	into
an	clean		is
and	cold	gave	it
any	come	get	its
are	could	give	
around	cut	go	jump
as		goes	just
ask	did	going	
at	do	good	keep
ate	does	got	kind
away	done	green	know
	don't	grow	
be	down		laugh
because	draw	had	let
been	drink	has	light
before		have	like
best	eat	he	little
better	eight	help	live
big	every	her	long
black		here	look
blue	fall	him	
both	far	his	made
bring	fast	hold	make
brown	find	hot	many
but	first		may
	five		me

[1] E. W. Dolch, *Teaching Primary Reading* (Champaign, Ill.: Garrard Press, 1960), p. 255. Reprinted by permission. Coypright 1960 by E. W. Dolch.

much
must
my
myself

never
new
no
not
now

of
off
old
on
once
one
only
open
or
our
out
over
own

pick
play
please
pretty

pull
put

ran
read
red
ride
right
round
run

said
saw
say
see
seven
shall
she
show
sing
sit
six
sleep
small
so
some
soon
start
stop

take
tell
ten
thank
that
the
their
them
then
there
these
they
think
this
those
three
to
today
together
too
try
two

under
up
upon
us
use

very
walk
want
warm
was
wash
we
well
went
were
what
when
where
which
white
who
why
will
wish
with
work
would
write

yellow
yes
you
your

THE 95 MOST COMMON NOUNS[2]

apple

baby
back
ball
bear
bed
bell
bird
birthday
boat
box
boy
bread
brother

cake
car
cat

chair
chicken
children
Christmas
coat
corn
cow

day
dog
doll
door
duck

egg
eye

farm
farmer

father
feet
fire
fish
floor
flower

game
garden
girl
good-by
grass
ground

hand
head
hill
home

horse
house

kitty

leg
letter

man
men
milk
money
morning
mother

name
nest
night

paper
party

picture	school	stick	toy
pig	seed	street	tree
rabbit	sheep	sun	watch
rain	shoe		water
ring	sister	table	way
robin	snow	thing	wind
	song	time	window
Santa Claus	squirrel	top	wood

2 *Ibid.*, p. 257.

❧ INDEX